MOVIE NIGHTS

with

THE

REAGANS

A Memoir

MARK WEINBERG

SIMON & SCHUSTER

NEW YORK   LONDON   TORONTO   SYDNEY   NEW DELHI

Simon & Schuster
1230 Avenue of the Americas
New York, NY 10020

Copyright © 2018 by Mark D. Weinberg

First Simon & Schuster hardcover edition February 2018

SIMON & SCHUSTER and colophon are registered trademarks of
Simon & Schuster, Inc. For information about special discounts for bulk purchases,
please contact Simon & Schuster Special Sales at 1-866-506-1949
or business@simonandschuster.com.

The Simon & Schuster Speakers Bureau can bring authors to your live event.
For more information or to book an event, contact the
Simon & Schuster Speakers Bureau at 1-866-248-3049
or visit our website at www.simonspeakers.com.

Interior design by Ruth Lee-Mui

Manufactured in the United States of America

1 3 5 7 9 10 8 6 4 2

Library of Congress Cataloging-in-Publication Data is available.

ISBN 978-1-5011-3399-2
ISBN 978-1-5011-3401-2 (ebook)

FOR MY WIFE, ERIN

Because of her, I now understand what
Ronald Reagan meant when he said
he missed his wife when she was just in the next room.

FOR OUR CHILDREN, GRACE AND JAKE

Whose very existence thrills Erin and me beyond words
and who bring unending joy to us every day.

FOR MY PARENTS, JUDY AND HERB WEINBERG

Without whom I would not be here, but beyond that,
who were and are the embodiment of everything good in the world.

and

FOR NANCY AND RONALD REAGAN

Welcoming and warm, they allowed me the
greatest experience anyone could imagine.

CONTENTS

INTRODUCTION

NANCY REAGAN'S LAST GOOD-BYE

August 2015

My rental car and I are finding our way down the streets of Bel Air, on a trip I hadn't taken for years. Back then, when I worked for President and Mrs. Reagan, every one of these trips seemed important. Yet this one was perhaps the most important of all. I didn't know it for certain, of course, and I sure hoped it wasn't true. But I had a feeling this would be the last time I would see Nancy Reagan alive.

The pop-culture notion of the Reagans' former neighborhood is of multistory mega-mansions tucked behind elaborate gates and exotic foliage. There are, in fact, many homes like that—Elizabeth Taylor once lived nearby—but by no means does that image apply to all of them. That includes my destination that summer afternoon: the home of Nancy and Ronald Reagan.

With all due respect, if tourists were driving through Bel Air to ooh and aah over houses, they would not give the Reagan home a second look. "It's a very ordinary house," an onlooker said once when the former First Couple moved into their multimillion-dollar digs at 668 Saint Cloud Road in January 1989. By the time I make this drive again, the former president has been gone for more than ten years, but that doesn't matter. I still see the house as *theirs*. His widow clearly felt that way, too. She'd have never dreamt of abandoning the comparatively modest three-bedroom ranch house they shared a couple of miles from Century City, where the former president maintained his office after leaving the White House, and about an hour's drive from the Ronald Reagan Presidential Library & Museum in Simi Valley.

There's a nondescript metal mailbox in front of the gate, and at the appointed hour, I pull into the driveway, past the security station after having been cleared, and make the short drive to the front door.

In earlier days, whenever I came to the house, I'd knock on the large, round, brass door knocker, and either the president or Mrs. Reagan—or sometimes both—would open the door without pretense and show me in. Whenever I left, one or both always walked me to the door and stood there, waving, until my car was out of sight. So it was no surprise to me, on such a balmy day, that a smiling Nancy Reagan—at this point, largely confined to a wheelchair— was at the door to greet me again. Standing beside her were a home health care aide and her housekeeper.

As her health declined, Mrs. Reagan had allowed very few meetings like this one—which she knew in advance was an interview for this book. Her staff didn't want her to be overwhelmed with requests from former aides and old friends. So my visit was kept quiet. As I understand it, it was the last interview she ever gave.

I didn't know what to expect, but even at ninety-four, Nancy Reagan looked and acted like—well, Nancy Reagan. Her hair was a little less puffy than when she was First Lady, but still very nicely styled, and her makeup—essentially only lipstick—looked perfect. She wore an orange blouse and cream-colored pants, simple earrings, and her wedding band. Her eyes and smile were warm. And her voice, while slightly softer, was otherwise exactly as it had always been, warm and welcoming. Just hearing it immediately evoked so many fond memories of our many years together—especially when she laughed. As I saw her again, my thoughts returned to the first time I'd met her, when I joined the 1980 Reagan presidential campaign. We had not gotten off to the best of starts.

We had landed somewhere during our dizzying cross-country campaigning, and the Reagans were asked to stay aboard the plane for a short while because their motorcade was not yet ready. It was essentially just the two of them at the front of the plane, and I thought I saw an opportunity to ingratiate myself with Governor Reagan's influential wife.

I walked up the aisle, presented her with some trinkets I had found in a hotel gift shop, and said, "These might be fun for your grandchildren."

Mrs. Reagan accepted them, looked at me, and said "Thank you" in a perfunctory manner.

I strutted to the back of the plane, feeling cocky because I had made myself known to the candidate's wife.

As soon as I got off the plane, however, another staff member came up to me. "You're a fool," he said.

"What do you mean?"

"Don't you realize, Mrs. Reagan doesn't have any grandchildren?" He explained that the "grandchildren" were the children of Michael

Reagan, a son from the governor's first marriage to the actress Jane Wyman. My heart sank. Needless to say, I never mentioned grandchildren to the First Lady again.

Mrs. Reagan did not hold that incident against me. That may surprise some people who bought into the caricature—created by some critics and carried out in the press—portraying her as some sort of Cruella de Vil. Over the years, I'd learn many times how very wrong and unfair that characterization was.

"I'm not really walking very much anymore," she confessed as we met for that final time in California, "so I hope you'll forgive me for not opening the door."

"Of course," I replied, and leaned down to kiss her on the cheek. "I brought you something." An orchid, one of her favorite flowers.

"Oh, how beautiful. Thank you, Mark." She held it for a second, until the housekeeper reached down to take it to her bedroom.

Probably by design, the house still felt as if the president might be just down the hall, walking into the room at any moment, with a quip or story on hand. This was very much the house, after all, of a woman still mourning a husband who, because of Alzheimer's disease, was tragically lost to her long before he actually died.

"Where shall we go?" Mrs. Reagan asked. "How about in here?" She motioned toward the den. Outside the room hung Norman Rockwell's famous painting of the president, done in 1968 when Reagan was governor of California, which had been there for as long as I could remember.

The den, too, was precisely the way it was the day the Reagans moved into the home. Two of the walls were lined with bookshelves holding many leather-bound collections of books on various topics. There were a few decorative silver plates and framed photos interspersed among the shelves: Mrs. Reagan with Queen

Elizabeth II—the two had become good friends over the years—and another of the Reagans with Pope John Paul II at the Vatican.

The den had dark paneling, but the room was very bright because one wall was glass and looked onto the backyard. There was a small fireplace tucked into one wall and a TV hidden by the paneling. On the large red-and-white couch sat an embroidered pillow that bore a map of the United States, highlighting the forty-nine states Reagan won in 1984 (all but Minnesota, Democratic opponent Walter Mondale's home state), the words "You Ain't Seen Nothing Yet"—one of the '84 reelection campaign slogans—and an embroidered inscription, "Love, Fran and Ray." The pillow was a gift from Fran and Ray Stark, he the legendary Hollywood producer who, many lifetimes ago, discovered Barbra Streisand, and gave her a film career. Ray Stark was involved with dozens of motion pictures, including *West Side Story, The Misfits, Funny Girl, The Way We Were,* and *Steel Magnolias.* In front of the couch stood a very large coffee table, piled high with videos of movies in which Ronald Reagan had starred.

Nearby was a round wooden table, on which sat a beautiful orchid plant and some hand-painted enamel boxes.

The home health care aide gently wheeled Mrs. Reagan to this table, and I took a chair right next to her.

After I updated her—at her insistence—on my wife and children, we came to the reason for my visit. I reminded her that I was writing this book: the story of the Reagan presidency through the movies we watched at Camp David, the presidential retreat nestled in the wooded hills of Maryland, about an hour northwest of Washington, DC.

"I know you are," she said, smiling.

Her eyes sparkled when she talked about our weekends at Camp David. For all that has been written about the Reagans over the years, it was an aspect of their lives about which little was, or is, known. She seemed eager to relive the memories and to see them live on in print.

"That was such a special time."

Indeed it was. Which is the reason I wanted to write this book. It had been thirty-four years since I was a twenty-three-year-old White House press aide assigned to travel with the Reagans to Camp David for the weekends, and became one of the few members of the administration who saw them off guard and up close.

The idea of having a Press Office staffer accompany the president to Camp David was White House Press Secretary Jim Brady's. He thought it was essential that there be a point of contact with the chief executive at all times—someone who could act as his eyes and ears "just in case." Because Jim and his two deputies were married with young children, the role fell to the two assistant press secretaries: David Prosperi and me. For the first year of the administration, we alternated weekends, but after David left the White House staff for a big job in the private sector, word came that "the missus is comfortable with Mark," so I was more than happy to go every weekend.

I was assigned to a small cabin called Sycamore, located down the path from Aspen Lodge, the presidential residence, and just a stone's throw—literally—from Laurel Lodge: the main and largest building, where there was a big living room with a brick fireplace, conference room, presidential office, and dining room for senior staff.

Almost every weekend, a small number of the staff spent our evenings with the Reagans doing one of the things they loved best: watching movies. Over the eight years, we watched nearly every major motion picture of the 1980s—from 9 to 5, to E.T., to Back to the Future, to Raiders of the Lost Ark, to Ferris Bueller's Day Off. The last film we saw together, the 363rd in their eight years—was Cattle Queen of Montana. The last wasn't an eighties film but one of the president's "golden oldies," as he liked to call the films he'd starred in, and yes, we did watch other films in the Reagan repertoire: *Knute Rockne All American, Hellcats of the Navy,* and *Bedtime for Bonzo.* And we were very glad to do so.

The official "call time" for the movie in Aspen Lodge was always 8:00 p.m. But invitees knew to gather at 7:40 because, without fail, at 7:45 the front door would open, and President Reagan would usher in his guests, which usually included his personal aide, physician, military aide, Camp David commander, senior Secret Service agent in charge, Marine One pilot, senior White House Communications Agency (WHCA) officer, and me. Mrs. Reagan was usually standing in front of a roaring fireplace or near a large picture window, depending on the season, of course, and as soon as she saw us, she would wave us in with a big smile and say, "Come in, come in. Get out of the cold [or heat]. So glad you're here."

If it was a Friday night, the president's hair would look much softer and shinier than usual, because he had washed it that afternoon. (He did *not* dye it, nor did he slick it down with grease.) When I first saw it, I was struck by how nice it looked and told him so. He smiled, winked, and then did a spot-on imitation of the old TV shampoo commercial featuring an actress saying "I just washed my hair, and I can't do a *thing* with it." Everyone had a good laugh. Mrs. Reagan—never a fan of the wet look—motioned me over and whispered, "Keep telling him that. Ronnie needs to hear how nice it looks." I obliged every Friday thereafter.

Invariably, one person would be running a little late, so the group would stand near the fireplace and talk with the Reagans about such innocuous topics as the weather or sports. Once the straggler arrived, everyone would take his or her regular seat in the living room. The president and Mrs. Reagan sat on the couch with two ottomans, the personal aide and I were in easy chairs with ottomans next to the couch, and everyone else was in comfortable chairs behind the Reagans' couch.

Once everyone was seated, a screen would automatically come down from the ceiling, the lights dimmed, and the movie started. It was just like in a commercial theater. There was a projection room behind the dining room in Aspen Lodge, but the "window" through which the film was shown was hidden by a framed print, which was removed just prior to the showing of the film. A projectionist operated a state-of-the-art projector and ran the reels, which had come in the typical metal "cans" in order. About thirty minutes into the film, the presidential food service coordinators from the Navy White House mess who attended the Reagans wherever they went served popcorn in individual baskets, first to the Reagans and then to the guests. Water was also served. I once considered asking for a beer but did not have the nerve. After the president was diagnosed with diverticulitis, nuts and seeds were eliminated from his diet, and popcorn was banned. So on Fridays, a few hours before departure, I walked to a candy store across the street from the White House and purchased a large box of smooth-center chocolates, which the president liked. I thought about going back there one day and telling the nice ladies who'd carefully packed the box each Friday that their chocolates had been for the leader of the free world, but I never did.

Once the movie was over, everyone stood up, reassembled near the fireplace, and shared views on the film for a few minutes. The president always spoke first. Not because he insisted on it, but because the guests all wanted to know what he thought. If the movie was one that either the president or Mrs. Reagan had been in, the conversation could go on for quite a while, as all of the guests had lots of questions. Both Reagans were more than happy to regale us with tales of their days in Hollywood, which were always interesting.

Their memories were razor sharp, and they made us feel as if we were actually on the soundstages with them. If it was a Friday night, the president would dismiss his guests with a cheery "See you at noon tomorrow," which was the time of his weekly radio address to the nation.

The Reagans scrutinized every one of those films—watching them without moving their eyes from the screen—like students of the artistry of filmmaking. At the end of each movie, the president would immediately look at his watch to note the running time (he would track his radio addresses the following morning the same way). During the first couple of movies, I ended up watching the Reagans watching the films more than watching the films themselves.

Even though some of us younger folks in the "Aspen Movie Club" (which is what the regulars dubbed ourselves) were usually skeptical about the older movies the Reagans sometimes favored, we were always anxious to see films that the president and/or Mrs. Reagan had been in. Ronald Reagan said that watching his old movies was like "looking at a son I didn't know I had." To watch them with him was almost surreal.

As I sat with the president and Mrs. Reagan in their cabin at Camp David on our many movie nights, I was privileged to get a rare glimpse into their inner lives. I saw a small part of what made them tick—what resonated with them and what didn't. I saw what merited their glowing praise and what was gently cut down with their trademark good humor. It was during our weekends at Camp David, and especially as we watched movies together over the eight years the Reagans were in the White House, that I got to know them.

It did not take long before I realized that, for the Reagans, the movies weren't just pleasant distractions from the burdens of office. It was the world from which they originated during the prime of their lives, the language in which they sometimes communicated, the profession that changed their lives' trajectory, and the source of many life lessons. Old habits die hard. Sometimes, when asking for a Saturday radio speech text, for example, the president would call it a "script." And from time to time, he referred to me as his "publicity man."

"We were introduced to a whole new world and so many new people," Mrs. Reagan recalled, when I asked her about her Hollywood days. "You learned how to develop a tough skin and how to protect your privacy."

Those of us who knew President Reagan understood keenly that his years in the motion picture industry were probably the most enjoyable of his life. That is not to say he did not enjoy the presidency, but it did seem that he had more plain old fun making movies. Who wouldn't?

Though his political opponents routinely sought to diminish him as a "B-movie star," Ronald Reagan was never embarrassed about having been an actor. In fact, he was quite proud of being in "the motion picture business," as he called it. During our White House days, I remember once joking with a colleague that if Ronald Reagan could carve his own tombstone, it might read:

RONALD REAGAN

Movie Star
(Who Later Served in Public Office)

I have always felt that part of what he loved most about Hollywood was that that was where he met Nancy in 1949 and where they began their life together. Mrs. Reagan made that point as well. "It brought us together," she told me. "Ann Straus, who worked in publicity at Metro [Metro-Goldwyn-Mayer, or MGM Studios], suggested we meet. I thought that was a nifty idea."

To the consternation of his staff, Ronald Reagan would sometimes say he did not see how someone could do the job of president without having been an actor. Critics seized on that as evidence that he was shallow, insincere, and just playing a role. Ridiculous. I asked him about it once, and he told me what he meant: that because of television (there was no internet during the Reagan years) the modern-day US presidency required an understanding of how to influence public opinion in a new way. He was keenly aware that most people formed their opinions based on what they saw on-screen, and that a simple gesture, expression, or image could have far more impact than a perfectly crafted policy platform or speech.

He also was acutely aware of the fact that when people saw their president on television, they expected to see a person who conducted himself or herself with dignity because the president represented the American people. He viewed himself as a symbol and knew that what people in other countries thought about the US president was what they thought about America. Yet he did not obsess about details of these events. He wisely left that to the staff, whose expertise he respected as fellow professionals. It was nice to work for someone who understood and appreciated the technical requirements of the presidency, such as lighting, camera angles, and backdrops, which he had learned about in Hollywood.

Some of us on his ever-cautious, ever-worried Washington press team would have preferred the commander in chief downplay his Hollywood years. We thought there was something frivolous about the movie business, but Ronald Reagan did not. He viewed it as an honorable profession, one that required talent and hard work, and he often reminded us that, as a business, the motion picture industry was quite successful. I remember him pointing out on more than one occasion that the export of American culture and values—primarily through movies—was how many countries got to know and form opinions of the United States.

It's true that Ronald Reagan was most animated when recounting his Hollywood days, which led to unfair and unflattering stories about his lack of interest in more weighty matters of policy. But in fairness, his film career was what people asked him about most often. It was a lot more interesting to hear about being on a soundstage with Errol Flynn than it was talking about budget negotiations with bland politicians.

Reagan's friends and detractors alike often described the president's elusive nature. That he was, as many put it, a hard man to get to know. Sometimes I think that's true, and sometimes I think that's total nonsense. But his Hollywood career does provide some explanation for it.

In 1965, long before he entered the White House, Reagan entitled his first memoir *Where's the Rest of Me?* This was a famous line from one of his movies—the dark 1942 drama *Kings Row*—in which he played a man injured in a railroad accident who wakes up from surgery to discover to his horror that his legs have been amputated. Reagan worked for days on end to perfect that delivery. And the line stuck with him for years thereafter. "No single line in my career has been as effective in explaining to me what an actor's life must be," he wrote in the book. "So much of our profession is taken up with pretending . . . that an actor must spend at least half his waking hours in fantasy, in rehearsal or shooting."* That life also encouraged actors to keep to themselves, since every few months

*Ronald Reagan with Richard G. Hubler, *Where's the Rest of Me?* (New York: Duell, Sloan and Pearce, 1965), 6.

or so, they'd have to make friends with a whole new cast and crew, shoot a film, and then move on to something else.

"My world contracted into not much more than a soundstage, my home, and occasional nights on the town. The circle of my friends closed in. The demands of my work—sometimes as much as fourteen hours a day—cut me off even from my brother, Neil, who lived within half a mile of my apartment."* President Reagan had a very warm relationship with his only sibling, his older brother, Neil, who went by the nickname "Moon." They both went to Eureka College, and Neil also began his career in Hollywood. He was a radio director, an actor, and a television director. Even though he never appeared with his brother, Neil directed him in the television series *Death Valley Days*. Neil eventually went on to become a successful advertising executive.

The Reagans became accustomed to short, though often valued and memorable friendships, and depended more and more on each other for support and comfort. That was one of the secrets to their great love and enduring marriage.

Together, of course, they starred on the greatest and most important stage in the world. And they did it using all of the skills they'd honed during their many years in Hollywood—particularly a belief in the importance of telling a story. Which, of course, is the goal of every film.

Each movie I selected for inclusion in this book—from a list of the hundreds we watched together—tells a story of its own. Each occurs at a particular moment in time in the Reagan presidency and provides a view of what was going on in the administration behind the scenes. For example, we watched *Rocky IV* during a crucial turning point in the Cold War. Each film also tells us something about

*Ronald Reagan with Hubler, *Where's the Rest of Me?*, 6.

the 1980s, a decade many Americans still recall nostalgically. *Top Gun,* for example, is generally regarded as one of the definitive films of the era. And, just as important, each reveals new insights into the Reagans themselves.

Let me be clear at the outset: I am a proudly biased fan of President and Mrs. Reagan. I feel incredibly honored to have had the rare opportunity to work for them, travel with them, and share some of their deeply treasured time at Camp David with them. I hope this book enables readers to rediscover some of the most iconic movies in our country's history through the eyes and experiences of two of its most memorable public figures, who were also two deeply proud artists of the craft of filmmaking. I hope, too, that this book gives some more insight into their life together at Camp David, the White House, and afterward, and offers some understanding of what the Reagans were like behind the scenes. And I hope you enjoy reliving these memories at least a fraction as much as I did.

MOVIE NIGHTS

with

THE REAGANS

1

9 TO 5

———— ◆ ————

Starring: Jane Fonda, Lily Tomlin, Dolly Parton
Directed by: Colin Higgins
Viewed by the Reagans: February 14, 1981

———— ◆ ————

The Film That Made the Reagans Angry and
Propelled a First Lady's Crusade

It was February 14, 1981, and Ronald Reagan, less than one month into his presidency, was faced with a dilemma. With the press chronicling his moves and Secret Service agents trailing him everywhere, how was he going to surprise his wife with a Valentine's Day card?

Earlier that week, the president had told his security detail that, like most married men, he had personally selected a card every year during their nearly twenty-nine years of marriage, and he intended to continue the practice. To their consternation, Reagan further informed the Secret Service that he wanted to leave the White House, head over to a nearby gift shop, and purchase a card for the First Lady of his life.

Ronald Reagan could be very stubborn, especially on a matter that he held important. And on this question, he held firm.

So, after a series of troubled glances and murmurs, the agents relented and drove the chief executive to the store, where he picked out an assortment of cards for his wife.* That was when Reagan fully absorbed just how much his life had changed.

The result of his excursion was not what the president expected: total pandemonium, as stunned customers milled around and a crowd of onlookers formed, causing discomfort for the agents.

"That was just about the last shopping expedition outside the White House," Reagan recalled later. "It caused such a commotion that I never wanted to do that to a shopkeeper again." Still, he was quite tickled that he could surprise Nancy with a card that Saturday at Camp David, on one of their first visits to the presidential retreat.†

The Ronald and Nancy Reagan love affair is, of course, legendary. I confess that I did not understand its intensity—or believe in its sincerity—at first. When I heard the president say once that he "could not imagine life without Nancy," I didn't get it. Admittedly, I was single at the time, but that seemed a bit much. Yet as I got to know the Reagans over the years, I realized he was telling the truth. (And once I got married, I got it.)

Contrary to my cynical impression, there was nothing fake or staged about their relationship. It was not just for the cameras. Everything seen in public was the same behind the scenes. They held hands, whispered to each other, exchanged glances, and were edgy when the other was gone. Their devotion was so complete, in fact, that it could be, at times, isolating for others.

---

*Ronald Reagan, *An American Life* (New York: Simon & Schuster, 1990).
†Ronald Reagan, *The Reagan Diaries*, ed. Douglas Brinkley (New York: Harper-Collins, 2007), 4.

That isn't to say the relationship was without hiccups. Some were typical: the president expressing annoyance that his wife was taking too long getting ready to go somewhere, for example. If Ronald Reagan had one long-standing complaint about Nancy, it was that she was on the telephone a lot. It was not uncommon when we would be getting ready to go somewhere for the president, all dressed and ready, to stand with the staff and Secret Service, waiting for Mrs. Reagan. He would look at his watch and grumble, "Nancy is on that damnphone"—he made it one word—"again."

One time at the White House, he was in his tuxedo waiting impatiently for her. She emerged finally in a beautiful gown, and we got into the elevator that would take us from the family quarters to the ground floor, where the motorcade was staged. The annoyance melted away. Mrs. Reagan said to her husband, "You look pretty, honey." A quizzical look crossed his face, and he said, "I'm trying to figure out if it's okay for a man to look 'pretty.'" I assured him that it was.

The first time I arrived at Camp David, that Valentine's weekend, I was not entirely sure the experience was real. Who was I to be on Marine One with the president of the United States and spending a weekend with him and the First Lady at this famed place? I expected a burly man in a dark suit to come up behind me at any moment, tap me on the shoulder, and say, "It's over; you know you don't belong here," as he escorted me to a waiting government sedan.

My first impressions of Camp David were "*Wow!* This is amazing!" and yet, shortly thereafter, a sense of "This is it?" The presidential retreat was both overwhelming and understated, which I later came to realize was the point. It was designed to be a contrast to what some saw as the cold formality of the White House, which was really a museum where the First Couple's lives were constantly on display. Here the president and the First Lady could kick back, relax, and just be themselves. The facilities were neither fancy nor rustic; comfort was the goal. The devoted and discreet staff at Camp David succeeded in ensuring that everyone felt at home.

Camp David, Mrs. Reagan recalled, offered "a tremendous feeling of release."* It helped the Reagans keep a perspective on things and have time to reflect. It was such a special place that they guarded it, being careful about who was allowed to join them there. It was not that the Reagans had anything to hide. It was just that they did not want or need a large entourage when they were at this quiet, picturesque place where they could just relax. And there was nothing that helped them relax more than watching a feature film.

As had quickly become the practice since the Reagans began traveling to Camp David, the small group of staff with them was invited to join them in their residence to watch what was usually the latest popular movie. President and Mrs. Reagan had a strong desire to provide some entertainment for aides like me who, as he put it, "have to go with us" to Camp David. (As if we had better options.) The president was sometimes criticized for leaving the Oval Office at five o'clock every day, contributing to the false impression among some in the pundit class that he was old and lazy. Actually, it was an intentional practice. He left then because he knew that if he was in the office, the staff would stay as long as he did. He wanted them to go home at reasonable hours and be with their families.

Once he got to the family quarters, he would spend several hours at work at his desk in an office adjacent to his and Nancy's bedroom. The Reagans also scheduled their December trips to California to begin after Christmas Day, so that staff, press, and Secret Service could be with their families for the holiday.

*Nancy Reagan with William Novak, *My Turn: The Memoirs of Nancy Reagan* (New York: Random House, 1989), 255.

That chilly February evening, Mrs. Reagan greeted all of us for the showing of the evening's film, the comedy *9 to 5*, which had been released to great success the previous December. The film grossed nearly $4 million in its opening weekend, a huge take at the time, and became the second-highest-grossing film of 1980 (behind only *The Empire Strikes Back* and *Superman II*). The combination of the movie's star power and timeless message helped to make it one of the first real hits of the Reagan era.

The critics, as is often the case, were tougher to impress. The *New York Times* found the social commentary ham-handed. "'Nine to Five' begins as satire, slips uncertainly into farce . . . and concludes by waving the flag of feminism as earnestly as Russian farmers used to wave the hammer-and-sickle at the end of movies about collective farming," grumbled Vincent Canby, who at the time was one of the preeminent film critics in the country. The legendary film critic Roger Ebert called the movie "a good-hearted, simpleminded comedy." But he praised the debut performance of the country music star Dolly Parton, calling her "a natural-born movie star; a performer who holds our attention so easily that it's hard to believe it's her first film."

Parton wrote and recorded the movie's theme song, also called "9 to 5," which became one of her biggest hits. One wag almost immediately renamed the song "9 to 10" to poke fun at President Reagan's age (he had just turned seventy) and his alleged love of naps, a recurring joke that would resonate throughout the Reagan years. A 1979 *Saturday Night Live* spoof joked about Reagan's "dentures," his need to eat soft foods such as rice pudding and cottage cheese, and his need for frequent napping during the day. Reagan himself would make jokes in this regard. But in fact, the president hated taking naps during the day and did so only when required by his doctors, such as after the March 1981 assassination attempt.

Shortly after Reagan left office, however, the mostly good-natured ribbing about his alleged dozing crossed a line. After all, at that point, he wasn't even around to be in on the joke himself. Word reached us at the postpresidency office in Los Angeles that some on George H. W. Bush's White House staff were still cracking sleep jokes. Specifically, we had heard that on an overseas trip that began very early in the morning, a staff member said laughingly to the press, "Can you imagine the Gipper up at this hour?" It was understandable for a new president to want to establish his own identity, but taking a crack at his predecessor seemed mean-spirited to us.

Somehow word got back to Mrs. Reagan. One of the offending staffers wrote an apology note to her (which was answered by the staff). I spoke about it with President Bush's press secretary, Marlin Fitzwater, who had been my boss during the last two years of the Reagan administration and was a friend. He was certain that the crack came from a place of genuine affection, but nonetheless, he promised to take the matter to the top. True to his word, Marlin walked into the Oval Office and told President Bush of our conversation. Bush immediately handwrote Ronald Reagan a note (which began "Dear Ron" and mentioned Marlin and me by name) assuring President Reagan that he had nothing to do with such comments and that he'd ordered his staff to say no such things anymore. He added that he had the greatest respect and affection for the president and Nancy. When the note reached Los Angeles, President Reagan read it and completely accepted his successor's apology. He put Bush's note in his desk drawer, and that was that. Silly political squabbling never bothered or even interested Ronald Reagan. To this day, I wish I had asked him if I could have that note.

9 to 5 centers on the lives of three career women: a widow played by the comedian Lily Tomlin, a recent divorcée played by Jane Fonda, and a southern secretary played by Parton. Jane Fonda's

role in the film, and others that we viewed in the 1980s, was problematic, especially for the military members who traveled with the president to Camp David. Memories were still fresh over her role as "Hanoi Jane" during the Vietnam War, where she was seen, at least by conservatives, as a traitor to the nation. As a result, some members of our small Camp David staff expressed reluctance to watch anything in which she appeared—but did so as a courtesy to the Reagans. Ms. Fonda was then married to the liberal activist and fierce Reagan critic Tom Hayden, but if that bothered the president, he did not mention it. That was politics. I think he just wanted to see a funny film.

In the movie, all three women cope with lecherous sexual advances and other forms of discrimination from their male boss, played by the talented character actor Dabney Coleman. When Coleman's character, Franklin Hart Jr., discovers that Tomlin and the other women had accidentally poisoned his coffee and then attempted to cover it up, he sees an opportunity for blackmail. An outlandish series of events then leads the women to hold Mr. Hart hostage at his home until they can prove his own criminal misdeeds.

It is a silly but fun plot. Looking back, it is amazing how dated it is. The film shows what was then a state-of-the-art Xerox machine that takes up a whole room. The women are still being called secretaries and use giant electric typewriters that they cover every night. There are rotary telephones and what would now seem like over-the-top creepy bosses, such as the one played by Coleman, who wear three-piece suits and mustaches, and refer to their female employees as "girls."

Still, there was plenty of laughter throughout, including from the Reagans. However, one scene left the president angry. Early in the movie, the three women strengthen their friendship by sharing revenge fantasies against their boss while smoking marijuana. This scene would have been "truly funny," Reagan said, "if the three gals had played getting drunk, but no, they had to get stoned on pot." The president found that to be a distasteful endorsement of pot smoking.*

The scene caught Mrs. Reagan's attention, too, so much so that she cited it during the launch of her most visible and important initiative during her husband's presidency: her antidrug campaign, which was dubbed in the press as "Just Say No." "Just Say No" was never envisioned as a slogan, but rather it was the answer to a question Mrs. Reagan gave to a child who wanted to know what to do when urged to use drugs. Mrs. Reagan's answer was, "Just Say No!," which became part of pop culture. "When I am out talking to kids, more and more often they ask me why the media glamorizes drugs, and I'm afraid I don't have an answer," she said in a speech on her initiative. "However, the fact must be faced that, all too often, the media—and here I'm talking about those in entertainment, advertising, and news—present the idea, perhaps unconsciously, that drugs are acceptable. Well, drugs are not acceptable. Drugs injure individuals and shatter families." Referring to the film, without naming it, she went on to describe "a scene in a popular movie" in which three female coworkers "get hilariously high on pot." This kind of drug use in entertainment, she said, would only support "the notion of drug acceptability" to American youth.†

The film presented other themes that resonated with the Reagans. Tomlin and Fonda were prominent feminists and supporters of the Equal Rights Amendment (ERA). First introduced in 1923,

---

*Ronald Reagan, *Reagan Diaries*, 4.
†Donnie Radcliffe, "First Lady Says Some Media Glamorize Drugs," *Washington Post* online, April 24, 1982, www.washingtonpost.com/archive/life style/1982/04/24/first-lady-says-some-media-glamorize-drugs/16f2c36f-3e70 -44da-a0ac-c967b43f1a97.

and re-introduced several times thereafter, the ERA is a proposed amendment to the United States Constitution designed to ensure equal rights for all citizens, regardless of gender. It failed to be ratified by the required number of states within the time frame allowed. Over time *9 to 5* itself became something of a cause célèbre for women during the Reagan era. It was especially played that way by feminists against a Republican administration that some prominent women's rights groups tended to oppose. In 1983, for instance, the National Organization for Women (NOW) declared that Reagan's reelection the following year would constitute "a crisis for American women."

When it came to women, Ronald Reagan had an interesting (some might say contradictory) pattern of behavior. He never viewed women as anything less than men. To him, there was no job a woman could not do. From what I saw, those who influenced him the most—and those for whom he had the greatest respect and relied upon most heavily—were women.

Prime Minister Margaret Thatcher of Britain was every bit as influential on the fortieth president as any man was. Maybe even more so, because she did not have designs on his job or an agenda to enhance her status in American politics. Nor, of course, did his wife, who was indisputably the most influential and relied-upon person in his life.

Ronald Reagan knew Nancy had the best instincts of anyone in his inner circle and that her *only* agenda was his success. He valued her counsel. Sometimes he sought it, and sometimes it was "volunteered." In different ways, his two daughters were also significant influences on him. Maureen, his oldest child, from his marriage to Jane Wyman, shared her father's interest in politics. She served as cochairman of the Republican National Committee, sought elective office, albeit unsuccessfully, and became a trusted advisor to the president. And while he and his first child with Nancy, daughter Patti, often did not agree on political issues, he listened to her with an open mind—even when she was staunchly opposed to something he might have said or done—and was proud that she was passionate about things.

Because Ronald Reagan never judged people on the basis of gender, he was bothered that historically in America women had been denied certain opportunities simply because of that. In that sense, some of the themes of 9 to 5 undoubtedly struck a chord with him.

During his 1980 campaign, he'd said that if elected president, he would seek out the most qualified woman and nominate her to the Supreme Court. He did not pretend otherwise. That's not to say he was willing to compromise standards so that a woman could serve on the high court. He just believed that among jurists "qualified" to serve on the nation's highest court were many women, and it was high time one was appointed. He kept his promise just six months into his first term by nominating Sandra Day O'Connor to replace retiring justice Potter Stewart.

Women occupied many staff positions at the White House in the Reagan administration. Ronald Reagan was the first president to have a female military aide. At his insistence, the White House Military Office identified a woman with the background and skills to be one of those who walk a few paces behind the president carrying a briefcase—the "football," with the codes for launching a nuclear strike. Her name was Vivien Crea.

Many times over the years, Reagan shared an anecdote he'd heard. In one such story, there was an accident. The victim was stretched out, and a man elbowed his way through the crowd that had gathered. Seeing a woman bending down over the victim, the man shoved her aside, saying, "I have had training in first aid. Let me take care of this." He then started doing all the techniques he'd learned. Finally, the woman tapped him on the shoulder and said, "When you get to that part about calling the doctor, I'm right here."

While I never knew him to judge people on the basis of gender, Ronald Reagan did not treat women the same way he treated men. While with men he could share and appreciate a salty story or joke, he would *never* do so in the presence of women.

Once, former President Reagan and I were in the car on the way to a portrait unveiling at a swanky club in New York City, and I thought I would be very clever with him. "Sir," I said, "have you looked at your remarks in the briefing sheet for this event? You know the club is hanging a very fine portrait of you, and it's very important to be well hung." Without missing a beat, he looked in the front of the car to make sure there were no women agents present, then at me, and with that Reagan twinkle in his eyes, said, "Well, Mark, I've never had any complaints!" Even the Secret Service agents in the front of the car broke up in laughter. He would never have said that had there been a woman in the car.

The one exception to that rule was his mother-in-law, the actress Edith Luckett Davis. "The president and Edith had a special relationship," Mrs. Reagan's stepbrother, Dr. Richard (Dick) Davis, told me. "When the Reagans would visit Loyal [Nancy's stepfather] and Edith in Phoenix, the president and Edith would retreat someplace and exchange Hollywood gossip—Edith knew everyone—and off-color jokes."* (Nancy's mother divorced her biological father and later married Loyal Davis, who adopted Nancy when she was fourteen.) He always insisted that women precede him when doors were held open. That became an issue years later when, as a former president, he was announced onstage for a speech. If any woman accompanied Reagan, he would insist that she walk in front of him.

---

*Author conversation with Dr. Richard Davis via phone, summer 2016.

A booming voice would intone, "Ladies and gentlemen, the fortieth president of the United States," the curtains would part, and out would walk a woman no one had ever seen before, smiling awkwardly. Eventually, when women were doing the advance work in such circumstances, they would slip away just before President Reagan was announced onstage.

Getting back to the movie, 9 *to* 5 ends with a sort of feminist wish fulfillment: each of the women proves her value; they move on to new adventures through their merit; and the evil Mr. Hart is transferred to South America, where he's never heard from again. The American Film Institute named the film one of the top movies of all time, and it is continually referred to as a Reagan-era symbol "for women seeking equal treatment in the workforce." Whether it should be or not.

2

OH, GOD! BOOK II

Starring:	George Burns, Suzanne Pleshette, David Birney
Directed by:	Gilbert Cates
Viewed by the Reagans:	March 7, 1981

The Film That Starred One of the Reagans' Dearest Hollywood Friends, Who Modeled How to Joke About Old Age

The first full weekend of March 1981 came on the heels of one of the biggest media events in years. On Friday, March 6, the iconic CBS News anchor Walter Cronkite, who for three decades had covered eight US presidents and delivered the news to Americans during times of war, crisis, and assassination, signed off the air for the last time. President Ronald Reagan was one of his final guests.

The Cronkite interview was a high point for any White House press aide. But for a midlevel press aide like me, I was finding that the White House wasn't always glamorous.

Shortly after settling into my cabin one of the early weekends at Camp David, I received a call from the camp commander.

"Mark, I wanted you to be aware of a problem we had with one of *your* press photographers."

I knew from his referring to the press photographer as mine, it would not be a great conversation.

I asked him what was up. One of the photographers had relieved himself on a rock, the commander reported.

"What are you talking about?" I asked.

"He pissed on a rock near the duck blind," he replied, indicating the area on the grounds of Camp David where wire service photographers could witness the arrival and departure of Marine One in case we crashed. The commander said this behavior could not be tolerated. I promised to admonish the offending photographer. I picked up the phone in my cabin and requested to be connected with the White House in Washington. I asked the operator there to track down the photographer.

The White House operators were the best in the world. They could find anyone anywhere anytime. But like many of the people who worked at the White House, they had a unique way of doing things, with a language all their own. Whenever I asked the White House operator to find a reporter, photographer, or anyone else, she would ask, "Sir, would you like to take the ring?" I had no idea what that meant. It turned out that "take the ring" means that when the White House operator places a call for a staff member, she dials the number and then allows the staff member to announce himself or herself, as opposed to having the White House operator announce the call. As time went on, I took advantage of the willingness of White House operators to announce calls to people I wanted to impress, mostly old friends from college.

Once the offending photographer was on the line, I told him that I had heard from the commander of Camp David that he had peed on a rock.

With no hesitation or tone of remorse, the man said, "Yes, that's true, I did, and here's why: I told the marine escort that I really had to go to the restroom, but he refused to take me to one. I had no choice. I'm sorry, but they sure weren't very nice about it."

It was not exactly the type of "media relations" I expected to handle when I joined the White House staff.

The Cronkite interview, of course, presented no such awkwardness and went off without a hitch. Cronkite himself was the consummate gentleman, and his sit-down with the president during his final week on the air showed that he was going to remain a model of journalistic professionalism until his last moment on America's screens. Sitting in the Oval Office, the president and the veteran CBS anchor talked about Cold War issues such as the administration's support for the nation of El Salvador against Marxist guerrillas, and what some viewed as its controversial policies and statements toward the Soviet Union.* President Reagan had caused a stir when he was asked about the USSR in a late-January press conference and said that "the only morality they recognize is what will further their cause, meaning they reserve unto themselves the right to commit any crime, to lie, to cheat, in order to attain that, and that is moral, not immoral, and we operate on a different set of standards."

Asked about that remark by Cronkite, the president pointed out that the Communist ideology did not profess belief in God. "Their statement about morality is that nothing is immoral if it furthers their cause, which means they can resort to lying or stealing or cheating or even murder if it furthers their cause, and that is not immoral."

---

*Ronald Reagan, "Excerpts from an Interview with Walter Cronkite of CBS News, March 3, 1981," American Presidency Project, www.presidency.ucsb .edu/ws/?pid=43497.

It was an honest statement by Reagan but did little to appease the hand-wringing diplomatic corps.

No doubt it was a coincidence, but the themes of morality and faith fit nicely with Mrs. Reagan's movie selection for that weekend: George Burns's *Oh, God! Book II*, which had the beloved cigar-chomping eighty-five-year-old comedian taking on the title role.

The film was a sequel to the surprise hit *Oh, God!* This was a Warner Bros. production, and the minute its iconic blue-and-gold shield hit the screen, I suspect the president smiled and made a mental note of it. I soon came to notice that whenever he talked about Warner Bros. there was a twinkle in the president's eye. After all, it was the film company that first signed Reagan to a picture deal when he was just a radio announcer from Des Moines with a crew cut and thick glasses. It was obvious that being at Warner Bros. had been a happy time for him. He would often talk about it being like a family and having a comforting feeling of belonging.

The president occasionally talked about that first film job, which he almost sabotaged before it began. In 1936, while on a trip to Hollywood to cover the Chicago Cubs, who at that time held their spring training in California, Reagan did a screen test for Warner Bros. Told that it might be several days before studio head Jack Warner could view his filmed audition, Reagan decided not to wait around. He headed back on the train to Iowa. Reagan later recounted, "I had done through ignorance the smartest thing it was possible to do. Hollywood just loves people who don't need Hollywood."*

The Warner Bros. logo on the George Burns film propelled the president to give it greater gravity. The first *Oh, God!* movie, which premiered in 1977, also starred the popular singer John Denver and was one of the year's most successful films. (Denver did not take

*Ronald Reagan with Hubler, *Where's the Rest of Me?*, 74.

part in the sequel.) The poster for *Book II* showed the bespectacled Burns, as God, riding a motorcycle, and the tagline demonstrated the film's gentle humor: "That's right. I made another movie. You know me, I can't stop creating."

In the movie, the Almighty appears before a twelve-year-old girl named Tracy Richards. Burns puts forth his usual funny remarks and inside Hollywood jokes that had made him a popular stand-up comic. At one point, Tracy tells him that "somehow I thought you'd look holier and more fancy . . . I mean, like, with a crown and a long beard and a flowing white robe." Burns responds, "You're thinking of Charlton Heston." (Heston had previously played Moses in *The Ten Commandments* [1956] and John the Baptist in *The Greatest Story Ever Told* [1965].) God then asks the little girl to think of a slogan that would encourage more people to believe in him again. "Sometimes," Burns tells her, "you just have to believe in things you can't see."

The cutesy premise did have some dark moments. After Tracy does what God asks, her parents think she is delusional. A psychiatrist who administers a series of tests and a brain scan declares Tracy a psychotic who should be institutionalized. God comes to her defense, one-liners at the ready.

As you might guess, this was not an eighties movie that proved popular over the years. Roger Ebert, the film critic, called it a "third-rate situation comedy" and noted that "the movie's screenplay was written by no fewer than five collaborators, but they were so bankrupt of ideas that some scenes have a quiet desperation to them."*

Yet the Reagans were destined to like the film (they later screened

---

*Roger Ebert, review of *Oh, God! Book II*, January 1, 1980, RogerEbert.com, www.rogerebert.com/reviews/oh-god-book-ii-1980.

the somewhat better 1984 follow-up, *Oh, God! You Devil*) for one reason only: it starred their longtime friend.

Born Nathan Birnbaum, George Burns was the ninth of twelve children of Jewish immigrants. Burns was just seven years old and working in a candy shop when he was "discovered" as a singer. From there he began a ninety-year entertainment career, first in vaudeville, and then radio, and then as an actor in films and television. His partner in this was his wife and costar, Gracie Allen. She and he were a duo, with Burns in the straight-man role, on radio, TV, the stage, and in film for more than forty years. (Gracie Allen retired in 1958, and died of heart disease in 1964. Her husband lived to be one hundred, dying in 1996.)

"He was really a simple man, not full of himself or of being in pictures," Mrs. Reagan once told me. "And he was always happy."

"Sounds like someone else we know," I replied.

"Yes, yes it does," she said, and smiled.

By the time Reagan sought the presidency, Burns, a once-fading actor, was undergoing a late, unexpected revival. Many viewed him this way after his acclaimed performance in the 1975 film *The Sunshine Boys*, in which he played an aging ex-vaudeville comedian, a role that earned him an Academy Award. As Burns put it, in a line Reagan might well have used himself, "If you stay in the business long enough and get to be old enough, you get to be new again."[*]

Reagan was very happy about his friend's renaissance. Burns was among the few Hollywood stars with whom he carried on a semi-regular correspondence throughout his presidency. One of his closest friends in the business, the leading man Robert Taylor, had died

---

[*]Jere Hester and Don Gentile, "George Burns Is Dead at 100," *New York Daily News*, March 10, 1996, www.nydailynews.com/entertainment/george-burns -legendary-entertainer-dead-100-1996-article-1.719988.

in 1969, long before the Reagans moved into the White House. The Reagans and the Taylors had been extremely close for many years, even serving as godparents to each other's children. Tessa Taylor, Robert's daughter and the Reagans' goddaughter, told me that even after many decades, she could still remember what it sounded like when "Uncle Ronnie" would rub her earlobe as a little girl—a "rustling" sound with an echo, "like when you put a big seashell up to your ear"—and the kindness of "Aunt Nancy," as Tessa's own mother struggled with dementia. When Robert Taylor died, Reagan, then governor of California, delivered the eulogy and even included it in a collection of speeches he published later.

With Robert Taylor gone, their remaining friendships from the old days, like that with George Burns, became even more precious. I didn't know at the time how much George had influenced Ronald Reagan's post-movie-star life. I found out years later that, for one, he was a source of work. Nancy recalled that when it became clear that her husband's film career was waning, by the early 1950s, he was able to "get by" by guest-starring on TV programs such as the popular *Burns and Allen Show*. (In the show's third season, Reagan played himself.)*

Burns also advised Reagan about performing onstage, which he started to do in the 1950s as a master of ceremonies. Rather than just relying on his movie star pedigree, Reagan figured he needed to have something funny to say when he went before audiences. "George Burns once expounded on truth being the basis of all good comedy," Reagan recalled, "and he was right."†

To the delight of his audience, Reagan decided to make fun of himself and his lack of experience as an MC onstage. Self-deprecation

---

*Nancy Reagan with Novak, *My Turn*, 125.
†Ronald Reagan with Hubler, *Where's the Rest of Me?*, 250.

became a hallmark of his humor. His successful appearances led executives at sponsor General Electric to ask him to host a weekly television program, *General Electric Theater*, in the mid-1950s. Like most movie stars at the time, Reagan was wary of appearing on TV, thinking it would diminish his career. But he didn't have many options. What intrigued him was the chance to go around the country and speak at GE plants about politics and events of the day—the "mashed potato circuit," Reagan called it, because at many political dinners, the menu included mashed potatoes, regardless of the poorly prepared entrée. Sometimes he called it the "rubber chicken circuit," because roast chicken was frequently served.*

As a politician, Reagan, echoing Burns, proved a master at delivering jokes and telling humorous stories based on truth. Such as their advancing ages. "When I was a kid," Burns once quipped, "the Dead Sea was only sick." He could also be a bit more risqué: "Sex at ninety is like trying to shoot pool with a rope."†

Reagan, too, poked fun at his age, which usually had the advantage of easing people's own concerns about electing to office the oldest president in American history. "I never drink coffee at lunch," the president said once. "I find it keeps me awake in the afternoon." He also loved to use his friend George as a foil: "the only man in America older than I am." At another point, Reagan once described Burns's morning ritual: "He'd get up, go down to the porch, and get the paper. Then he'd look through the obituaries. And if he's not in it, he goes back into the house to get a cup of coffee." Reagan claimed Burns had complained about the Stars and Stripes to Betsy Ross, saying, "Personally, I think the pattern's a little busy, but let's run it

---

*Ronald Reagan with Hubler, *Where's the Rest of Me?*, 250.
†"George Burns, Quotes," Goodreads, www.goodreads.com/author/quotes/43259.George_Burns.

up the flagpole and see if anyone salutes it."* But perhaps his best line ever about his age came in the 1984 debate against Walter Mondale. When asked if being the oldest president in history (he was seventy-three) might be a detriment, Reagan, with a totally serious expression, replied, "I will not make age an issue of this campaign. I am not going to exploit, for political purposes, my opponent's youth and inexperience." Even Mondale laughed out loud, and it defused the age issue for the remainder of the campaign.

Reagan's jokes and stories often had a purpose. They allowed him to make points in a subtle way or sometimes avoid making one at all. One time the president and the First Lady invited Mrs. Reagan's stepbrother, Dr. Dick Davis, and his family to an event at the White House. A Russian pianist performed in the East Room, after which there would be a "surprise." Following the performance, the guests made their way upstairs to the family quarters. The president and Dr. Davis waited at the elevator until everyone had gone up. As they did, Reagan made small talk with his brother-in-law by pointing out the presidential seal above the Blue Room and remarking how Harry Truman changed the eagle looking from spears of war to the olive branch of peace.

When they got to the family quarters, the president and Dr. Davis stood at the back, where the guests had gathered. In the front, an easel covered in velvet cloth had been set up. With great flourish, Dr. Davis remembers, his stepsister, Nancy Reagan, unveiled her official portrait. In it, she was dressed in a full-length bright-red gown, with a pearl necklace. President Reagan whispered to Dick, "Well, Dick, what do you think?" Clearly seeing the similarity to what a cardinal might wear, Dick replied, "Well, sir, it does look a

---

Dean Martin Celebrity Roast of George Burns, NBC-TV, May 17, 1978, www .youtube.com/watch?v=_Qt5BD6ANqk.

bit ecumenical." The president launched into a joke about a man who was drunk at a party, then approached a person, and asked for a dance, to which the person said, "No. First of all, you are slightly intoxicated, second, the orchestra is not playing, and third, I am a cardinal of the Roman Catholic Church." Dick interpreted that to mean that his brother-in-law shared his view about the painting and its resemblance to clerical garb.* But did he? Who knows?

For the most part, Reagan and Burns shared gentle humor—which is also what drew the Reagans to the *Oh, God!* films. What made the movies particularly appealing to some in the often cynical 1980s was their overt defense of spirituality and faith. But the films didn't preach to audiences, and they weren't divisive. Burns's God, as the film critic Roger Ebert put it, was "a sort of ancient Will Rogers on a Christmas card by Norman Rockwell."†

That was just fine with the president. Although Reagan owed his victory in the 1980 election, in part, to the participation of the so-called religious right—large groups of evangelical voters who supported issues such as allowing prayer in school and prohibiting abortion—he was not one to Bible thump. In the ten years I worked with him, I never heard the president talk about his religion or try to impose his faith on others. He respected people of all faiths—as well as atheists, of which his son, Ron, is one—and did not presume any superiority.

Reagan received criticism in some quarters for not attending church during his time in the White House. The charge was that he mined the votes of the faithful for the election but didn't share a deep, abiding belief in God. That was untrue. The president told me

*Author conversation with Dr. Richard Davis via phone, summer 2016.
†Roger Ebert, review of *Oh, God! Book II*, January 1, 1980, RogerEbert.com, www.rogerebert.com/reviews/oh-god-book-ii-1980.

on a number of occasions that one of his biggest regrets about life in the White House was his inability to attend regular Sunday worship services, as he had before his election.

He made the decision for a variety of reasons. The Secret Service told the Reagans that the churchgoers would have to pass through metal detectors if he were there, something he thought was very intrusive, and he worried that his presence at a church might make it a target and thereby pose a risk to other worshippers. The president also didn't want pastors to feel pressured to include political issues in their sermons. (However, on one occasion he did go—unannounced—to Easter services at a church near the ranch he owned in California, which the Secret Service thought was safe.)

Both Reagans missed their regular church attendance. When they returned to Los Angeles after the presidency, they attended worship services regularly again, starting with their first weekend, at which they received a standing ovation from the congregation at the Bel Air Presbyterian Church. "We probably won't be doing that every Sunday you come," said the pastor, the Reverend Donn Moomaw.

Religious though they were, like many in Hollywood, the Reagans could be a bit superstitious. I have always been a nervous flier, which Ronald Reagan didn't know until many years into our time together. Once, after his presidency, we were on a small, private jet on the way back to Los Angeles after a speech somewhere. It was around six o'clock, and it had been arranged that dinner would be served in flight, even though it was a short hop. President Reagan sat in a captain's chair at a table and faced the front of the airplane. I sat opposite him at the table and faced the rear. We took off from the runway but did not gain much altitude—or at least it seemed that way to me. The president looked at his watch, then peered into the cockpit, to which the door was open, then at his watch again and then back to the cockpit.

"They seem to be doing something with a flashing red light in there," he announced to us in the passenger section. I about passed out. "Yep, they're working on something up there that has their attention," he explained. He looked at his watch again. Then back to the cockpit. "Good Lord, they're still at it," he said with a tone of exasperation.

At that point, I had heard enough. "Will you please stop it?" I said to him in a firm, loud voice. He looked surprised and bewildered. One of the Secret Service agents immediately explained, "Mark is a bit of a nervous flier, Mr. President." He smiled, touched my hand, and said, "Me too. That's why I always wear these lucky cuff links," which he showed me. They were square gold replications of a calendar page of March 1952, with Tuesday the fourth being marked by a purple stone. That was the date of the Reagans' wedding anniversary. "So don't worry, we'll be fine. I was just getting concerned that if they did not fix whatever that light was, we would run out of time for dinner." Dinner? Seriously? *That's* what he was worried about?! I was genuinely annoyed.

From then on, every time we flew somewhere, he made a point of showing me that he had on his "lucky cuff links." Once, however, he forgot to wear them, and as soon as we boarded the plane and were seated, he turned toward me and said, "Say, I owe you an apology. I wore some other cuff links today. But don't worry, it's a nice day out."

"Couldn't you have told me after we safely returned home?" I asked. He laughed. We had a lot of turbulence on the flights that day.

My fear of flying was not restricted to small private planes. I could get nervous on the White House press charter and even on Air Force One. I used to imagine that if—God forbid—Air Force One went down while I was on board, the headline in my hometown paper, *The Cleveland Plain Dealer,* would read "Air Force One Crashes; Weinberg, All Others Killed."

Superstitious or not, Reagan believed in heaven and in the afterlife. Mrs. Reagan did, too, especially after the president's passing. As their daughter, Patti, recalled, during her eulogy for her mother in 2016: "In the weeks after he died, my mother thought she heard his footsteps coming down the hall late at night. She said he would appear to her long after midnight sitting on the edge of the bed. I don't know anything about the possible passages between this world and the next, but I do know her faith in these visits eased some of her loneliness. They made her feel that he was close by."*

Quite unexpectedly, the president once told me his views about death and the afterlife in 1990, when I informed him that I was thinking about moving on to another job. It had been more than ten years. The time seemed right. He told me he had "been wondering" when I would want to move on because he understood that "people at your age need to do other things.

"Besides," he told me, "I won't be here forever."

I knew what he meant, but decided not to play along.

"Well, I know that one day you may want to close this office and work from home."

He shook his head and said, "No, Mark, I mean *here.*"

"Oh, Mr. President, please don't say that," I protested. I admired and liked him so much, I didn't even want to think about him not being on Earth to share his point of view or tell a story.

---

*"Patti Davis Delivers Heart-Rending Eulogy at her Mother Nancy Reagan's Star-Studded Funeral," *New York Daily News* online, March 11, 2016, www .nydailynews.com/news/politics/patti-davis-moving-eulogy-mom-nancy-reagan -funeral-article-1.2561715.

"But, Mark," the president said firmly, "I am not afraid of that." He smiled. "In fact, I am looking forward to it."

I may have turned green. I asked him not to tell anyone else that.

But on that evening in March 1981, the little group at Camp David was enjoying a much more lighthearted vision of the afterlife, courtesy of Reagan's old friend George Burns. However, as Burns's God helped young Tracy navigate her family's problems, a very real family drama was unfolding halfway across the country, setting in motion a chain of events that would come to personally affect all of our lives.

That very evening, a troubled young man arrived in Denver to meet his mother and father. Upon the advice of a psychiatrist, the parents decided to give their son some money but refused to allow him to return home.* "You're on your own," his father told him. "Do whatever you want to do."† This, as it turned out, was "the greatest mistake of my life," the man's father would reflect later.‡ The young man's name was John W. Hinckley Jr.

---

*Stuart Taylor Jr., "Hinckley's Mother Tells Jury of Forcing Son from Home," *New York Times* online, May 7, 1982, www.nytimes.com/1982/05/07/us/hinckley-s-mother-tells-jury-of-forcing-son-from-home.html?pagewanted=all.

†Gregory Gordon, United Press International online, "Breaking into Tears, John W. Hinckley Jr.'s Father Told . . . ," May 12, 1982, www.upi.com/Archives/1982/05/12/Breaking-into-tears-John-W-Hinckley-Jrs-father-told/3366390024000.

‡Judi Hasson, United Press International online, "John W. Hinckley Jr. Rushed Out of the Courtroom . . . ," May 12, 1982, www.upi.com/Archives/1982/05/12/John-W-Hinckley-Jr-rushed-out-of-the-courtroom/8690390024000.

3

RAIDERS OF THE LOST ARK

---◆---

Starring: Harrison Ford, Karen Allen
Directed by: Steven Spielberg
Viewed by the Reagans: July 10, 1981

---◆---

The Film That Revealed the President's Greatest Hollywood Regret

The weekend capped off a busy few days for President Reagan, who had announced his first Supreme Court appointment: Sandra Day O'Connor of Arizona, the first woman ever nominated to the court. He was fending off complaints from the right for her suspected tolerant views on abortion.

Earlier in the day, the president met with Pierre Trudeau, the Canadian prime minister, over issues such as acid rain. Some claimed that pollutants in the air caused by industries were damaging the environment. Then it was off to Camp David.

As he arrived in the Catoctin Mountains that Friday, he noted in his diary that "almost upon arrival, the relaxing began. What a joy that beautiful spot is getting to be."*

President Reagan had come to love Camp David for many different reasons. It was not his nature to be cooped up inside all day. He much preferred the outdoors, such as the horseback and Jeep rides he took at the California ranch he'd bought in 1974 and renamed Rancho del Cielo—Spanish for "Ranch in the Sky." As long as I knew him, he enjoyed taking visitors to his office or home to look out the window.

"With Ronnie," Mrs. Reagan once told me, "it's always about the view." Camp David gave him the expansive view of America that brought him peace.

Camp David was also a safe place for Mrs. Reagan, and safety had become a much more urgent priority since the March 30 assassination attempt. The shooting, the first time a sitting president had been shot since John F. Kennedy, had shocked the entire world, including Reagan's friends and former colleagues in Hollywood. The 1981 Academy Awards ceremony, scheduled for that evening, was postponed. There is a certain irony to this given how Reagan felt about his treatment by the American Academy of Motion Picture Arts and Sciences. When the show was televised twenty-four hours after its original air time, host Johnny Carson told viewers that the old Hollywood adage "The show must go on" didn't seem all that appropriate.† "The president is in excellent condition, as of the last reports," Carson announced on the air. There was a long, sustained applause from the audience—a rare note of bipartisanship in liberal Hollywood.

---

*Ronald Reagan, *Reagan Diaries*, 55.
†"The Opening of the Academy Awards in 1981," *53rd Annual Academy Awards*, ABC-TV, March 31, 1981, www.youtube.com/watch?v=Rq4jfI-ItAU.

As we all arrived at Camp David, where weekends had been so important in the president's recovery over the past few months, the shooting was still fresh in my mind. How couldn't it be? It changed my life at the White House considerably, since my boss, Press Secretary Jim Brady, a wonderful man for whom I'd worked on the 1980 John Connally presidential campaign, was permanently incapacitated from the bullet that damaged his brain.

I was in my office, just off the White House Press Briefing Room in the West Wing, when the call came in that there had been a shooting outside the Washington Hilton hotel, where President Reagan had just delivered a speech. My colleague David Prosperi reported that the president was on his way to the hospital for what they thought at the time was a "precaution." But, he added in a very serious tone, "Jim has been hit" and was being taken to George Washington University Hospital. I couldn't believe it. I raced up the hallway to Jim's office, grabbed his secretary, Sally McElroy, who had already called the White House garage to have a car come get us, and we hustled downstairs to West Executive Avenue (the small street between the White House and the Old Executive Office Building) to await our car. Once inside, we asked the driver to take us to the Bradys' house in nearby Arlington, Virginia, where we picked up Jim's wife, Sarah, and drove to the hospital.

My mind raced. It was Jim who had brought me to the Reagan campaign. He was hired as a senior advisor (but not press secretary) to Reagan shortly after Connally withdrew from the race. A few months later, Jim recommended me to Reagan's press secretary, Lyn Nofziger, who gave me a job as a press assistant on the campaign "tour." Lyn assigned me to the traveling staff, and I had a permanent seat on the Reagan campaign plane. Jim and I got back together right after the election in the Washington office of the president-elect, where Brady was the chief spokesman. My main job was to write the press releases announcing President-elect Reagan's Cabinet and senior White House staff selections. I would take a draft to Jim, he would make some edits, call the president-elect on the phone, read it to him for approval, and then it would be issued. More than once Jim looked at me and said, "Kid, getting things approved will *never* be this easy again."

Between Election and Inauguration Days, one of the most popular Washington parlor games, especially among those of us in the Press Office, was to guess who President-elect Reagan would choose to be his White House Press Secretary. Jim wanted the job and was well qualified. But the president-elect took his time in making up his mind. It was not that he did not want Jim; it was just that he had higher-profile jobs to fill first, such as Cabinet secretaries, and he wanted to make the best possible decision. Almost every day, there would be a rumor about another "leading candidate" for the position of White House press secretary, complete with reports from California about people the president-elect was supposedly interviewing for the job.

At this early stage of the incoming Reagan administration, there were already false rumors popping up about Mrs. Reagan's supposed dominating style. One of the most outrageous had to do with my boss, Jim Brady. There were rumblings that he did not "look the part" to Mrs. Reagan—that she wanted someone more youthful and handsome. Absolute garbage. Neither the president nor Mrs. Reagan ever judged people on the basis of their looks. (I would point out that Reagan's longtime press secretary, Lyn Nofziger, was intentionally not a matinee idol—and proud of it. But he was a favorite of the Reagans who appreciated his loyalty and talents.) Nancy Reagan heard the silly rumor and was so amused by it that she once signed a picture to Jim calling him her "Y&H," meaning youngest and handsomest. It was a sign of true affection because she knew that a lot of

Reagan people fondly referred to her husband as the "O&W," meaning oldest and wisest.

When we arrived at the hospital, I accompanied Mrs. Brady to the emergency room entrance. Hospital staff took Sarah to her husband's side.

I waited in a hallway, still not knowing that the president had been shot. The initial news reports were that he'd escaped unharmed. Without warning, around a corner came an entourage of people surrounding a gurney on which the president was lying. Surrounding him were doctors, nurses, Secret Service agents, military personnel, policemen, and, of course, Mrs. Reagan, who looked panic stricken. They walked briskly toward the suite of operating rooms.

I found out later that the president had insisted on walking into the hospital but then collapsed once he made it through the entrance. Upon examination in the emergency room, he was found to have been shot in the chest, suffering a collapsed lung, and was prepped immediately for surgery.

I spent that night at the hospital going between where President Reagan was in recovery and where Jim was in recovery.

In its own way, the shooting was another example, in this case a cruel one, of Hollywood playing an outsized role in Ronald Reagan's life. The gunman, John Hinckley, was reportedly obsessed with the young actress Jodie Foster after watching the 1976 film *Taxi Driver* and, in his bizarre, damaged mind, thought an assassination attempt would get her attention and elevate his social status.*

During the course of Jim's long recovery, both of the Reagans agonized over what they could do to help the Bradys. They also were

---

*American Experience, PBS online, http://www.pbs.org/wgbh/americanexperience/features/biography/reagan-hinckley/.

heartbroken over the fact that a Secret Service agent and a Washington, DC, policeman were injured in the attempt. The president felt guilty that Jim was injured because of a gunman shooting at him. The Reagans helped set up a trust fund so that the Brady home could be renovated to accommodate Jim's use of a wheelchair. Jim's injuries were severe, deeply impacting his mental abilities. But, the president refused suggestions over the years that followed to remove Jim as his press secretary due to his impairment. A doctor had told President Reagan that keeping Jim in the position was crucial to his recovery. He explained that Jim needed a goal to strive for, even if he would never resume the job, and urged the president not to replace him. Astonished, Reagan said, "Why, I was never planning to make a change there at all." Despite Jim's inability to resume his role leading the White House press office, he retained the title of Press Secretary to the President until the last day of the Reagan administration.

Much has been written over the years about how the president was affected by the shooting. In his 2015 book *Killing Reagan: The Violent Assault That Changed a Presidency*, the TV news personality Bill O'Reilly alleged that Reagan became mentally incapacitated after the assassination attempt—a slow descent that led him to watch soap operas all day, among other ridiculous claims—and that Mrs. Reagan became his minder, deciding "whom Reagan will and will not see."* Many Reagan historians have disputed this completely. I was there every day and can state without question that the president did not change much from the shooting at all. He remained

---

*Annelise Anderson, "Killing the Reagan Legacy," review of *Killing Reagan: The Violent Assault That Changed a Presidency*, by Bill O'Reilly and Martin Dugard, *National Review*, September 26, 2015, www.nationalreview.com/article/424663/killing-reagan-legacy-annelise-anderson.

energetic, of good humor, optimistic, engaged, and involved in policy making. He was out of the hospital in less than two weeks and back in the Oval Office within a month. And I *never* knew him to watch soap operas.

It *is* true that Mrs. Reagan changed, but not as O'Reilly contends. She was much more concerned about her husband's safety and worried whenever he was away from her. That's why Camp David proved more and more of a sanctuary, especially in the summer months, when they could take walks, ride horses, and swim without fear. It made our movie nights even more of an escape for a woman who now lived practically every minute fearful on some level that another assailant was out there waiting for her husband.

The feature film that topped off our weekend was the action-adventure movie *Raiders of the Lost Ark*, the highest-grossing film of 1981 and one of the most successful Hollywood productions ever. *Raiders* introduced viewers to the dashing archaeologist Indiana Jones, played by Harrison Ford, fresh from his popular role as Han Solo in the *Star Wars* series. The brilliant yet crusty daredevil would go on to star in three sequels: *Temple of Doom*, *The Last Crusade*, and *The Kingdom of the Crystal Skull*. It was an overt return by Hollywood to the action-adventure series of the past.

Raiders of the Lost Ark, set in 1936, was the most successful and popular of the four. In the film, Indiana Jones travels to the South American jungle to find a golden statue. Returning to America, Dr. Jones learns about the existence of an artifact called the Ark of the Covenant, which, according to legend, was the receptacle for the Ten Commandments. Chancellor Adolf Hitler, methodically building up Nazi Germany's military in preparation to dominate Europe and ultimately the world, has dispatched agents to bring him the artifact. He believes that its supernatural powers will make

Germany invincible. Jones, also traveling in search of the ark, runs into an old flame from his past, Marion Ravenwood, played by the actress Karen Allen, whose life is in jeopardy after she associates with the wrong people.

I suspect what most impressed the Reagans about *Raiders of the Lost Ark* was that the film, with clear-cut heroes and villains, peppy theme song, and litany of engrossing seat-of-your-pants adventures, was as close to a golden oldie—as Reagan called the films from his era—as a movie in the 1980s could come, marking an overt return to action-adventure films such as *High Noon*.

"My dad was generally discomfited by more modern films with their profanity, sexuality, gritty realism, and less than sunny political perspective," his son Ron recalled. "He preferred the more predictable tropes of cinema from the thirties and forties, where heroes wore uncomplicated white hats and women were 'the gals.'"*

The president believed that the films of yesteryear were far better than anything Hollywood made in the modern era. He would press this view on anyone he could find, particularly the service members posted at Camp David who would occasionally join us for an evening's film.

"He would say this as if revealing an important truth," Ron told me, "seemingly unaware that young soldiers agreeing—or at least pretending to agree—with their commander in chief was a foregone conclusion."†

Raiders of the Lost Ark undoubtedly kindled many memories in the president, and a wistful yearning or two. The movie was in effect a modern update of the classic Western, with a daring hero battling villains such as the Nazis. The president spoke passionately about

*Author conversation with Ron Reagan via email, summer 2016.
†Ibid.

the Nazis and the evil they brought to the world. He told us that for a long time, he kept a film of American soldiers liberating Nazi concentration camps so that he could show actual evidence to anyone who questioned the reality of the Holocaust.

President Reagan also loved any movies with scenes of horseback riding, which was one of his favorite pastimes at Camp David. And he was outspoken in his love for those animals. Once, when we watched an action movie that featured scenes of horses falling during battle, Reagan stood up and offered a long monologue on how much was done behind the scenes to ensure the animals' safety.

Harrison Ford's portrayal was drawing comparisons to one of Reagan's most famous costars. One review called Ford "Hollywood's slickest swashbuckling hero since Errol Flynn."* The *New York Daily News*, too, noted that Ford evoked Flynn at the height of his movie stardom. Others suggested that director Steven Spielberg modeled Indiana Jones on the legendary actor. Spielberg himself explained that he saw Ford's character as "a remarkable combination" of Flynn and Humphrey Bogart.

As it happened, Reagan had a vivid memory of Flynn, who was his costar in the 1940 Western *Santa Fe Trail*. Flynn played the future Confederate general Jeb Stuart; Reagan played George Custer. The film's other big stars were Olivia de Havilland, as the love interest Kit Carson Holliday, and Raymond Massey, who portrayed the abolitionist John Brown. Reagan's interactions with Flynn, one of the biggest stars of the day, taught him many lessons about humility and the fleetingness of fame. The handsome actor, whom Reagan

---

*"People in the News: Reagan Always Dreamed of Swashbuckler-Type Roles," *Eugene (OR) Register-Guard*, January 28, 1985, 2A, www.news.google.com/news papers?nid=1310&dat=19850128&id=E9tVAAAAIBAJ&sjid=ieEDAAAAIBAJ &pg=6454,6178278&hl=en.

once called "a beautiful piece of machinery," was such an A-lister that just being associated with an Errol Flynn film boosted Reagan's stature. "Suddenly there were people on the lot greeting me who hadn't previously acknowledged my existence," he recalled.* His association with Flynn also helped him put his own image in perspective. Reagan (and everyone else on the set) was acutely conscious of Flynn's preening, which to the future president became a reminder to keep his own feet firmly on the ground.

Reagan remembered Flynn, then thirty years old, with thick, dark hair and a thin mustache, as a "strange" and "needlessly insecure" person who was nonetheless very "aware" of his stardom.† At one point, Flynn flew into a rage on the set when he hadn't been called for a shoot for four straight days. Reagan surmised that Flynn believed this meant his role in the film wasn't as big as he'd been told.‡

The president recounted a story about Flynn that he'd retold many times over the years. In one scene in *Santa Fe Trail*, Reagan was standing next to Flynn around a campfire. Flynn then walked over to the director, had a whispered conversation, and came back to the group. Within seconds, the director moved Reagan away from the star. It turned out that Flynn had wanted to ensure he was the tallest individual on film. He didn't want Reagan, who was roughly the same height, in his camera shot.

Reagan purposely moved dirt with his feet and built up a little mound, so that when the camera went to a wide shot, he stood taller than Errol Flynn. He wasn't too sure that Flynn enjoyed what he did, Reagan recalled, but the other actors on the set sure did. The

---

*Ronald Reagan with Hubler, *Where's the Rest of Me?*, 95.
†Ibid., 96.
‡Ibid.

president had an impish side to his character on occasion, and he especially liked to deploy it against people who displayed a grandiose sense of themselves.

The truth is, as Reagan would later admit, he had envied the type of role that Flynn and, later, Harrison Ford, made famous. He longed to play the same type of character in various movies. But, as he noted, he was usually typecast in "the light-drawing-room comedy-type pictures."* He had a running battle with Warner Bros. for years on that score.†

Ronald Reagan always preferred playing heroes. During his entire acting career, spanning dozens of roles, he recalled playing a bad guy only twice. The first time was in high school, where Reagan played the villain in George Bernard Shaw's play *Captain Applejack.* The second, and much better known, instance was in the violent 1964 film *The Killers,* his last movie. Reagan played a gangster and in one scene even slapped around the actress Angie Dickinson. His character, a Mob boss, was named Jack Browning. John Cassavetes and Lee Marvin were also in the film, which was based on an Ernest Hemingway short story.

This was the only villainous role in his professional film career, one reviewer noted, "and he plays it shockingly well."‡

"I'm afraid they took advantage of an actor's ego," Reagan recalled about when he agreed to do the film. They told him, "But

*"People in the News: Reagan Always Dreamed of Swashbuckler-Type Roles," *Eugene (OR) Register-Guard,* January 28, 1985, 2A, www.news.google.com/news papers?nid=1310&dat=19850128&id=E9tVAAAAIBAJ&sjid=ieEDAAAAIBAJ &pg=6454,6178278&hl=en.
†Ibid.
‡Gary Susman, "Ronald Reagan's Five Most Memorable Movies," *Entertainment Weekly* online, last modified June 7, 2004, http://ew.com/article/2004/06/07 /ronald-reagans-five-most-memorable-movies.

you've never played a villain before," which made it seem like an interesting challenge. But Reagan knew it was not a role for him, and his audience did, too. "A lot of people kept waiting for me to turn out to be a good guy in the end and dispatch the villains in the last reel," he reflected later, "because that's the way they had always seen me before."

The lesson for the future president was simple: "Heroes are more fun." He quoted a man named Eddie Foy, a well-known actor and vaudevillian, who once said, "Sing pretty, act pretty, pretty things they enjoy."* These were lessons that informed Reagan's views as "the Great Communicator." As he remarked to us many times in the White House, people like to be uplifted, and they responded to leaders who appealed to their hopes and aspirations. As such, the president insisted on using language that was affirmational. America was "the shining city on a hill." In one speech I wrote for him, I used the phrase "never forget," and he changed it to "always remember." Not wanting to hurt my feelings, he made a point of telling me that he liked the speech a lot but always wanted to be positive rather than negative.

Indiana Jones, of course, was a hero, which was why the Reagans, like most of America, responded so positively to him. At first glance, Dr. Jones was cynical, distant, maybe even a little self-interested. But he could be counted on to defend the red, white, and blue, as well as the woman he loved. That was a role Reagan liked but did not get to play very often in Hollywood.

On a handful of occasions, however, Reagan did get his wish. Perhaps the most interesting was his role as Jeff Williams in the 1951 film *Hong Kong*. The plot, described on the film website IMDb, sounds eerily like an Indiana Jones film: "The theft of a jeweled

---

*Ronald Reagan with Hubler, *Where's the Rest of Me?*, 38.

treasure is within an adventurer's grasp; he is restrained by his love for a good woman."

Many years later, various commentators tried to equate the Indiana Jones films with the Reagan era. The film historian Douglas Brode noted that Ford played "a rugged individualist [who] could face off against evil empires and defeat them"—not unlike President Reagan himself. On the other side of the world, the Australian academic Katherine Biber argued that Indy "represented the political and cultural sentiments of the Reagan era." I'm certain the president didn't see it in those terms. I think he just found it a fun movie.

The *Indiana Jones* films would, of course, cement Harrison Ford in the pantheon of top action stars. All of us who watched *Raiders of the Lost Ark* enjoyed a scene that became an iconic fan favorite, in which Indiana Jones is chased through a variety of obstacles, several of which almost cost him his life. After getting through that, he is confronted by an intimidating swordsman who proceeds to do a long, impressive routine with a scimitar and challenges Ford to a fight. Initially, Indiana Jones plans to battle him with his whip. Then, with a look of exhaustion, he calmly, and comically, pulls out his revolver and shoots the guy dead. The scene, apparently, was improvised. On set, Harrison Ford had suffered through dysentery and didn't have the stamina for a long, drawn-out fight sequence, such as the one that had been planned, so he suggested this abrupt ending instead.*

As an actor, Reagan had used a gun before, but that was not the only time he used one. In fact, he owned a gun as a private citizen.

---

*"Harrison Ford Reveals the Truth About That Famous 'Raiders of the Lost Ark' Scene," news.com.au, accessed September 15, 2017, www.news.com.au/enter tainment/movies/harrison-ford-reveals-the-truth-about-that-famous-raiders-of -the-lost-ark-scene/news-story/a43b77b997ae3d2cbe9ac6c109f2ea59.

Once, when he lived in Iowa, he'd used a .45-caliber pistol to foil a robbery at a boardinghouse. He was renting a room there and heard a commotion outside his second-story window. Reagan grabbed his gun and called out to the robber from the darkness, "Drop it! I've got a .45 up here and I'm going to blow your head off."

Even then, Reagan was a good actor and a great communicator. What the robber didn't know was that the gun didn't have any bullets.*

---

*"People in the News: Reagan Always Dreamed of Swashbuckler-Type Roles," *Eugene (OR) Register-Guard*, January 28, 1985, 2A, www.news.google.com/news papers?nid=1310&dat=19850128&id=E9tVAAAAIBAJ&sjid=ieEDAAAAIBAJ &pg=6454,6178278&hl=en.

4

ON GOLDEN POND

Starring: Henry Fonda, Katharine Hepburn,
Jane Fonda
Directed by: Mark Rydell
Viewed by the Reagans: September 26, 1981

The Film That Hit Close to Home

An aging couple so devoted to each other that there often seemed to be little room for anyone else. A rebellious daughter with a notoriously difficult relationship with her father. This was the essence of the Academy Award–winning *On Golden Pond*. At the time, some people were saying the same about the Reagan family.

As the Reagans entered their first autumn in the White House, their daughter, Patti Davis, was making headlines. Smart, headstrong, and outspoken, Patti, then twenty-eight, was a proud liberal who saw little need to hide her political views simply because her father was president of the United States. For most of her life, and by her own admission, she'd been dramatic and willful. When she was fourteen, Patti made plans to run off with a dishwasher working at the private school she attended. She dropped out of college and lived with the guitarist Bernie Leadon of the Eagles.* "I was pretty feisty," she recalled in a 1981 interview. "My idea of beauty was total beatnik: black turtleneck and black skirt, black around the eyes and white lipstick. I thought I looked ravishing." Her casual attitude toward drug use—"I don't think pot is such a terrible drug," she once said—deviated sharply from her parents' views.[†]

Shortly after the president's election, Patti, an aspiring actress, signed a six-figure contract with NBC.[‡] In May 1981 she filmed one of her first roles, as the girlfriend of a male stripper in a TV movie entitled *For Ladies Only*. Asked about whether or not such a role might embarrass her parents, Patti told reporters that she was a professional actress and didn't pick roles based on the impact they might have on her famous parents.[§] Patti admitted that she was taking advantage of the opportunities presented to her as First Daughter. "It's the biggest break I've ever had," she told *People* magazine. "People are interested in me—maybe not for the right reasons, but they're interested. There are a lot of starving actors and actresses, some of them real talented, whom you'll never hear of because they didn't get the right break. But any of these people, if they had the break, would

*Ronald Reagan, *Reagan: A Life in Letters*, eds. Kiron K. Skinner, Annelise Anderson, and Martin Anderson (New York: Free Press, 2003), 44.

†David Sheff, "A Reagan by Any Other Name, Star-Elect Patti Davis Hopes for Her Own Landslide," *People* online, last modified January 12, 1981, http://people.com/archive/a-reagan-by-any-other-name-star-elect-patti-davis-hopes-for-her-own-landslide-vol-15-no-1.

‡Albin Krebs and Robert McG. Thomas, "Notes on People: The President's Daughter Puts In a Long Day," *New York Times* online, May 20, 1981, www.nytimes.com/1981/05/20/nyregion/notes-on-people-the-president-s-daughter-puts-in-a-long-day.html.

§Ibid.

take advantage of it."* (Her agent, Norman Brokaw of the powerful William Morris talent agency, had represented Marilyn Monroe as well as Patti's mother when Nancy was under contract to MGM.)†

A month later, Reagan wrote a letter to his friend William F. Buckley Jr., editor of the conservative *National Review*, in which he confided his troubles with his outspoken daughter.‡ He thanked Buckley for providing information rebutting the assertions of the antinuclear crowd, and shared that information with his daughter "during a good, long discussion" at the Reagan ranch in California.§ The president had even enlisted his science advisor, Jim Keyworth, to talk to Patti about her nuclear concerns.¶

But it wasn't Patti's advocacy that worried the president. He wrote Buckley: "I think my biggest problem is, believe it or not, her friendship and admiration for Jane Fonda and Tom Hayden." Ms. Fonda had married Hayden, a longtime liberal activist, in 1973. (They divorced in 1990.)

Like other members of the administration, the president was uncomfortable with Jane Fonda's controversial activities during the Vietnam War. She was a regular participant in demonstrations against the war, but her activism sometimes crossed the boundaries of normal protest. In 1973 she attacked returning American prisoners of war as "liars and hypocrites" when they recounted being tortured by their captors.

The previous year, she made a high-profile visit to Hanoi. At one point, she posed for a photo while sitting in a Vietcong antiaircraft

*Sheff, "Star-Elect Patti Davis."
†Ibid.
‡Ronald Reagan to William F. Buckley Jr., July 15, 1981, in Ronald Reagan, *Reagan: A Life in Letters*, p. 63.
§Ibid.
¶Ibid.

vehicle, which outraged many and was widely viewed as a propaganda victory for Communist North Vietnam. As a father—not just as a politician—Reagan was concerned about such a person holding influence over his daughter. "I told her bluntly I could not share those feelings because both [Fonda and Hayden], in my mind, were traitors to their country," he wrote Buckley. "I didn't really try to argue the point with her because I know there's nothing harder than driving a wedge between friends—and she believes they are friends."*
His clear intimation was that Ms. Fonda was taking advantage of Patti to further her own political agenda.

This could have made the viewing of *On Golden Pond*, which starred Ms. Fonda and two acting legends—her father, Henry Fonda, and Katharine Hepburn—much more interesting. I knew little about the inner workings of the Reagan family at the time. When I saw the film, I paid attention to the story but didn't have a clue about the other, more personal subtexts the film offered the president and First Lady. Of these, there were many.

As it happened, Henry Fonda and Katharine Hepburn were longtime friends of the Reagans. The president had known Fonda from Reagan's days as head of the Screen Actors Guild (SAG), the union for film actors (Reagan was president of SAG from 1947 to 1952 and again in 1959–1960), though they tended to be on opposite sides of debates. Reagan was a Democrat then. He was a very effective union president who fought hard to win concessions for actors regarding payment and residuals, and even organized a famous 1960 actors strike, the first such action in the history of Hollywood.

Mrs. Reagan was close to Hepburn for many years. The blunt and vivid Hepburn had been a friend of Nancy's mother, Edith Luckett Davis, an accomplished Broadway actress, and had occasionally

---

*Reagan to Buckley Jr., *A Life in Letters*, 63.

visited the Davis home. Another frequent visitor was Spencer Tracy, Ms. Hepburn's paramour on and off the screen, whom Nancy remembered as "the most charming man I have ever known."[*] When Nancy's stepbrother, Dick Davis, came home from college to stay with his parents during those years, he woke up one morning to find Ms. Hepburn having coffee in the kitchen. "She was in Chicago because Spencer Tracy, who had a drinking problem, was hospitalized by my dad," Dick recalled. "She was so dynamic, extremely bright, with such a good sense of humor."[†]

When Nancy moved to California, Hepburn had even loaned Nancy the use of her car, a late-1930s "wooden convertible," as Dick called it, with a braking system of questionable reliability.[‡] The Davises knew about and disapproved of Hepburn's long-running secret affair with the married Tracy, which would span twenty-six years, up until his death in 1967. Nancy became friends with Tracy's wife and once allowed their deaf and disabled son to stay on her couch when he visited New York. "He enjoyed musicals," Mrs. Reagan remembered. "Somehow he sensed the music through the vibrations he felt."[§]

Despite her misgivings about Tracy's and Hepburn's scandalous romance, young Nancy came to admire Hepburn as an actress. When Nancy first considered an acting career, she went to Hepburn for advice.[¶] Ms. Hepburn sent her a long, candid letter warning her that she knew only the glamorous parts of the job. It was a hard profession, Hepburn noted. Most would-be actresses ended

[*]Nancy Reagan with Novak, *My Turn*, 79.
[†]Author conversation with Dr. Richard Davis via phone, summer 2016.
[‡]Ibid.
[§]Bob Colacello, *Ronnie & Nancy, Their Path to the White House—1911 to 1980* (New York: Warner Books, 2004), 186.
[¶]Nancy Reagan with Novak, *My Turn*, 78.

up as waitresses and receptionists, not the stars her mother had befriended.*

Undaunted, Nancy went to New York to pursue her ambitions and occasionally visited Hepburn at her Eighty-Ninth Street apartment for dinner. Ms. Hepburn hated to go out, Nancy remembered. Dining in public made her nervous and sick to her stomach. The two women remained close for years until the relationship went sour— inexplicably, at least, to Mrs. Reagan. Hepburn had decided to cut off ties once she learned that Nancy was a Republican.†

In the years that followed, Mrs. Reagan heard from her former friend only periodically, although Hepburn was not above using her prior relationship with the Reagans to lobby for a cause. On Christmas Eve 1981, for example, the star fired off a terse telegram to the First Couple demanding that they intervene in plans to destroy—or "ruthlessly toss away" as she put it—the Morosco, a landmark theater on Broadway.

On Golden Pond was the second-highest-grossing film of the year (after *Raiders of the Lost Ark*), bringing in more than $100 million.‡ The film centered on the dysfunctional relationships between Henry Fonda's Norman Thayer Jr., a retired University of Pennsylvania professor, his wife, Ethel (Hepburn), and their estranged daughter, Chelsea (played by Jane Fonda).

The plot centers on the aging Norman and Ethel spending the summer at their family lakeside cabin. The summer marks an important milestone for Norman—his eightieth birthday—which only seems to make him more glum and cantankerous. For the occasion,

---

*Nancy Reagan with Novak, *My Turn*, 79.
†Ibid.
‡"On Golden Pond," Jane Fonda Official Web Site and Community, accessed September 16, 2017, www.janefonda.com/on-golden-pond.

their daughter, Chelsea, comes to visit for the first time in years. Her fiancé, Bill, a dentist played by Dabney Coleman, and his young son, Bill Jr., accompany her. Over the weeks that follow, Norman and Billy bond over fishing. When Chelsea returns, she is angry and jealous that the teenager has formed an attachment with her father that she never could, leading to a pivotal and long-overdue confrontation between father and daughter.

Jane Fonda knew this role would be her last chance to appear on-screen with her father, who was in declining health. A passion project for her, she purchased the rights to the play on which the movie was based. Ms. Fonda was taken so much with the idea of the film because the parts that she and Henry Fonda would play— the conservative, private father and the headstrong daughter clamoring for his love and attention—echoed their real-life relationship.[*] "Imagine a woman with a difficult relationship with her father finds a play in which the father and daughter so paralleled real life," she said once about the film. "And I was able to buy the rights!"[†]

On Golden Pond would, in fact, turn out to be Henry Fonda's last film and the last major one for Hepburn, who was suffering from a pronounced neurological condition that caused involuntary tremors. True-to-life aging was a major theme of the film. Fonda's character, Norman Thayer Jr., suffered from heart palpitations and memory loss, and viewed the passage of time with fear and bitterness.

The differences between the characters in the film and the

---

[*]Eleanor Quin, "On Golden Pond," Turner Classic Movies online, accessed September 16, 2017, www.tcm.com/this-month/article/161287%7C0/On-Golden-Pond.html.

[†]Stacy Wilson Hunt, "Jane Fonda Opens Up About Her Father, Her Return to Acting, and the Lesson She Learned from Warren Beatty," *Hollywood Reporter* online, last modified December 7, 2011, www.hollywoodreporter.com/news/jane-fonda-warren-beatty-women-entertainment-268529.

Reagans themselves were stark. Reagan was never preoccupied with his age, except to make light of it. He joked frequently about taking naps during Cabinet meetings, even though the president did not nap.

That wasn't always the case with his staff, however. One weekend at Camp David, we saw the 1951 musical *Show Boat*, and with all due respect to Kathryn Grayson, Ava Gardner, and Howard Keel, it was the most boring movie ever shown at Camp David. By far. But the Reagans loved it. At least, I *think* so. After a few minutes, I dozed off and woke up only when the lights came back on. Naturally I did not say anything during the post-movie comment period, and was almost out the door when the president tapped me on the shoulder and said with a wink and a big smile, "Guess you were pretending it was a Cabinet meeting."

Like most of his supporters, I didn't really think of Ronald Reagan as "old." But looking back years later at the experience of watching *On Golden Pond* with him, with its poignant story of aging, I recalled one of the few times that Reagan's advanced age did hit me.

As a former president, Ronald Reagan traveled to Dallas for an event requiring an overnight stay in a hotel. Every time we would go to Dallas, whether during the White House years or after, Reagan's Secret Service detail seemed nervous. I thought maybe I was just imagining it, but I finally asked a senior agent if what I sensed was correct. He admitted it was, and I asked why. He explained that there were some mentally ill people "out there" who would be thrilled to pull off a copycat-type killing of a president, at least in terms of locale, so the agents were always especially happy to be leaving Dallas without an incident.

On this particular trip, Fred Ryan, the chief of staff, had to stay back in Los Angeles, and President Reagan's longtime executive secretary, Kathy Osborne, came with us. We did whatever was scheduled in the evening and escorted the president to his suite. Kathy told the president she would pick him up at his suite at a certain time the next morning. I would meet them in the holding room near the speech site.

The next morning, just as I was done shaving and showering, the phone rang. It was Kathy, who sounded distressed. She had gone to the president's suite at the appointed hour, knocked on the door—hard, several times—but received no reply. She asked the Secret Service agent stationed outside if he'd heard any rustling, and he had not. Kathy was worried and thought it would be better for a male to enter the suite under these circumstances, just in case. I dressed, raced to the suite, and asked the agent to open the door. I entered a pitch-black sitting room and stumbled my way into the bedroom. I could make out a shape in the bed but could not tell if he was breathing. So I approached the foot of the bed and said in a loud voice, "Mr. President. Mr. President." Nothing. I did it again, even louder. Nothing. I then yelled, "Ron! Ronnie!" several times. No response.

Finally, I summoned the courage and shook the foot of the bed. The president moved, sat up groggily, and said, "Yes?"

"It's Mark. Sorry to wake you, sir, but it's time to get started."

He put on his glasses, looked at the clock on the nightstand, and said, "Oh, good Lord. I'm sorry. I took out my ears [meaning his hearing aids] last night and guess I did not hear the alarm." I told him not to worry about it and that Kathy and I would be right outside whenever he was ready.

Coping with aging was not the only theme of *On Golden Pond*. A major theme was about healing relationships, especially between parents and their children, something the Reagans understood well.

The film contained one poignant, pivotal scene. After several instances in which Norman and Chelsea fail to connect with each other and hurt each other's feelings, the daughter makes one last tearful effort to reach her father.

"Norman, I want to talk to you."

"What seems to be the problem?"

"It occurred to me that we should have the relationship that a father and daughter are supposed to have."

"What kind of relationship is that?"

"It just seems that you and I have been mad at each other for so long."

"I didn't know we were mad. I just thought we didn't like each other."

In the scene, Chelsea puts her hand on her father's arm. It may be the first time she's touched him in years. "I just want to be your friend," she says through tears.

Henry and Jane Fonda had rehearsed this scene many times, but she'd never touched him during those practice runs. Ms. Fonda recalled later she wanted to save that moment until it could be captured on film, so she could get her father's honest reaction. When Jane Fonda as Chelsea touched her father, the tears that welled up in his eyes came from both Norman Thayer Jr. and Henry Fonda himself. "The emotions hit him, tears came to his eyes, then anger again as he tensed up and looked away," Jane recalled.*

The message of that scene was that despite all the differences between father and daughter, there was still great love there. I can't be certain what was going through the Reagans' minds when we watched that scene at Camp David, but I have to imagine they

---

*Quin, "On Golden Pond."

couldn't help but think of their own daughter. The same forces of love and tension played on that relationship as well.

That Ronald and Nancy Reagan deeply loved their daughter is without question.

Some thought Ronald Reagan was a cold or distant parent. The infrequency of Patti's visits to the White House was cited as evidence. I always felt that Ronald Reagan was a loving father and quite capable of expressing it. In 1954, when she was twenty-one months old, Ronald Reagan wrote a letter to his infant daughter while he was off filming *Cattle Queen of Montana*. He apologized for being away from her. "You see we always want you to be surrounded with love so you'll know how important it is," he wrote.*

When Patti was fifteen, Reagan was again the attentive father, admonishing his daughter for smoking at her Arizona boarding school, a violation of the rules. "There are two issues here, dear Patti," he wrote. "One is the fact that for two years you broke not only school rules but family rules, and to do this, you had to resort to tricks and deception." He added, "We are concerned that you can establish a pattern of living wherein you accept dishonesty as a fact of life."

But he made a point of reaching out in ways that he hoped would be helpful. Knowing of her interest in screenwriting, in April 1968, when Patti was sixteen years old, Governor Reagan sent her a page from the script for the recent hit *Bonnie and Clyde* so that he could discuss with her the art of screenwriting. Patti is a gifted writer, a skill I suspect she inherited from her father.

And there is no doubt Patti deeply loved her father. In 1981, when he was shot, Patti flew to Washington to be at her parents' side. She held her father's arm as he left the hospital.

---

*Ronald Reagan to Patti Reagan, July 12, 1954, in Ronald Reagan, *Reagan: A Life in Letters*, 52.

Like Jane Fonda, Patti was also working out her complicated relationship with her father on the public airwaves. Just around the
time that we watched *On Golden Pond* that fall, Patti was interviewed on a California local radio program hosted by, of all people,
Tom Hayden and Jane Fonda. Both women avoided discussing politics, but instead commented on being the "child of a national monument." Noting that as the daughter of Henry Fonda, she had been
drawn into "some alienations and rebellions," Ms. Fonda asked Patti
if anything like that had happened to her.

"Yes," said Patti, "and I think there's a tendency to go overboard
with that because you encounter a situation of your identity being
threatened; your individuality being threatened just by people per-
ceiving you as someone's daughter. And so the tendency is to go
'But I'm me.'" She admitted that she could be "a little headstrong"
and that she had occasionally been difficult to deal with as an ado-
lescent. But she added, "I think now we've worked through a lot of
that."* As it turned out, that was wishful thinking. In the years that
followed, Patti would write a roman a clef that painted her father as
cold and removed and her mother as a controlling, hectoring drug
addict.

While Patti's estrangement with her parents would continue on
and off throughout her father's presidency and afterward, her friend
Jane Fonda appeared to have found some peace from her work on
On Golden Pond. The film brought Henry Fonda his only Oscar,
which many viewed as long overdue. Since he was too ill to attend
the ceremony, Jane Fonda accepted the award on his behalf for a

---

*Albin Krebs and Robert McG. Thomas, "Notes on People: Two Actresses Dis-
cuss Life with Fathers,"*New York Times* online, August 28, 1981, www.nytimes
.com/1981/08/28/nyregion/notes-on-people-two-actresses-discuss-life-with
-fathers.html.

film she had made happen. It was "the happiest moment of my life," she recalled.

"My father is so happy," she said in her acceptance speech. "He feels so fortunate to have been able to play the role of Norman Thayer, a character that he loves a lot and understands very well." She headed right to his bedside to hand him the Oscar.

Henry Fonda died of heart disease five months later at age seventy-seven. As befit his private nature, the actor requested that no funeral be held, and he was promptly cremated. In a statement, President Reagan remembered him as "a true professional dedicated to excellence in his craft. He graced the screen with a sincerity and accuracy which made him a legend."

Jane Fonda had finally reached an understanding with her father. "I was grateful for having had *On Golden Pond* with him and that I'd managed to tell him I loved him before it was too late," she recalled. "I could feel myself making peace with the fact that though he hadn't given me all I needed from him, he'd given me plenty."* Hopefully Patti has come to the same conclusions.

The last time I saw Patti was at her mother's 2016 funeral. She spoke movingly about her parents and her feelings of separation from them, which she put in perspective:

"My parents were two halves of a circle, closed tight around a world in which their love for each other was the only sustenance they needed," she said. "While they might venture out and include others in their orbit, no one truly crossed the boundary into the space they held as theirs."†

---

*Quin, "On Golden Pond."
†"Patti Davis Delivers Heartrending Eulogy at Her Mother Nancy Reagan's Star-Studded Funeral," *New York Daily News* online, March 11, 2016, www .nydailynews.com/news/politics/patti-davis-moving-eulogy-mom-nancy-reagan -funeral-article-1.2561715.

Of her mother, she said: "I tried her patience, and she intimidated me. We were never mild with one another. Whether we were distant and angry or bonded and close, our emotions burned up the color chart. Nothing was ever gray, but there were moments in our history when all that was going on between us was love. I choose to remember those moments."* Of which, I'm sure there were many.

*"Patti Davis Delivers Heartrending Eulogy."

5

CHARIOTS OF FIRE

———◆———

Starring: Ben Cross, Ian Charleson, Sir John
Gielgud
Directed by: Hugh Hudson
Viewed by the Reagans: October 3, 1981

———◆———

The Film That Inspired a President

With the cool autumn winds threatening to close in on Camp David, soon to be followed by ice and snow that could blanket the riding trails, the president decided to take his horse on a new adventure one October weekend. For the last ride of his first year in office, he would take a different route than usual. He rode out of the back gate of the secured Camp David compound into the surrounding Catoctin National Forest. He followed an old road that led to the remnants of a summer hotel, the Valley View Manor, with a notable history. Once owned by the attractive socialite Bessie Darling, it was the scene of her murder on Halloween night 1933 at the hands of a jealous lover. A decade later, during the Second World War, it became a lodging for visiting dignitaries before closing down and falling into disrepair.

The stories fascinated Reagan; he wanted to see the place for himself. "It's a tumbled ruin now," he recorded.* Parts of a staircase and an old stone wall were among the fragments still standing. A cold wind blew among the trees, and after spending some time at the grim setting, the president turned his horse homeward, toward the comforts of Aspen and movie night.

This weekend's offering, *Chariots of Fire,* would be the second film the Reagans watched that week. Earlier, at the White House, they had screened *The French Lieutenant's Woman,* starring Jeremy Irons and Meryl Streep. This movie was something of a racy offering for them, involving affairs, adultery, and story lines from two different time periods. The president found it a "beautiful and unusual film."†

That was faint praise compared with his thoughts on *Chariots of Fire,* which had been released in the United States only about a week before. The film, which went on to win the Oscar for best picture, would quickly become one of President Reagan's favorites. It tells the story of athletes competing as runners for Great Britain in the 1924 Summer Olympics, centering on two of the greatest in British history: Eric Liddell (played by Ian Charleson) and Harold Abrahams (Ben Cross). Both men were driven not just by national pride and competitive spirit but also by their faith.

Liddell was a devout Christian, a child of missionaries who later became a missionary himself, and treated his natural athletic talent as a gift from God. He earned his victories not for his own glory but for God's. He even refused to race on Sunday, leading to a dramatic situation in the film.

---

*Ronald Reagan, *Reagan Diaries,* 71.
†Ibid.

Harold Abrahams, however, was Jewish, and as such, experienced prejudice despite his admission to the elite ranks of students at Cambridge University. In an early scene, Abrahams must confront a bigoted college student but soon settles into Cambridge life. He pushes himself as a runner to triumph over those who look down on him—to "run them off their feet."

The film follows the parallel stories of Liddell and Abrahams, and their competition against each other in various races over the years. Both qualify to represent Britain in the 1924 Olympics, each overcoming his own hurdles to win gold medals. *Chariots of Fire* had many picturesque scenes, none more so than the runners training on a beach. It was filmed on the North Sea in the charming university town of St. Andrews, Scotland, and quickly became an iconic moment of the film. The unorthodox modern, heavily electronic score by the Greek composer Vangelis, by turns haunting and triumphant, helped drive the drama, and the opening theme became a number one single.

The movie's title came from the hymn "Jerusalem," which was itself based on a poem by William Blake and has become a revered national hymn in Great Britain. One verse reads:

Bring me my Bow of burning gold;
Bring me my Arrows of desire:
Bring me my Spear: O clouds unfold!
Bring me my Chariot of fire!

Chariots of Fire not only celebrated Britain's past athletic glory in the 1924 Olympics but also was a movie of its time. The early scenes, set at Cambridge in 1919, show a Britain still under the shadow of World War I. The new students, including Harold Abrahams, are regaled by an inspirational speech from their college master, who pays tribute to the young men of the previous generation who "died for England and all that England stands for." He then calls on Abrahams and the others to "discover where your true chance of greatness lies . . . and let no power or persuasion deter you in your task"—setting the challenge before them of helping shepherd their country out of the devastation of the war years.

So it was in 1981, when Britain was again finding its way out of a period of gloom, this time economic. In the late 1970s, Britain's flagging economy and double-digit inflation had earned it the epithet "sick man of Europe."* But in 1979 the Conservative Party was elected into power, and a new prime minister took office with a plan to grow the economy with unapologetic free-market reforms: Margaret Thatcher. Already by 1980, inflation was dropping precipitously. When *Chariots of Fire* was released the following year, it looked as if Britain was once again entering a period of prosperity. Indeed, the movie seemed to reflect the Thatcherite themes of self-reliance, faith, and optimism to overcome serious obstacles.

Thatcher's election paralleled Ronald Reagan's one year later. Both the United States and the United Kingdom had elected conservative leaders; believers in the free market who weren't afraid to stand firm against the Soviet Union.

Reagan and Thatcher were well matched politically and personally, leading to one of the strongest periods of cooperation between the United States and Britain, and one of the most influential partnerships between world leaders since the end of World War II.

Though I had few interactions with Margaret Thatcher (she was one of the first foreign leaders the Reagans honored with a visit to Camp David), from my observations, the two had an easy rapport and

---

*Hugh Pym, "Margaret Thatcher: How the Economy Changed," BBC News online, last modified April 8, 2013, www.bbc.com/news/business-22073527.

high regard for each other. Thatcher was smart and serious. Reagan fascinated her. He shared her basic philosophy but couldn't be more stylistically different. Thatcher biographer Charles Moore points out that Reagan's "easygoing ways" contrasted with the prime minister, a "hyperactive, zealous, intensely knowledgeable leader, who injected energy into all her doings but also displayed what Reagan considered to be the elegance of a typical, gracious English lady."*

These differences were on display in planning the first state dinner of the Reagan administration, held just a few weeks after he took office, in honor of Thatcher's visit to Washington. White House aides were eager to show the style of the new First Couple. One goal of the event was to showcase the look of the new administration and throw off the grungy, downtrodden style that some associated with the Jimmy Carter White House. Career diplomat Jim Rentschler, who served on the National Security Council staff for both presidents and was involved in the planning, recalled:

"Some of the Carter people used to walk about the White House in bare feet. As soon as Reagan came in, out went the memos banning jeans, banning sandals, and requiring everyone to wear a suit. *Glamour* was a word often used, and *class* too."†

What better opportunity to demonstrate the difference than with a glittering state dinner? It was decided to make it a white-tie affair—the ultimate in formal occasions—and "infused with Hollywood glamour," as Rentschler remembered.‡ (He was appointed US ambassador to Malta by President Reagan in 1982.)

As it turned out, Mrs. Thatcher was not comfortable with such

---

*Charles Moore, "Margaret Thatcher's First Visit to Washington of the Reagan Presidency," *Huffington Post*, accessed September 16, 2017, www.huffington post.com/charles-moore/margaret-thatchers-first-_b_3308679.html.
†Ibid.
‡Ibid.

Hollywood glamour. According to Charles Moore, she requested that the attire for the dinner be downgraded to black tie instead of white, concerned that "some of her people would not have the requisite clothing." Indeed, she had her own personal and political problems with the aesthetic: "She was the grocer's daughter. She didn't want to come over here dressed up like that. It was an impoverished time in Britain, after all."* The Reagans understood and were happy to settle on black tie.

On the night of the dinner, Reagan toasted Thatcher by praising the "special relationship" between the United States and the United Kingdom and their shared tradition of democracy. He promised Thatcher, "Together we'll strive to preserve the liberty and peace so cherished by our peoples. No foe of freedom should doubt our resolve."† In those early days of the Reagan-Thatcher partnership, when the outcome of the Cold War was still far from certain, Reagan invoked the humor of Winston Churchill in another trying time:

"[I]n the dark days of World War II, he could call attention to the fact that the enemy had threatened to wring the neck of the United Kingdom. And after the Battle of Britain, as he was speaking, who will ever forget him leaning over that podium and saying, 'Some chicken. Some neck.'"‡ The dinner attendees erupted in laughter.

In her toast, Thatcher quoted a writer who, she said, had visited London just after World War II. "He wrote that 'in spite of the homesickness, the hunger, and annoyance at socialist bumbling, my farewell to London held its measure of regret. There were friendships

*Moore, "Margaret Thatcher's First Visit to Washington."
†Ronald Reagan:"Toasts of the President and Prime Minister Margaret Thatcher of the United Kingdom at the State Dinner, February 26, 1981,"American Presidency Project, www.presidency.ucsb.edu/ws/?pid=43466.
‡Ibid.

made and cherished to this day.'" Then she made her big reveal: "Mr. President, you were that homesick and hungry author," she said to Reagan, and promised him that on his next visit he could expect two things: "The first is the friendship of the British people, and the second, that the years of socialist bumbling are at an end."*

The visit was an undisputed success, and a history-making partnership began. Reagan and Thatcher got along better than anyone could have imagined. There were no glitches, and the chemistry was exactly as one would have hoped. Jim Brady, my boss in the Press Office, joked, "We needed a crowbar to pull them apart."†

In Margaret Thatcher, Ronald Reagan found a person whose brilliance he respected, whose world vision he shared, whose strength and courage he admired, and whose company he enjoyed. And the feeling was mutual. That summer, during a G7 summit meeting they both attended in Canada, Mrs. Thatcher observed the president doodling—an eye, a male torso, several heads, and a possible self-portrait. He left the piece of paper on the conference table. She took it, put it with her papers, and brought it back with her to her flat at 10 Downing Street.‡

Reagan had spotted Thatcher's leadership skills early on. He often told the story about their first meeting in 1975 in England, before he was elected president and before she was elected prime minister. Later an Englishman asked him what he thought of the rising star of the Conservative Party. Ronald Reagan replied she would make an excellent prime minister. The questioner looked aghast,

---

*Ronald Reagan, "Toasts of the President and Prime Minister Margaret Thatcher."
†Moore, "Margaret Thatcher's First Visit to Washington."
‡Associated Press, "Papers Reveal Thatcher Kept Reagan's Doodles," CBS News online, March 16, 2012, www.cbsnews.com/news/papers-reveal-thatcher-kept-reagans-doodles.

frowned, and in a disapproving tone that suggested the idea was unimaginable (at least to him), said: "A woman? Prime minister?" To which Ronald Reagan replied, "Well, you had a queen named Victoria once, who did rather well." The questioner said sheepishly, "By Jove, I'd forgotten all about that." It's a sweet story, and a fitting prelude to the Reagan-Thatcher era, but Reagan's biographer Lou Cannon notes that it may well be apocryphal.*

What is unmistakable to Cannon, and to anyone else who knew Reagan well, is that he was an "ardent Anglophile." According to Cannon, "It was widely believed that Reagan's Anglophilia was a product of World War II, when Hollywood was ardently pro-British," but he speculates further that "Reagan's admiration for Britain may have been formed during his Illinois boyhood rather than in Hollywood." The staunchly British hero of an antiwar play called *Journey's End* may have inspired young Reagan.† A 1928 drama, *Journey's End* was about the officers in a British Army infantry company in northern France in World War I. It chronicles the experiences of Captain Denis Stanhope, originally played by Sir Laurence Olivier, who turns to alcohol to help him cope with the stresses of battle.

Reagan's appreciation for British culture was not limited to its movies or its Conservative political leaders. He and Mrs. Reagan also formed a personal connection with one of the long-standing pillars of British society: the monarchy. A close camaraderie developed between the Reagans and the royal family. The president admired the queen's lifetime of service to her country and her sensible, unpretentious style when they were together. But I believe it was her love of horses, which he shared, that helped establish the bond

---

*Lou Cannon, *President Reagan: The Role of a Lifetime* (New York: Simon & Schuster, 1991), 407.
†Ibid.

between them. Ronald Reagan was known to say that riding with the queen at Windsor Castle in 1982 was one of his fondest memories of his time as president.

I had not been sure what to expect when I met Queen Elizabeth II myself, but I found her delightful. Her Majesty was gracious, pleasant, and so much more "real" than I imagined. She was not at all fussy, and looked at life with a keen sense of humor and a taste for adventure. When she and her husband, Prince Philip, Duke of Edinburgh, visited the Reagans at the ranch, a terrible rain blanketed the whole Santa Barbara area, causing several last-minute logistical adjustments to the planned program. She was not bothered a bit. (Incidentally, in *Chariots of Fire*, her uncle Edward, who became king in 1936, only to abdicate the throne later that year to marry an American divorcée, attempts to persuade Eric Liddell to race on a Sunday.)

Prince Philip, on the other hand, was known to be temperamental. It was hearsay, but I was told he could be impatient and even unpleasant about logistical matters such as when motorcades would be moving, and who would and would not be allowed to ride with the queen and him. In fairness, he did seem to have taken on the tough job of making sure the operation surrounding the queen ran smoothly while she remained the center of attention— the "bad cop" in the relationship, as it were. And always a step behind her.

The queen and Prince Philip always received the Reagans when they were in London. One special day in 1989, former president Reagan visited the queen to receive his honorary knighthood. Officially it was known as Honorary Knight Grand Cross of the Most Honorable Order of the Bath. The queen presented it to him at a private luncheon at Buckingham Palace. No kneeling or swords were involved. When the queen and Prince Philip were showing the Reagans out of the Palace afterward, Her Majesty noted that the president was not holding on to the box containing his insignia tightly. "Oh, please don't drop it," she cautioned. Luckily, he didn't!

Mrs. Reagan became true friends with the queen in her own right over the years. This relationship blossomed when Queen Elizabeth and Prince Philip visited the West Coast in 1983, and the First Lady joined the royal couple for dinner at the legendary San Francisco restaurant Trader Vic's, accompanied by some fifty members of the White House and royal staffs. Everybody loosened up. The queen had a gin martini (Tanqueray) before dinner, and it was vodka and orange juice for Mrs. Reagan. Dinner, the press reported, was "Indonesian lamb, finishing the meal with rum ice cream topped with pecans."[*]

Some White House staff members present were shocked by Prince Philip's salty language in front of the queen and Mrs. Reagan, but neither woman seemed to notice or care. One Trader Vic's bartender told the press, "The queen was laughing a lot. A Secret Service man said it was the first time he had seen her smile."[†]

The Reagans also had a special relationship with the queen mother, a fixture of the British monarchy for more than a century. At one state dinner at Buckingham Palace in 1984, Reagan provided some impromptu entertainment by reciting the poem "The Shooting of Dan McGrew" by the British-Canadian poet Robert W. Service. As it turned out, the queen mother shared Reagan's love for Service's writing. Mrs. Reagan recalled that during the president's recitation

---

[*]Joan Goulding, United Press International online, "Queen Dines at Trader Vic's," March 3, 1983, www.upi.com/Archives/1983/03/03/Queen-dines-at -Trader-Vics/7330415515600.
[†]Ibid.

at that dinner, the queen mother piped up and fed him several of the lines.*

On one postpresidency visit to London, the Reagans called on the queen mother and Princess Margaret at Clarence House, where the queen mother was then living. I, along with two other staffers who had accompanied the Reagans, waited in a nearby parlor. After less than ten minutes, word came that the queen mother wanted to visit with the Reagan staff, and we were shown into an ornate drawing room full of beautiful furniture. Exquisite art hung on the walls. There was also a large grand piano, on top of which sat an opened box of Ritz crackers.

As soon as we entered, the queen mother came to us and asked if we had been to London before, and how we were enjoying the trip. She said we must try some "of our wonderful restaurants," and I asked if we could use her name if we had trouble getting in. She laughed. Since then, I've often thought of her whenever I snack on a Ritz cracker.

The Reagans were equally fond of Charles, Prince of Wales, and his wife, the then-princess Diana—and vice versa. Charles is smart, savvy, and politically astute. He hired a former Reagan aide, Robert Higdon, to run his American foundation. On the few occasions that I saw Princess Diana, she seemed shy. It's not that she was standoffish, she just wasn't as gregarious as her husband. I remember one trip to London in particular when the Reagans called on Charles and Diana and their young family at Kensington Palace. As we were leaving, I saw the two young princes, William and Harry, in their pajamas watching us from the window.

*James F. Clarity and Warren Weaver Jr., "Briefing: Reagan the Reciter," *New York Times* online, October 6, 1985, www.nytimes.com/1985/10/06/us/briefing -reagan-the-reciter.html.

Over the years, Mrs. Reagan became quite close to Prince Charles. In a rare gesture of respect and friendship, the prince traveled to Washington for the state funeral when President Reagan died. Before the formal ceremony, he called on Mrs. Reagan at Blair House, the presidential guest house, located across the street from the White House, and handed her a handwritten letter of sympathy from his mother, the queen—another example of the extraordinary relationship between the Reagans and the Windsors.

In England and America, Reagan invoked *Chariots of Fire* to conjure up images of freedom and the divine source from which he firmly believed it flowed. In 1984, at the Conservative Political Action Conference (CPAC) in Washington, he urged the audience to "unite, shoulder to shoulder, behind one mighty banner for freedom," offering this encouragement:

> And in those moments when we grow tired, when our struggle seems hard, remember what Eric Liddell, Scotland's Olympic champion runner, said in *Chariots of Fire*. He said, "So where does the power come from to see the race to its end? From within. God made me for a purpose, and I will run for His pleasure."
>
> If we trust in Him, keep His word, and live our lives for His pleasure, He'll give us the power we need—power to fight the good fight, to finish the race, and to keep the faith.*

Reagan himself kept that faith throughout his presidency. In 1988, as his time in office was drawing to a close, he addressed the Royal Institute of International Affairs, in London, just days after he and

---

*Ronald Reagan, "Remarks at the Annual Conservative Political Action Conference Dinner, March 2, 1984,"American Presidency Project, www.presidency.ucsb.edu/ws/?pid=39591.

Soviet leader Mikhail Gorbachev had "exchanged the instruments of ratification" of the Intermediate-Range Nuclear Forces (INF) Treaty, putting the agreement into effect and ushering in significant arms reduction in both the United States and the Soviet Union.* Reagan hailed this step as a victory for civilization, as some progress made "ever so slowly but ever so relentlessly and lovingly to a moment when the will of man and God are as one again." He closed with "one last story that can remind us best of what we're about."

> It's a story that a few years ago came in the guise of that art form for which I have an understandable affection: the cinema. It's a story about the 1924 Olympics and two British athletes: Harold Abrahams, a young Jew, whose victory—as his immigrant Arab Italian coach put it—was a triumph for all those who have come from distant lands and found freedom and refuge here in England; and Eric Liddell, a young Scotsman, who would not sacrifice religious conviction for fame. In one unforgettable scene, Eric Liddell reads the words of Isaiah: "He giveth power to the faint, and to them that have no might, he increased their strength, but they that wait upon the Lord shall renew their strength. They shall mount up with wings as eagles. They shall run and not be weary."

Reagan called this faith that drives so much of *Chariots of Fire* "our formula for completing our crusade for freedom . . . the strength of our civilization and our belief in the rights of humanity."†

As it turned out, echoes of *Chariots of Fire*, which Reagan first

---

*Ronald Reagan, "Remarks to Members of the Royal Institute of International Affairs in London, June 3, 1988," American Presidency Project, www.presidency.ucsb.edu/ws/?pid=35906.
†Ibid.

watched at Camp David in October 1981, would be felt decades later in his last appearance in the public eye. In 2004, at Ronald Reagan's funeral service at the Washington National Cathedral, the choir sang a version of "Jerusalem"—the hymn that gave the film its title. As the *Washington Post* reported, "[T]he organ roared to life, and the boy sopranos floated their ineffable descant into the ether."* Just a few moments after the last notes of "Jerusalem" faded away, the assembled mourners heard the first of the tributes to the fallen president. It was delivered by Lady Thatcher, who, though too ill to speak on her own, had recorded a video message for the event. "We have lost a great president, a great American, and a great man," she said, "and I have lost a dear friend."

---

*David Von Drehle, "The Funeral: Reagan Hailed as Leader for 'the Ages,'" *Washington Post* online, June 12, 2004, www.washingtonpost.com/wp-dyn/articles/A35593-2004Jun11.html?nav=headlines.

6

E.T.
THE EXTRA-TERRESTRIAL

———◆———

Starring: Henry Thomas, Drew Barrymore,
Peter Coyote
Directed by: Steven Spielberg
Viewed by the Reagans: June 27, 1982

———◆———

The Film That Made the Reagans Cry

A lot of what was happening on Earth in the days before the president and Mrs. Reagan hosted a screening of *E.T. the Extra-Terrestrial* at the White House probably made a science-fiction movie about life on another planet appealing to many of the people there.

It started with Israeli prime minister Menachem Begin's visit to Washington. Ronald Reagan was unalterably committed to the well-being of Israel and its people. He understood the alliance's strategic importance to the United States, but well beyond that, he understood the historic significance and imperative of the right of the state of Israel to exist in peace. Israel's safety was nonnegotiable to him. But Menachem Begin was not the easiest man to like, even for strong supporters of Israel. The discussions President Reagan had with the prime minister that day were exasperating.

The administration's concerns about Israel's strong response to the Palestine Liberation Organization (PLO) shelling of Israeli villages was the issue. In retaliation for repeated attacks by PLO forces in southern Lebanon, Israel invaded and briefly occupied southern Lebanon until the PLO left. The president's public comments after their meeting telegraphed the tension. In uncharacteristically brief remarks to the press, Reagan said that it had been merely "worthwhile" to have Begin at the White House again. Ouch. Everyone knew that was diplomat speak for contentious.

Reagan's private diary entries offer more illumination. The president described himself as being "pretty blunt" about his concerns but that Begin came back with a "defense." Sounds like an argument. The president's notes went on to refer to the matter as "a complex problem," saying: "In the larger meetings with his people and ours, we went at it again. He's adamant against our proposal to sell arms to Jordan. My argument is we're trying to create more 'Egypts' who'll make peace with Israel. He refuses to believe another Arab state will do what Egypt did." Ronald Reagan's last word on that meeting says it all: "Frustrating." That was Monday. Quite a beginning to the week.

Storm clouds arrived that Wednesday. The president met with Secretary of State Alexander Haig, whose arrogance, constant complaints, and refusal to cooperate with the White House staff had become a problem. From his bizarre (and constitutionally incorrect) behavior announcing himself "in charge" in the White House after the president had been wounded by a would-be assassin's bullet, to his whining about what helicopters he was assigned to ride, Haig had alienated virtually everyone at 1600 Pennsylvania Avenue. The president knew a change had to be made and wrote in his diary, "I was prepared for Al to resign." But Haig did not make it easy, complaining to the president about a number of things, almost all of which related to perceived slights and other minor issues. Reagan referred to it as "a bill of particulars," which he promised to review. In a rare, but telling, note of exasperation, Ronald Reagan penned in his diary for that day: "I'm ready for Camp David."

Friday was a predictably grim day at the White House, as the president accepted Haig's resignation. The drama was over. There were no wet eyes among the White House staff when Ronald Reagan walked into the Press Briefing Room that afternoon to announce Haig was out and former labor and treasury secretary and Office of Management and Budget director George P. Shultz would replace him. The president was gracious to Haig in his public statements, but in his diary, he referred to the ordeal as "a heavy load." Although Ronald Reagan respected the service that the highly decorated veteran of both the Korean and Vietnam Wars had rendered to his country, enough was enough.

Some may consider George Shultz to have been a terrific Secretary of State, but he was not always nice to the president's staff, at least not the mid-level and junior staff. Simply put, he could be rude. He often treated me and others like we were furniture. Not worth acknowledging.

I am certain the Reagans were not aware of how Shultz treated us. Had they been, I am sure they would have passed the word to him to behave appropriately. Regardless, I eventually got to tell Mrs. Reagan about it and was more than happy to do so.

In 1989 or 1990, we were on an airplane traveling somewhere, and Mrs. Reagan mentioned George Shultz's name. I either rolled my eyes or curled my lip to indicate my dislike, which Mrs. Reagan saw and chose not to ignore. "Mark," she said in a tone a bit less than warm, "what's the issue with George?" I knew she liked him (he kissed up to her shamelessly), so I took a deep breath and decided to tell her. "Well, Mrs. Reagan," I began, "you know how no matter how busy or preoccupied you or your husband could be, that you never, ever failed to smile and say hello to people when you saw them?" She smiled and said, "Yes."

"George is not that way." She raised her eyebrows and said "Oh?" in a very skeptical tone. So I explained: "Yes, George walks right by people and ignores them, even if they say hello. Sometimes he just looks at people and says nothing. Nothing. Even if they say hello first. That is, unless you happen to be a pretty woman or someone very powerful. Then he has all the time in the world for you," I said. She laughed.

"But Mrs. Reagan," I said, "if the most important and busy man and woman in the world always had time to be courteous to people, why couldn't he?"

She paused. "Yes, well, you may have a point." From then on, every time we were with George Shultz, Mrs. Reagan would look at me, raise her eyebrows, and smile.

As Ronald Reagan entered the second year of his presidency, his widespread popularity among the American people had begun to decline. This leveling was common after a president's first year in office, but it reminded Reagan of how fleeting a sense of unity in America could be. Undeterred, he looked for new opportunities to transcend typical partisan divisions and inspire the nation. He identified one such opportunity in the Space Shuttle Program in the summer of 1982.

To maximize its impact, Reagan wanted the American people to feel that the Shuttle Program belonged to them rather than to the government. This task was well suited to his unique gifts as a communicator. His speech declaring the first space shuttle operational could have easily been given from the Oval Office or the press room at NASA's headquarters, but he delivered it instead on the tarmac at Edwards Air Force Base in California after the space shuttle *Columbia* landed from its test mission.

He made sure it happened on the Fourth of July, when people would be off from work and feeling their most patriotic. The event turned into a remarkable spectacle. A half million Americans came to the Southern California desert to watch the *Columbia* land, including forty-five thousand who overflowed onto the ramps and taxiways at the Dryden Flight Research Center to hear the president speak.

The White House advance team had worked hard to create an event that would showcase the best of the president's onstage skills as a communicator, with a little bit of drama. Some might call it a Hollywood touch. In addition to christening *Columbia*, the purpose of the event was to introduce America to its second space shuttle, the *Challenger*. When Reagan reached the part in his speech referencing the future of the Shuttle Program, a jetliner carrying the *Challenger* on its back thundered overhead with precision. As the crowd roared, he leaned into the microphone and boomed, "Where we're going to go in the future is something that depends on you." His message resonated deeply with a country already transfixed on the wonders of space.

Following America's victory in the space race of the 1960s, defined by our being the first (and only) country to land men on the moon and bring them back safely, the United States and the Soviet Union had spent a decade trading off on a series of remarkable achievements, from orbital space stations, to unmanned Mars landings, to flybys of Jupiter and Saturn. As these captured the attention of the public, an appetite developed for movies, music, and books that could transport anyone, not just NASA astronauts, into the far reaches of space. Perhaps the most notable cultural touchstone from the era was *Star Wars*, which broke the record for highest-grossing film of all time upon its release in 1977. Five years later, however, *Star Wars's* record would be surpassed by another film—one that, as if to complement Reagan's own efforts, took all the mystery and enchantment of space and placed it in the heart of the American suburbs.

On June 27, 1982, one week before the event at Edwards Air Force Base—and the day of *Columbia's* launch—a star-studded group of Washington and Hollywood veterans sat with the Reagans at the White House to watch a new film titled *E.T. the Extra-Terrestrial*. This was an unusual occurrence, as the president and Mrs. Reagan customarily watched movies at Camp David with a small circle of aides.

Its director, Steven Spielberg, and members of the cast were there. Neil Armstrong, the first man to walk on the moon, and several other astronauts were also in attendance, as was the newest Supreme Court Justice, Sandra Day O'Connor. Several of the guests and luminaries had brought their young children. The atmosphere in the White House that evening was almost whimsical. *Columbia's* successful launch hours earlier had been the perfect prelude, and now these influential Americans were gathered not for a stuffy state dinner but to watch a family film about a homesick alien.

In *E.T. the Extra-Terrestrial*, a lonely middle child named Elliott discovers an equally lonely alien hiding in the shed in his suburban backyard. With the help of his teenage brother and younger sister, he brings it into his house and hides it from his mother. Over time Elliott's friendship with the creature, which he names E.T., grows into a mysterious telekinetic connection in which he gets sick when E.T. is sick, sad when E.T. is sad, and even intoxicated when E.T. discovers beer in the family refrigerator. After government agents in full astronaut suits capture the alien, the children manage to help him escape just in time to meet the spaceship that's come to take him home.

After the audience took their seats, Spielberg stood and introduced the film, calling it an ode to his childhood. He then sat beside the Reagans. As the film played, the president seemed enchanted, laughing at the charming dialogue and turning occasionally to whisper into Nancy's ear. By the time the film reached its stirring emotional send-off, both he and the First Lady were crying, as were many others in the audience.* Spielberg later recounted that the president was so moved toward the end that he "looked like a ten-year-old kid," leaning forward in his seat as he watched.

E.T. struck me as fundamentally Reaganesque in tone and approach. Its wholesome depiction of Middle America, its impish sense of humor, and its subtle placement of the protagonist in opposition to the government aligned with his identity. After the closing credits, President Reagan stood and faced the crowd, searching from face to face for a moment to read reactions. "I wanted to thank you for bringing *E.T.* to the White House," he said. "We really enjoyed your movie." He paused before saying with a completely straight face: "And there are a number of people in this room who know that everything on that screen is absolutely true."†

---

*Janet Maslin, "Nation's First Film-Goer Gets a Front-Row Seat," *New York Times* online, April 21, 1983, www.nytimes.com/1983/04/21/us/nation-s-first -film-goer-gets-a-front-row-seat.html.

†Alejandro Rojas, "Spielberg Confirms Reagan's Extraterrestrial Comment," OpenMinds, last modified June 6, 2011, www.openminds.tv/spielberg-con firms-reagan-705/10057.

The audience broke out in laughter, but the seriousness of his delivery went on to spark rumors among self-proclaimed "UFOlogists" that Reagan had let slip a state secret about an alien encounter. The rumors persist to this day. In an interview in 2011, Spielberg confirmed the comment but stated, "I'm sorry to say I think he was simply trying to tell a joke."

One guest at the event, Morgan Mason, had an interesting take on what Reagan was doing. I believe Morgan was the only Hollywood movie veteran to serve on Ronald Reagan's White House staff. The son of Academy Award nominee and acclaimed actor James Mason and actress-screenwriter Pamela Mason, both born in England, Morgan had appeared in *Hero's Island,* along with his father, when he was just seven, and in *The Sandpiper* with Elizabeth Taylor and Richard Burton three years later. In 1979 he joined Ronald Reagan's presidential campaign, despite his father's advice to the contrary—"Oh, my dear boy, don't be ridiculous; he doesn't have a chance"—and, following Reagan's decisive victory over incumbent president Jimmy Carter in 1980, was appointed deputy chief of protocol of the United States. Shortly thereafter, the president asked him to join the White House staff, where he served as special assistant to the president for political affairs. Morgan is married to Belinda Carlisle, lead vocalist of the all-female rock group the Go-Go's. Their son, Duke, is also active in politics.

The Reagans liked Morgan so much that when he left the White House staff, they came to his farewell party at the home of Mike Deaver. Despite his pedigree, Morgan was neither pretentious nor arrogant. He was like a young Ronald Reagan: handsome, smart, charming, politically savvy, courteous to everyone, and had a wonderful sense of humor. Unlike many on the White House staff, Morgan was a person about whom no one had an unkind word.

And he was clever. Morgan once gave the Reagans a unique

anniversary gift: the business card of the famed divorce attorney Marvin Mitchelson framed behind glass with a small hammer and a sign reading "Break in Case of Emergency!" Both Reagans howled with laughter when he presented it. On one occasion, Morgan was playing tennis on the White House court when Chief of Staff James A. Baker III called him. Baker was peeved that Mason was recreating instead of working at his desk. Baker told Morgan that he had "just been with your boss," meaning White House Political Affairs Chief Edward J. Rollins. Without missing a beat, Mason replied, "Well, I was just with yours," meaning Nancy Reagan. That was that.

Mason told me, "When I first got to the White House, one of my jobs was to arrange screenings in the family theater for movies such as *E.T.* and *Victory*," which takes place in a Nazi POW camp during WWII. The camp commander (Max Von Sydow) organizes a soccer match between his German soldiers and the Allied POWs. It was directed by John Huston and also starred Michael Caine.

"We tried to get the key people to come—Steven Spielberg, Sylvester Stallone, Kirk Kerkorian, who on three separate occasions owned MGM Studios—like that. There was always an informal dinner afterward. Everyone was relaxed and had fun. I seem to recall that after seeing *E.T.*, the president said something about how can we be one hundred percent sure that there are not other forms of life out there? A few people looked startled, and a few laughed politely, but I remember thinking how open-minded it was of him to acknowledge that possibility and not buy into the arrogance that we were the only living creatures ever."

My view was that the president's comment was almost certainly intended to draw laughter, but his serious delivery also made me think he was giving a gift to the children in the audience. Similar to the way a parent might confirm the existence of Santa Claus, Reagan was lending extra weight to the magic of the film for all those who wanted its magic to be real. He was also giving a wink to the filmmakers, indicating that their aim to inspire audiences was also his aim.

E.T., of course, did succeed—wildly. And not just in ticket sales but also in leaving a sizeable cultural footprint. It introduced to science fiction the idea that alien visitors need not be evil conquerors but might instead be cosmic companions.* This seemingly new concept was a refreshing twist for many filmgoers who were drawn to the subject matter of space and extraterrestrials but burned out by the pervasive darkness of such films.

Spielberg's intention, however, was never to revolutionize science fiction. It was to capture the essence of childhood. He was inspired to make *E.T.* by experiences he had in his own childhood after his parents' divorce, when he was beset by feelings of loneliness and would cope by retreating into his imagination. The choice of an alien companion at the film's center—as opposed to, say, a golden retriever or an orca whale, as in other children's films with similar narrative arcs—was a function of the space-crazy era in which the film was released.

"I wanted E.T. to become a kind of conscience and companion to kids growing up in the eighties," Spielberg said once. "In the fifties, I had Jiminy Cricket and Winnie-the-Pooh as imaginary sidekicks and preceptors. They were creatures who outlived their original contexts, and I hope the same thing happens with E.T."†

Spielberg used a variety of techniques to pull the audience back into childhood, including shooting most scenes from a low vantage

---

*"New Releases: E.T. the Extra-Terrestrial," *Christian Science Monitor* online, March 22, 2002, www.csmonitor.com/2002/0322/p14s01-almo.html.

†Gary Arnold, "'E.T.: Steven Spielberg's Joyful Excursion, Back to Childhood, Forward to the Unknown," *Washington Post* online, June 6, 1982, www.wash ingtonpost.com/wp-dyn/content/article/2005/06/22/AR2005062201424.html.

point. He also took the time to develop the ancillary characters in Elliott's family. They span different ages and filter the story's central theme—Elliott's attachment to E.T.—through their own complex points of view. This multigenerational approach gives older audience members a way to relate to the story without relying exclusively on their memories of being Elliott's age.

Watching Elliott, we witness his first-time struggle with feelings of loss and abandonment. E.T.'s role in Elliott's life grows from being like a pet, to like a friend, to like a stand-in parent or mentor. When E.T. appears to have died and his telekinetic connection with Elliott seems severed, Elliott says, "I must be dead, because I don't know how to feel."

Meanwhile, Elliott's teenage brother, Mike, allows us to see the events unfold from a slightly older perspective. Mike has a scene in which he's talking with one of the scientists who set up shop at the family's home. He explains Elliott's connection with E.T. this way:

SCIENTIST: You said it has the ability to manipulate its own
             environment?
MICHAEL: He's smart. He communicates through Elliott.
SCIENTIST: Elliott thinks its thoughts?
MICHAEL: No. Elliott feels his feelings.

After this exchange, Mike withdraws into a closet full of stuffed animals, toys, and comics that he's clearly outgrown. With tears in his eyes, he pulls his knees up to his chest and falls asleep on the floor, having retreated one more time into the comfort of childhood.

In the film's emotional final scene, even adult characters such as Elliott's mother and the government agents become teary-eyed at the relationship between Elliott and E.T. They watch as the two stand outside the spaceship and labor through an anguished good-bye. E.T. points a glowing finger at Elliott's forehead and says, "I will be right here." The audience senses that Elliott is saying good-bye to part of his childhood as much as to a friend. We see even the cold and anonymous government agents won over by E.T.'s magic.

As the highest officeholder in the United States government, President Reagan had to have identified with the government agents portrayed as antagonists throughout the film. His infamous comment about everything on the screen being true showed how aware he was that, in the minds of many Americans, he was the ultimate authority on whether the government was hiding anything about its knowledge of space.

He viewed the movie, however, not just from the perspective of a sitting president but also as a veteran of the movie business. In a conversation after the screening, President Reagan told Spielberg that *E.T.* had left him feeling nostalgic, not about childhood but about a simpler time in filmmaking.

"I only have one criticism of your movie," he said. "How long were the end credits?"

"Oh, I don't know," Spielberg replied. "Maybe three, three and a half minutes."

Reagan was unimpressed. "In my day, when I was an actor, our end credits were maybe fifteen seconds long. Three and a half minutes, that's fine—but only show that inside the industry. Throughout the rest of the country, reduce your credits to fifteen seconds at the end."

His point was that people in the filmmaking business would be interested in seeing their names and those of their colleagues, but the rest of the country would not.

Nancy intervened before Spielberg had the chance to respond. "Oh, Ronnie," she said. "They can't do that. You know that."

"Oh, yes, yes," the president sighed. "I suppose."*

It's a humorous conversation in hindsight, but it also showed the way Reagan's mind worked when viewing films. He watched them as a student of the craft. He came from a less technically advanced time in moviemaking, when crews didn't consist of the visual effects artists and hordes of specialized technicians needed to make *E.T.* Spielberg, on the other hand, was of a new generation in Hollywood. He understood that big effects were the draw for audiences, even if the smaller human moments were still what kept them in their seats.

As the director intended, the science-fiction elements of the film connected it to kids growing up in the eighties. He further appealed to them with references to other popular sci-fi space adventures throughout. In an early interaction between Elliott and E.T., Elliott shows off a series of *Star Wars* action figures. Later on, E.T. is trick-or-treating, disguised by a white sheet, and tries to chase after a child in a Yoda costume, saying "Home . . . home . . . home." Near the film's end, Elliott explains to a neighborhood boy that E.T. needs to get to a spaceship. "Well, can't he just beam up?" the boy asks, in reference to existing sci-fi clichés. Elliott's impatient reply: "This is *reality*, Greg."

A sense of reality, it seems, is what audiences were craving from the science-fiction genre.

The flight of the space shuttle one week after the screening of *E.T.* was a moment of unity for the country. It continued to inspire Americans in the coming years, and the administration kept searching for methods of involving the American people, including children, in the program.

*Rojas, "Spielberg Confirms Reagan's Extraterrestrial Comment."

The Shuttle Student Involvement Program was one such method. It gave students the opportunity to propose experiments to be performed by astronauts in space. Reagan also had far bigger ideas. He was determined to see a civilian launched into space before the end of his second term. He believed that was a way to truly give the American people a stake in the Shuttle Program.

In 1984 he proposed the Teachers in Space Project. "I am directing NASA to begin the search in all of our elementary and secondary schools," the president said, "and to choose as the first citizen passenger in the history of our space program one of America's finest: a teacher. I can't think of a better lesson for our children and our country."

After more than eleven thousand applied, a high school social studies teacher from Concord, New Hampshire, named Christa McAuliffe was selected. What followed would be one of the greatest tragedies of the Reagan presidency. On January 28, 1986, just seventy-three seconds after it had launched, the *Challenger* exploded, killing Christa and the six other astronauts on board.

It was the worst disaster in NASA's history and a heavy blow to the US space program. Yet with Christa on board, the deepest wound was to the American people. The shuttle that had been a source of inspiration since it first thundered overhead at Edwards Air Force Base in 1982 had become a source of heartbreak. The millions who had watched Christa's training unfold suddenly felt no desire to follow in her footsteps. Reagan understood the challenge before him. This was a human tragedy more than a scientific disaster, and he needed to respond in kind.

He wanted, first of all, to speak to the millions of schoolchildren who had watched the disaster happen live. For many, it remains one of their earliest and most vivid memories. The gifted speechwriter

Peggy Noonan went to work and drafted what would become defining words.

"I want to say something to the schoolchildren of America who were watching the live coverage of the shuttle's takeoff," the president said in his now-famous speech the evening of the disaster. "I know it is hard to understand, but sometimes painful things like this happen. It's all part of the process of exploration and discovery."

He also wanted to remind people that the Shuttle Program would remain a public endeavor, one for all to share in and experience. "We don't hide our space program," he said. "We don't keep secrets and cover things up. We do it all up front and in public. That's the way freedom is, and we wouldn't change it for a minute. We'll continue our quest in space. There will be more shuttle flights and more shuttle crews, and, yes, more volunteers, more civilians, more teachers in space. Nothing ends here; our hopes and our journeys continue."

7

RETURN OF THE JEDI

◆

Starring: Mark Hamill, Harrison Ford, Carrie
Fisher, Frank Oz
Directed by: Richard Marquand

WARGAMES

◆

Starring: Matthew Broderick, Ally Sheedy,
Dabney Coleman
Directed by: John Badham

Viewed by the Reagans: June 2–4, 1983

◆

The Films That Stirred the President's Imagination

The year 1983 saw some of the tensest moments in the Cold War
since the Cuban Missile Crisis. The president, long a fervent
anti-Communist, bluntly and repeatedly made plain his view of
the Soviet Union and its dangerous ambitions. He spoke often of

his deep and abiding concern for the well-being of the American people and our way of life, his fear that Soviet expansionism was like a cancer that could eventually rob millions of their freedoms, and his belief that if he could just get his Soviet counterpart in a room and talk to him man-to-man, he could convince him that the United States had no hostile intentions, and there was no need for the nuclear brinksmanship that had characterized the relationship for so long.

On March 8, 1983, Reagan dubbed the Soviet Union "an evil empire."* That speech, which seemed to wipe away decades of US policy seeking a long-term peaceful coexistence with the Soviet Union, changed the course of the Cold War more than any other, and probably more than any speech ever delivered since Abraham Lincoln spoke at Gettysburg and Franklin Delano Roosevelt responded to Pearl Harbor. It outraged many of the president's political opponents, who called it dangerous warmongering. It also outraged the Soviets, who feared such an obvious departure from the policies and views of Reagan's immediate predecessors. A new Soviet president, the stern-faced former KGB chief Yuri Andropov, who replaced the late, long-serving Leonid Brezhnev in 1982, did not ease concerns about a blistering standoff between the United States and the Soviet Union. He may have been disappointed, but Ronald Reagan was undeterred.

Two weeks later, in a historic address from the White House, the president announced his support for research and development of the Strategic Defense Initiative (SDI), a missile defense system

---

*"March 8, 1983: 'Evil Empire' Speech" (transcript), University of Virginia Miller Center online, https://millercenter.org/the-presidency/presidential-speeches/march-8-1983-evil-empire-speech.

that Reagan hoped would render nuclear weapons obsolete.* The total elimination of nuclear weapons and their potential to destroy the world was something to which Ronald Reagan was devoted. It bothered him that some people viewed him as anything less than committed to achieving that goal.

Critics such as Senator Ted Kennedy of Massachusetts attacked the vision as "reckless *Star Wars* schemes." Reporters soon dubbed the missile shield Reagan's "Star Wars" plan. The idea was to associate the plan with wacky science fiction. Of course, it also connected it to one of the most beloved film franchises of all time. It just so happened that the third and latest outing in the *Star Wars* universe, *Return of the Jedi*, was being shown in the presidential lodge at Camp David the first weekend of June.

The president had grown quite comfortable with the routine and rhythms of Camp David as well as with the personnel who spent so much time with him. In warmer months such as this, he and Mrs. Reagan often enjoyed going to the swimming pool behind Aspen. This was where one of the great Camp David traditions during the Reagan era—essentially a "rite of passage" for new Secret Service agents joining the Presidential Protective Division—took place.

Whenever a new agent joined the detail, he was told to bring a bathing suit to Camp David and to be ready to stand post.

When the president went poolside, the new agent would put on his bathing suit and get ready to go. At that point, before the new

---

*"March 23, 1983: Reagan Proposes 'Star Wars' Missile Defense System," *New York Times* Learning Network, last modified March 23, 2012, http://learning.blogs.nytimes.com/2012/03/23/march-23-1983-reagan-proposes-star-wars-missile-defense-system/?_r=0.

agent left the Secret Service cabin, a senior agent would stop him and hand him a pair of goggles, a snorkel, and fins.

Too nervous to ask any questions, the new agent would put them on and waddle out to the pool, in full view of the president.

The first time this happened, as an agent headed toward Ronald Reagan dressed like a deep-sea diver, the chief executive was startled. But he was too polite to say anything. So he greeted the agent, asked his name, where he was from, and so on.

Later, Reagan asked the senior agent in charge, "What's with the new guy?"

Once he was informed that this was a prank for every new agent, the president was amused (and relieved) and looked forward to a new one waddling along.

The first few times the prank happened, the president had been by himself at the pool. Mrs. Reagan was in Aspen Lodge, probably on the phone or reading. But eventually the prank took place in front of the First Lady. After observing an agent waddle by in goggles and large flopping flippers, she whispered to the president, "Honey, what was that?" Without looking up from his papers, he replied, "New guy."

Jedi was intended to close out the *Star Wars* trilogy. (This was many years before producer-director-writer George Lucas filmed three prequels.) It reunited the main cast—Harrison Ford's Han Solo, Carrie Fisher's Princess Leia, and Mark Hamill's Luke Skywalker—and was a guaranteed blockbuster even before its release. The film earned $500 million worldwide.

Its main competition that summer was expected to be the soon-to-open *Superman III*, a lackluster "threequel" to the two more popular *Superman* films, starring Christopher Reeve in the title role.

Coincidentally, Reeve had been invited to attend a White House reception the following weekend honoring the Special Olympics, which was also being used as a vehicle to promote *Superman III*.*

The visit caused some White House aides concern. Reeve, a supporter of the Special Olympics, was one of the most vocal anti-Reagan celebrities in Hollywood and that was a high standard to meet. In a 1982 interview in *Playgirl*, a magazine neither of the Reagans read, Reeve declared, "I don't think Reagan knows what he's doing. I don't think he has a clue. He's provoking the Russians in a terrifying way. It seems to come from some sort of misplaced pioneer spirit."†

Reeve said that he was an advocate for a unilateral nuclear freeze. That was a popular position of many on the left. They wanted the United States to end its nuclear missile deployment and development regardless of the Soviets' escalating buildup.‡ He also labeled Reagan, as did many in Hollywood, as insensitive to the poor—or, as he told the interviewer, the president was "raping poor people in this country."§

Reeve did appear with Reagan at a Special Olympics event the following weekend. The president seemed to have charmed him—as he did with many opponents. Reeve, in fact, called Reagan—whose name he pronounced "Reegan"—"a wonderful person."

The president himself later reflected on the visit in his diary: "He's done some acrimonious interviews about me being a cold fish with a heart only for the rich. I'm just optimistic enough to think he might have changed his mind." Tellingly, the Reagans had watched

---

*White House Briefing Paper, June 10, 1983.

†Henry Schipper, "Christopher Reeve," *Playgirl*, December 1982, www.chris reevehomepage.com/sp-playgirl1982interview.html.

‡Ibid.

§Norman D. Sandler, "Politics Ignored in White House Guest List," United Press International online, June 12, 1983, www.upi.com/Archives/1983/06/12 /Politics-ignored-in-White-House-guest-list/6639424238400.

Superman II at Camp David with their son, Ron, in 1981. But they skipped the viewing of *Superman III*.

Ronald Reagan liked many aspects of the Superman view of the world—specifically, truth, justice, and the American way—as well as the *Star Wars* films, in which good vanquished evil. *Star Wars* echoed his messages of patriotism perfectly, though it may not have been a message Hollywood or the film's creator intended. By many accounts, George Lucas held views similar to Reeve's. He even revealed his true intentions in a 2005 interview with the *Chicago Tribune*, asserting that the first *Star Wars* film "was really about the Vietnam War, and that was the period where Nixon was trying to run for a [second] term." Years later, the *Los Angeles Times* observed: "For the counterculture, America itself was the Empire to be combated in the name of youth solidarity, just as the Death Star amounted to another name for the military-industrial complex." Darth Vader and the Empire could be seen as stand-ins for the US government—led by men like Nixon and Reagan—versus the small group of freedom fighters, who were stand-ins for the Vietcong.* The Soviets also shared this view. Its official news agency, Tass, compared Reagan to the villainous Vader, dark lord of the Sith.†

Perhaps what was most interesting about the kerfuffle with Reeve was what it said about the differences in the philosophies and outlook of the president and his critics. As Reeve noted in his infamous *Playgirl* interview, "Reagan seems to dig into this thing of believing in himself no matter what his critics say, which I think

---

*Kyle Smith, "How 'Star Wars' Was Secretly George Lucas' Vietnam Protest," *New York Post* online, September 21, 2014, http://nypost.com/2014/09/21/how -star-wars-was-secretly-george-lucas-protest-of-vietnam.

†Mathis Chazanov, "Reagan as Darth Vader," United Press International, June 12, 1983, https://www.upi.com/Archives/1983/06/12/Reagan-as-Darth-Va der/1123424238400/.

is a particularly American trait." Asked by *Playgirl* if he had "any problems with Superman's politics, his role as a defender of truth, justice, and the American way," Reeve responded, "The way I deal with that is to dismiss it completely."

"Don't you think he has any influence on the way kids see the world?" the reporter pressed.

"I certainly hope not," the actor replied.*

But that didn't come across to moviegoers, or to the Reagans. In a review that year of *Return of the Jedi*, the *Washington Post* noted how *Star Wars* "helped close some of the psychological wounds left by the war in Vietnam. *Star Wars* tapped into inspirational depths that transcend political allegiance. It reflected politically uncomplicated yearnings—to be in the right, to fight on the side of justice against tyranny."

The president was a fan of the films because in many ways they were, like *Raiders of the Lost Ark,* adaptations of his favorite Westerns, in which the villains were mostly unambiguous, and the good guys always won. And it was easy to see the appeal of Luke Skywalker: a good-looking, optimistic farm boy with big dreams who changes the world. Not much of a departure from Reagan himself. Leia and Han Solo were both quintessential Western characters: he, the swashbuckling daredevil with the heart of gold; she, the tough-talking, rugged pioneer woman determined to make it in a man's world. As the writer Charlie Jane Anders noted in 2015: "*Star Wars* starts out in the Wild West, the rough-hewn old frontier, and then it races upward, soaring and expanding its scope, until at last it becomes World War II. It's the story of drifters and dreamers, who find their purpose out in the absolute dead middle of nowhere, and end up leading the revolution against an Empire. You can't even

*Schipper, "Christopher Reeve."

imagine a more quintessentially American story than the original *Star Wars*."*

Return of the Jedi offered a special twist, because it included the redemption of one of the most evil characters in movie history, Darth Vader, who sacrifices himself and his ambitions out of love for his son. Reagan was a big believer in redemption stories, as were most people. I suspect he may have reflected on his own father, Jack, who had been tormented by alcoholism and died at age fifty-seven in 1941.

Contrary to some popular notions, *Star Wars* didn't give birth to Reagan's policies. His reference to the "evil empire"—in what sometimes was called "the Darth Vader speech"†—was not a phrase inspired by the films. If the line was inspired by anything, it was probably the 1952 anti-Communist book *Witness* by Whittaker Chambers, an American Communist sympathizer who, beginning in 1932, spied for Russia against the United States. In 1939 a disillusioned Chambers went to the US government and revealed the names of others in the spy ring in exchange for immunity from prosecution. Meanwhile Chambers wound up becoming a vocal critic of Communism and a darling of US conservatives. He was a senior editor at William F. Buckley's *National Review* in the late 1950s and died of a heart attack in 1961.

He referred to the Soviet Union as "the focus of institutionalized evil." (Reagan, in his famous 1983 speech, labeled the Soviets "the focus of evil in the modern world.")

---

*Charlie Jane Anders, "How Star Wars Helped Create President Reagan," *i09* (online blog), last modified December 7, 2015, https://io9.gizmodo.com/how -star-wars-helped-create-president-reagan-1746708591.
†Lily Rothman, "This Is the Ronald Reagan Speech That Just Showed Up on *The Americans*," *Time* online, last modified April 22, 2015, http://time .com/3831400/ronald-reagan-the-americans-speech.

Nor was his vision of a missile shield rendering nuclear weapons obsolete inspired by *Star Wars*. It came from his deep belief in the importance of ridding the world of the MAD (mutually assured destruction) policies that nuclear weapons enabled.

Although both Reagans liked United Press International's White House bureau chief and legendary reporter Helen Thomas personally, the president occasionally expressed annoyance when she referred to his defense system as "Star Wars."

"I wish whoever coined that expression would take it back again, because it gives a false impression of what it is we're talking about," he said once. In an interview with Soviet journalists, Reagan explained that the term was "based on a misconception," and distanced the actual missile defense system from the movies. "We're talking about seeing if there isn't a defensive weapon that does not kill people, but that simply makes it impossible for nuclear missiles, once fired out of their silos, to reach their objective—to intercept those weapons." His irritation with the "Star Wars" label only caused his "tormentors," such as ABC News's chief White House correspondent, Sam Donaldson, among others, to persist in calling it "Star Wars." (Reagan eventually gave in to the inevitable, at one point telling reporters that for supporters of the missile defense shield, "the force is with us.")

I have often been asked if the president was aggravated by Donaldson, who was perhaps the loudest and most provocative of the shouting questioners. Not at all. President Reagan got it that television was a performance medium and that Sam was just doing his job. Both Reagans liked Sam, and I think he liked them too.

The Reagans' feelings were not shared by everyone on the White House staff. On more than one occasion, I got dirty looks from some senior aides when reporters would shout questions at the president during Oval Office or Cabinet Room photo ops. A senior aide once asked me why I could not "control" the press and tell them not to shout questions at the president. I replied that it was fantasy to tell a reporter not to ask a question. Another time, toward the very end of the Reagan presidency, a top aide grabbed my arm during an Oval Office photo op when reporters were shouting questions about some supposedly sensitive national security issue. "Make them stop," he ordered me. I'd had enough. I had already accepted the Reagans' offer to join their post–White House staff in Los Angeles, so I was relatively fearless in answering. I turned to the person and said, "If you had adequately briefed the president, this would not be such an issue," and walked away.

Reagan understood the role that the press played in informing an American public that was still very tense in the later days of the Cold War. It is easy to forget now, but even in the 1980s, the specter of nuclear war still hung closely over the United States and the Soviet Union. President Reagan and all of us in his administration understood the stakes, as did the members of the press corps. We all had our jobs to do in keeping the country safe and informed.

But while Reagan may not have appreciated clever film-inspired nicknames for defense programs, this is not to say that films and dramatized depictions had no influence on his views regarding the Cold War. Anxiety over the prospect of a global nuclear war at the time was a common theme in acclaimed movies such as *Threads* in Great Britain and *Testament* in the United States. They were both stark depictions of people suffering and dying amid a global nuclear fallout.

One TV movie that reached the greatest audience was *The Day After*, a 1983 ABC-TV production watched by a record one hundred million people. The film, starring Jason Robards, JoBeth Williams, and John Lithgow, dramatized the nuclear destruction of Lawrence, Kansas, and Kansas City, Missouri. It shocked and depressed many, including Ronald Reagan. When asked his opinion of the film, he replied, "Any drama or any motion picture or any play is based on one thing. It isn't successful unless it has or evokes an emotional response."* And it definitely provoked one in the president. "It's very effective and left me greatly depressed," he recalled. "My own reaction was one of having to do all we can to have an effective deterrent and to see that there is never a nuclear war."†

Indeed, the commander in chief's determination to support a missile defense system may have been bolstered further by the second film we saw that weekend: *WarGames*, which had just hit movie theaters on Friday, June 3.

WarGames, starring a twenty-one-year-old Matthew Broderick in a breakthrough performance along with *9 to 5*'s Dabney Coleman, received glowing reviews. The film's premise was fanciful. An air force computer in charge of America's nuclear arsenal goes haywire and is on the verge of launching a preemptive missile strike against the Soviet Union, only to be averted at the last minute through the resourcefulness of a teen computer whiz played by Broderick.

Like most suspense films, the pacing brings viewers into the action. And it certainly did for us. At one point, a general standing in a conference room at the North American Air Defense Command (NORAD)—a photo of President Reagan visible on the wall behind him—picks up a red phone and barks, "Get me the president!" At that moment, everyone gathered in the Aspen living room to watch the movie, including President and Mrs. Reagan, turned to

---

*"Interview with Garry Clifford and Patricia Ryan of People Magazine, December 6, 1983," American Presidency Project, www.presidency.ucsb.edu/ws/?pid=40876.
†Ronald Reagan, *Reagan Diaries*, 273.

look at the phone next to where he was sitting. Laughing, we half expected it to ring.

There were other edge-of-the-seat moments, such as when Broderick's character has no money to make a crucial call from a pay phone. He improvises, using a ring top from an aluminum soda can, thereby saving the world from a nuclear holocaust.

When the movie ended, the entire Aspen cabin was uncharacteristically quiet. We rose from our seats, pondering the possibility of rogue computers triggering a global catastrophe.

Mrs. Reagan finally broke the silence, asking no one in particular, "Could that really happen?"

There were several high-ranking military people in the room who had watched the film with the Reagans. They kept their silence.

Then the president's doctor, Dan Ruge, a civilian, answered calmly, "Yes, that could happen." After a long pause, he added, "In fact, I've done it." Dr. Ruge, a distinguished neurosurgeon, had been a partner of Mrs. Reagan's stepfather, Loyal Davis, in Chicago. He and his wife, Greta, had known Nancy Reagan for a very long time.

There was another long pause, with stares and silence.

Then Dan said with a smile, "I've used a ring top to make a call at a pay phone."

The room erupted in laughter, with none heartier than the Reagans'.

The film's dire warning of the dangers of an accidental nuclear launch clearly made a lasting impression on President Reagan. Just two days later, as Lou Cannon describes in his biography, Reagan met with a group of Democratic congressmen to discuss his missile defense program. At one point, he put aside his notes and talked about *WarGames* and the dangers an inadvertent launch might pose to the United States. His concern, like the film itself, was dismissed by some in the room as far-fetched, even absurd. Yet only a few months later—on September 26, 1983, to be exact—the Soviet Union's early warning system malfunctioned twice, alerting Russian generals of a launch of US nuclear missiles. Fortunately, a senior official in the underground bunker near Moscow deduced that the computer was in error, and a nuclear crisis was averted. Life, it turned out, imitated art—and it might have had dire consequences.

8

CURSE OF THE
PINK PANTHER

———◆———

Starring: David Niven, Ted Wass
Directed by: Blake Edwards
Viewed by the Reagans: September 16, 1983

———◆———

The Film That Revealed Reagan's Biggest Disappointment

On Friday, September 16, 1983, the president held an event honoring Hispanic Americans in the Armed Forces and demonstrated yet
again how films affected his thinking. He told those gathered that
he'd recently seen "a wonderful film" called *Hero Street*, the story
of a street in a Hispanic neighborhood in Illinois. At the end of that
street, the president noted, is a monument to eight heroes who gave
their lives for America.

In fact, from twenty-two families on this block, eighty-four men
served in World War II, Korea, and Vietnam. In World War II
and Korea, fifty-seven came from that street. The two Sandoval

families sent thirteen sons: six from one family, seven from the other, and three of the Sandoval sons never came back. I think you will agree with one man in the film who says they so willingly defended America because it was for them, as for all of us, a place of opportunity. I think you will agree with his words when he said, "I don't think there's any more to prove than has been proven on this street." And perhaps you will understand why the name on Second Street in Silvis, Illinois, was changed a few years back. The new name is Hero Street.*

This story was exactly the sort the president loved because it reaffirmed his feelings about America. By telling it, he hoped it would encourage others to feel the same way.

Not that the country was in an optimistic mood at that moment. Two weeks earlier, the Soviet Union had shot down Korean Airlines Flight 007 after it had strayed inadvertently into prohibited Russian airspace while en route from Anchorage, Alaska, to Seoul, killing all 269 aboard, including a US congressman. After originally denying involvement, the Soviets claimed preposterously that the passenger airliner was a spy plane. The crisis over the shooting—the president called it "a crime against humanity that must never be forgotten"—was the closest the United States and the Soviet Union had come to armed confrontation since the 1962 Cuban Missile Crisis. That weekend, the president's weekly radio address offered some of the harshest rhetoric yet regarding the atrocity.

"Apparently [the Soviet Union's] contempt for the truth and for

---

*"Remarks at a White House Ceremony Honoring Hispanic Americans in the United States Armed Forces, September 16, 1983," Ronald Reagan Presidential Library & Museum online, www.reaganlibrary.archives.gov/archives /speeches/1983/91683a.htm.

the opinion of the civilized world is equaled only by their disdain for helpless people like the passengers aboard KAL Flight 007," Reagan said. "They reserve for themselves the right to live by one set of rules, insisting everyone else live by another. They're supremely confident their crime and cover-up will soon be forgotten, and we'll all be back to business as usual. Well, I believe they're badly mistaken."

The president's weekly radio addresses had begun in 1982 and have been a tradition of every president since. (President Barack Obama turned them into video addresses, available on YouTube.) Two events in Reagan's life probably influenced the idea for the weekly address: his memory of his idol Franklin Roosevelt delivering "fireside chats" throughout his twelve-year presidency and Reagan's own career in radio. The president took pride in his abilities as a radio sportscaster—sometimes even dramatizing play-by-plays of entire baseball games based solely on wire reports back when that was his profession.

President Reagan established the practice of delivering a weekly radio address to the nation at 12:06 p.m. every Saturday from wherever he was. He liked to do it live, rather than tape it in advance, unless logistics—such as time differences on a foreign trip—made that impossible. He did them from the Oval Office, the ranch, and, sometimes of course, from Camp David. Those involved in the broadcast, and those with no role whatsoever, all showed up at Laurel Lodge anywhere from 11:00 to 11:45 a.m. The White House Communications Agency (WHCA), an elite military unit that provides communications support to the president in his role as commander in chief, had technical oversight of the broadcast, under the strict supervision of the White House Television Office's director, Elizabeth Board, or Deputy Director Flo Grace. Representatives from the media were also always present to "feed" the broadcast to the US radio networks.

At first, when at Camp David, the president would deliver the address from a small table in the Laurel living room, but because more and more people felt they needed to be present, the broadcast site was moved to the Laurel conference room, which had a table large enough to accommodate the Cabinet and then some.

Shortly before noon, a Secret Service agent posted in Laurel would announce, "Imminent arrival," and everyone would snap into action. The WHCA team tested the microphones at the president's chair, the camp commander and the military aide checked their watches, the presidential food service coordinator placed a glass of bottled water on a napkin embossed with the presidential seal next to the president's microphones, the personal aide stood near the main door of the conference room, and I stood next to Mrs. Reagan's seat against the wall just behind the president. The Reagans entered Laurel through the front door and walked into the conference room. If they were going horseback riding that afternoon, the president would have his riding boots on. He frequently wore a baseball cap. Mrs. Reagan would always wear a nice shirt and usually jeans, plus a sweater or a Camp David jacket.

The president greeted everyone with a big smile and a "Hello, all. How do you do?" as Mrs. Reagan took her seat next to me. We'd whisper as we talked about whatever was on her mind. The chief executive made his way to his seat in the middle of the conference table, in front of the microphones, and looked through his script. Elizabeth or Flo sat next to him, and the personal aide next to her. Sometimes a White House staff photographer or official White House TV crew was present to record the broadcast. The camp commander, the military aide, and Secret Service personnel hovered near the doors at the end of the room. The president would chat with Elizabeth or Flo about such topics as the weather, the number of squirrels or deer seen on the walk to Laurel, or the movie shown the previous night, until the WHCA technician would ask for a voice-level check. The president would then go into "broadcast mode" and recite a few lines of the address, until the tech assured him all was okay. He would then resume chatting, very quietly, until Elizabeth or Flo shouted, "Thirty seconds!"—at which point a big "On the Air" sign would light up, and everyone would be silent. "Five seconds," Elizabeth or Flo said loudly, and they would count down on their fingers, pointing to the president at the precise moment he was to begin. "My fellow Americans" were the next words heard.

Elizabeth or Flo signaled the president every time a minute had elapsed so that he could speed up or slow down as necessary. That was because the former radio announcer prided himself on delivering the speech in *exactly* five minutes and had rehearsed it several times the day before, marking in bold black pen where each minute was, or should be.

When it was over, and the "We're clear!" was shouted by the WHCA technician, the president would look at his watch and ask Elizabeth or Flo how he had done in terms of timing. It was important to him to be exactly on the mark, and 99 percent of the time, he was. Then both Reagans rose from their chairs, thanked everyone, and off they went to lunch in Aspen.

There were some differences when the address was delivered from the White House. From time to time in the second term, Jim Kuhn, the president's personal aide, asked me to fill in for him on Saturdays when the president was delivering the weekly radio address from the Oval Office rather than Camp David. This involved waiting on the ground floor for the elevator from the residence to meet the president when he came down around eleven forty-five, escorting him into the Oval Office, making sure everything was all set up for the live radio address, and, when it was over, escorting the president back to the residence, including riding with him up in the elevator to the family quarters.

On one such occasion, President Reagan delivered his weekly radio address without incident, and everything seemed fine. The day before, Jim had asked me to get the president to sign some routine correspondence after the radio address. He handed me a folder before he left that Friday evening. After the radio address, rather than have the president do so in front of the people assembled in the Oval Office (radio network, military technicians, other staff, Secret Service, and so on), I thought it better to have him attend to the paperwork once we got upstairs. So I took the folder with me as we walked along the colonnade onto the ground floor of the White House and took the elevator up to the family quarters. I walked with the president into his personal office, which was located next to the Reagans' bedroom, and said, "Mr. President, there are a couple of routine letters we need to get you to sign," opened the folder, and handed him a pen. He signed the letters. I said, "Thank you very much, sir, have a nice weekend," and departed. I walked back to the West Wing, put the folder of signed letters back on Jim's desk, and went home for what was a quiet weekend.

On Monday, I arrived at the White House at the usual time, went to my office, and got down to work. At around ten, Jim called me on the private direct line between our offices and said, "He wants to see you." I said, "I'm sure he does," or something to that effect, because I thought Jim was scamming me. So I continued about my business.

An hour or so later, Jim buzzed me again and said in a more plaintive tone, "He really does want to see you." This time, I could tell he wasn't joking, so I said I would come by soon. Still, I could not imagine what the president would possibly want to see me about. It was completely out of character for Ronald Reagan to summon anyone to the Oval Office like that. Nonetheless, after about twenty to thirty minutes, I put on my suit coat and walked down the hall to the area outside the Oval Office, where Jim and the president's personal secretary, Kathy Osborne, had their desks.

Jim was not there, so I told Kathy that Jim said the president wanted to see me. She looked perplexed and said, "He does?" She got up from her desk, walked into the Oval Office, and then came back out no more than thirty seconds later. Sounding surprised, she told me that the president did indeed want to see me and that I should go right in. So I marched into the Oval Office. President Reagan was at his desk having his lunch and reading some briefing materials. I said, "Mr. President, I understand you wanted to see me, sir."

He looked up. "Oh yes, Mark, come in, please."

I approached his desk, and he said, "Say, on Saturday, you had me sign some letters, and"—at this point, I got a huge knot in my stomach because I was sure I had screwed up something—"I did so with the pen that you had given me, but I didn't give it back to you." He then opened the top drawer of the Resolute desk—used by several presidents, the iconic desk is a double pedestal partners' desk, made from wood from the British ship HMS *Resolute* and given to President Rutherford B. Hayes by Queen Victoria in 1880—took out the pen I had given him to sign the letters two days earlier, and said, "I didn't know if it was special to you for some reason or not, and I felt bad about having kept it over the weekend. I was going to call you about it, but I didn't want you to have to come back into the office to get it, so here it is. I'm sure sorry if it was something you needed or wanted to have." He then handed me the pen—a black felt-tip that I had bought at a local drugstore. I said, "Mr. President, thank you so much. It really wasn't, but I sure appreciate it." He smiled and said, "Well, all right." I mumbled something about my getting back to work and left the Oval Office. I wish I'd kept that pen.

The president's attention to the details surrounding the radio addresses was impeccable—but then, it had to be. Sometimes the topic of the addresses was a policy proposal to which the president wanted to give a special focus, and sometimes, like this weekend's address, it was on the most serious matters of life and death.*

As a break from the tension surrounding the downed Korean airliner, the Reagans had prepared a special treat. Tonight's feature was not a box office juggernaut but the Blake Edwards film *Curse of the Pink Panther*. The movie was an effort at a comeback for the once-popular Pink Panther series, but it was without its familiar and beloved actor Peter Sellers, who played the bumbling Inspector Jacques Clouseau. Sellers died suddenly of a heart attack in 1980 at age fifty-four. (Sellers had appeared in all five previous Pink Panther movies, although 1982's *Trail of the Pink Panther* was pieced together using footage of him from previous films.)

There was one, and only one, reason the Reagans wanted to see the film, though. One of the costars was their daughter. Patti, then a thirty-year-old actress whose credits included guest spots on TV shows such as *Fantasy Island* and *Hart to Hart*, played the character Michelle Chauvin, a French newscaster. Usually the Reagans preferred to watch movies in concentrated silence. But Mrs. Reagan broke the quiet when their daughter's name appeared on the screen.

She turned to the president, and in a voice loud enough for everyone in the room to hear, said, "See that, honey? Patricia *Davis*," in a slightly teasing manner. Davis, of course, was Mrs. Reagan's maiden name. There was an unmistakable tone of pride when she

---

*"Radio Address to the Nation on the Soviet Attack on a Korean Civilian Airliner, September 17, 1983," Ronald Reagan Presidential Library & Museum online, www.reaganlibrary.archives.gov/archives/speeches/1983/91783a.htm.

saw that her daughter was using it for her acting career. The president had no reaction.

I never spoke with him about it so I don't know if he wanted Patti to pursue an acting career, but my guess is he was proud of her. Still, family members in the same demanding profession can experience some difficulties. Even the president and Mrs. Reagan were not immune to them. Yet only once in the more than three decades or so that I knew them did I detect a sense of professional "rivalry" between them.

In the late summer of 1986, we were at the Reagan ranch, near Santa Barbara, when an NBC-TV news crew came to film a special on the First Lady, hosted by Chris Wallace. With the camera rolling, the president and Mrs. Reagan were having lunch together on the front patio of their small adobe home, as they often did. They were seated at a little round table, on which were some raw vegetables, sandwiches, chips, and soft drinks. Mrs. Reagan began the conversation with her husband about something innocuous—it could have even been the weather—but try as she might, she could not get him to engage on any subject. Earlier in the day, he had been his usual genial, witty self, but now he gave only polite one-word responses—"yep" and "nope"—to whatever she said, and then would munch on a carrot or celery stick. He did not seem interested in conducting a conversation. This uncharacteristic behavior went on for several minutes, until we escorted the NBC crew to another location on the ranch. Later that day, I asked another aide who had also witnessed the scene what was up. "He didn't want to be a costar in her show," he explained.

Like all married couples, the Reagans could have their disagreements and even bicker occasionally, but it was rare, really. In all the time I spent around them, I witnessed only one full-blown argument. In 1989, the seventy-eight-year-old former president had returned from the Mayo Clinic in Rochester, Minnesota, where he'd undergone head surgery to resolve a subdural hematoma caused by his being thrown by a wild horse a few months earlier. We were at their home in Los Angeles. Former president Reagan's doctors had told him to ease back into his routine but to take it slowly. He wanted to go to the barbershop, have a trim, and maybe get a manicure. Because the barber would have to touch the president's head, Mrs. Reagan was uncomfortable with the idea and did not think he should go just yet. But he was adamant. They argued about it in raised voices. They weren't screaming at each other—they never did that—but they *were* arguing. He said, "I put up with an awful lot around here, and I want to go because I enjoy it." She was exasperated and said finally, "Then do whatever you darn please." Needless to say, it was awkward as heck for me to be there, and I wanted to disappear.

The next day I was at the house again for some reason or another; probably for a meeting about upcoming events. The president pulled me aside just inside the foyer and said, "Say, Mark, you know those hostilities that you witnessed yesterday between Nancy and me, well, that's all over now." I replied, "Mr. President, I don't know what you mean."

"You know, the hostilities yesterday with regard to the barbershop and all," he said.

"Sir, I do not recall anything of the kind," I insisted, wearing a smile. He looked at me, winked, and said with a big smile, "Well, all right, then."

There were other times I found myself stuck in the middle of some awkwardness between Mr. and Mrs. Reagan. Once in the post-presidency years, we were getting ready to leave on a trip. In a few days, Ronald Reagan was to tape an interview with Barbara Walters of ABC News about his memoir, *An American Life*. He had often

The only regret I have about my years in the White House is that I was not married at the time, and thus could not share the experience with my wife and our children. But there is nothing I can do about that. I have shared with them many memories, and was thrilled beyond words when Mrs. Reagan received us at her home a few years ago. It is one of my most cherished days. I just wish RR could have been there. (*Left to right:* Nancy Reagan, Mark Weinberg, Erin Weinberg, Grace Weinberg, and Jake Weinberg) *Courtesy of the author*

I was glad, however, that my parents and siblings were able to enjoy my time in the White House. This picture was taken around the time of my father's sixty-third birthday. The president called him "kid." (*Left to right:* Mark Weinberg, Michael Weinberg, Herbert Weinberg, RR, Judith Weinberg, and Mary Ellen Weinberg)

To Mark—
About those leaks — !
Guess Who?

At some point in the first term, there was the predictable concern about "leaks." The very small group of staff who accompanied the president and Mrs. Reagan to Camp David on weekends prided ourselves on the fact that there were never any leaks from Camp David. Ever. And we made a point of telling people that. One could say we were a bit boastful. Somehow Mrs. Reagan heard about it, found this photo of me—outside the closed door of the conference room in Laurel Lodge—and signed it. It arrived in the interoffice mail one day! *Courtesy of the Ronald Reagan Presidential Foundation & Institute*

Camp David was nothing if not fun. Everyone enjoyed being there. I faked stealing the official sign, which did not amuse the humorless US Marine Corps guards one bit. At all. *Courtesy of the Ronald Reagan Presidential Foundation & Institute*

At Christmastime, we always had the Reagans pose for a photo in front of their "personal" tree in the family quarters of the White House. I looked forward to these photo ops because it was then that I would discreetly place my Christmas gifts for them under it. Ronald Reagan liked getting presents for his birthday, Christmas, etc. It wasn't that he wanted "things," he just delighted in receiving presents. (And he always either called or wrote—by hand—to say thanks.) I always reminded the president that they were to be opened on Christmas Day. Yet almost as soon as I turned to walk toward the elevator, I could hear him ripping off the wrapping paper! *Courtesy of the Ronald Reagan Presidential Foundation & Institute*

From time to time, the Reagans would spend weekends in Washington, and often in the second term, Jim Kuhn—the president's personal aide—would have me fill in for him in terms of handling the Saturday radio address, so that he could be at home with his wife and children. One aspect was to meet the president at the elevator in the residence and walk with him to the Oval Office. Often, there was paperwork (letters to sign, etc.) for the president to do while he was in the office. By the way, Saturdays were the only time Ronald Reagan did not wear a suit to the Oval Office and he did that so that the staff would not feel obligated to dress up.

Courtesy of the Ronald Reagan Presidential Foundation & Institute

The Reagans stopped in Alaska on their way home from China in 1984, where they met with Pope John Paul II, who was embarking on his own tour of Asia. It was raining, yet no one had an umbrella on Mrs. Reagan. She thanked me, but said, "Now, Mark, when the pope's plane comes here . . ." and before she could finish, I said: "I will disappear so there is nothing in the way of the picture." She smiled. *Courtesy of the Ronald Reagan Presidential Foundation & Institute*

I had a bet with the president about something—probably a sporting game—which I lost. I dutifully paid up. *Courtesy of the Ronald Reagan Presidential Foundation & Institute*

Even when at his beloved ranch, President Reagan insisted on delivering his weekly radio address live. It was at 9:06 a.m. Pacific time, which meant I had to leave Santa Barbara around 7 or so to be at the ranch on time. He was always happy there. This was taken in a temporary building erected near the Reagans' house. It was there that he made those now infamous remarks about "outlawing Russia forever . . ." *Courtesy of the Ronald Reagan Presidential Foundation & Institute*

The Reagans loved to take walks at Camp David, almost always together. Occasionally, the president would walk with the staff, in this case Jim Kuhn, his personal aide, the camp commander, and me. He was already in his riding gear. This was taken in front of Aspen Lodge. *Courtesy of the Ronald Reagan Presidential Foundation & Institute*

During the radio addresses, which the president delivered live from the conference room in Laurel Lodge at Camp David, I always sat with Mrs. Reagan and we talked about everything. With the president at the microphone is Florence Grace, the deputy director of the White House television office. *Courtesy of the Ronald Reagan Presidential Foundation & Institute*

referred to that project as "a monkey on my back," but he understood that his record of the White House years was important for history, and he spent hours with pen and pad writing it out. Now that it was published, the usual round of interviews was scheduled, including the sit-down with Walters due to take place when we got back. Late on the day before we left Los Angeles, Mrs. Reagan called me and in a very serious voice said, "Mark, Ronnie is talking with Barbara about the book in a few days, and you have to make sure he sees it before. He has to look at it on the plane tomorrow. There's plenty of time." "Of course, Mrs. Reagan," I replied.

After Reagan's speech—the topic and location are lost to me now—we got back on the plane for the long flight home to LA. In my briefcase was the book, and I knew what I had to do. I moved from my seat on a bench on the small plane to a seat right in front of President Reagan's, opposite a small table. He was reading a news magazine (and, as was his usual habit, removing the annoying subscription cards he found there). He knew I had come over to him for a reason but chose not to look up.

"Mr. President," I said meekly. Without putting down the magazine, he looked up and said, "Yes," in a very uncharacteristic "What the heck do you want?" tone.

"Well, sir, as you know, you are scheduled to talk with Barbara Walters next week about your book and—"

"So?" he interrupted with unmistakable irritation.

"Well, sir, I just thought it would be a good idea for you to see the book before that." I pulled it out of my briefcase and placed it in front of him on the much-too-small table between us. He glared at me. I wished I had a parachute.

Then I had an idea. I picked up the book and said, "Mr. President, do you see this book?"

"Yes, Mark, I see it," he answered with obvious annoyance.

"Sir," I said a bit more loudly and pointedly than probably necessary, "do you *see* it? Are you *looking* at it?"

Again, an icy glare. "Yes, darn it, I see it. What's your point?" he asked, in a rare tone of displeasure.

Pronouncing each word carefully and slowly, I then said, "Okay, so if anyone—for example, a lady who lives in Bel Air—asks, you have *seen* your book, right?" I held my breath.

He got it. Ronald Reagan smiled that smile, cocked his head, looked me in the eye, and said, "I sure have."

"Great, thanks, sir." I slipped the book back in my briefcase and returned quickly to my seat. He went back to reading his magazine, and I took a nap. Just before we landed, I sat down across from him again, looked him in the eye, and said, "Now, sir, if anyone asks, you've seen the book, right?" He winked and said, "You bet." Sure enough, just before the interview with Barbara Walters, Mrs. Reagan asked me if her husband had seen the book. "Yes, of course," I replied.

Even if they had the occasional moment of tension, the Reagans were loving parents, and they were nothing but proud to see Patti in her screen debut. That was certainly the highlight of that particular viewing. The *Pink Panther* movie, frankly, was not great. I won't bore you with the plot, such as it was. Reviews were not kind. "Not unfunny, and not really an offense to the memory of Inspector Clouseau," the *New York Times* opined. "It's merely a movie with very little reasons to exist."

Although her role was small, the *Times* could not help but be vicious toward Patti's performance. "Also in the large cast, inexplicably, is Patricia Davis, President Reagan's daughter, playing a French newscaster," the reviewer wrote. "Not even those undiscriminating enough to find this 'Pink Panther' film as charming as any of the others will imagine that this newscaster's French accent is genuine."

But something else about the film lingered in my mind. It offered a rare insight into the president's own feelings about himself. After the movie ended, being the loyal staff that we were, we all took our turn singing Patti's praises.

In a desire to please the Reagans, someone (not I) made the ridiculously fawning comment "She should get an Oscar for that performance"—a remark that pretty much everyone recognized for its absurdity. Including the Reagans.

Mrs. Reagan laughed politely. But the president said nothing. He looked a little surprised by the suggestion, and I sensed there was something about it that gnawed at him. Years later, I would learn why. The subject of an Oscar was a sore one for Ronald Reagan. He was realistic enough to know that none of his movie performances was of that caliber, although he was justifiably proud of his acting in many of his films. In the buildup to his first summit meeting with Mikhail Gorbachev, in Geneva, Switzerland, in 1985, the president had been bothered by references to him in the USSR media as a "B-movie actor." During a walk with the Soviet leader, Reagan asked that he tell one of Russia's leading critics of American culture, Georgi Arbatov, that his roles "weren't all B-movies." He suggested the Soviets see his performance in *Kings Row*.[*]

Arbatov was not the only person to speak critically about President Reagan's movie career. In 1987 the president welcomed Jim Harbaugh, the acclaimed quarterback for the University of Michigan Wolverines (and today their head coach), to the Oval Office. My school, the George Washington University, did not have a football program, so, by default, I became a fan of the University of

---

[*]Eleanor Clift, "Stars Salute Hollywood Alumnus 'Dutch' Reagan," *Los Angeles Times* online, December 2, 1985, http://articles.latimes.com/1985-12-02/news /mn-12659_1_ronald-reagan.

Michigan, where my sister went for her undergraduate degree. While in the White House, I was impressed by Harbaugh, who went on to a fourteen-year career in the National Football League as a player. At one point in the second term, I learned from our advance team that he was to be at some event President Reagan would be attending in Michigan. I hoped to meet Jim there. But as things turned out, his coach, the legendary Bo Schembechler, wouldn't allow him to miss practice. At least, that's what I was told.

I had read that Jim was disappointed by that. Knowing the president always enjoyed visiting with young people, especially college athletes, I took it upon myself to reach out to Harbaugh and invite him to come to Washington to meet President Reagan. Jim said he would be honored to do so and asked if he could bring some members of his family with him, specifically his mother and his grandmother. He explained that his father, a football coach at another college, had recruiting trips planned and could not join them. As someone who was very close to both of my grandmothers, I was impressed that Jim wanted to include his, and agreed. They were friendly, unpretentious, and wonderful people.

However, when I took them into the Oval Office to meet President Reagan, there was an awkward moment. The president and Jim had a very animated conversation about football, and Jim's mother was as pleasant as could be. His grandmother, who was delightful, wanted to do more than just pose for a photo. She told the president, in the most sincere and heartfelt way, that while she "never cared for you much as an actor, I think you are a great president."

I don't think anyone had ever said such a thing to him before, and I had a feeling it shocked him. But Reagan was gracious in his response. He gave the Harbaugh family presidential gifts and posed for photos, after which I escorted them out of the Oval Office. I later heard from his aide, Jim Kuhn, that the president was distressed to learn someone did not like him as an actor and wondered which movies of his she had seen. (I said I would find out but never did.)

President Reagan was never much of a complainer. But one day, after his presidency had ended, we were in his office in Los Angeles talking about Hollywood, and he said, "You would think that after what I've done—being the only one from that profession to do so—they would commemorate it in some way. But I guess their political agenda has taken over good manners." Reagan was a little bothered that Hollywood never officially acknowledged that one of their own had ascended to the presidency. He thought an honorary Oscar might have been in order—and felt that had he been a Democrat, he would have received one. Several of us on the former president's staff felt badly that we had not sought that for him once he was back in Los Angeles. We should have done so soon after we got there.

The popular impression of Ronald Reagan, especially as memories of his actual presidency continue to fade, was that he was an avuncular, nice guy who danced in the sunlight of life. He did. But he was a human being, with the ability to be hurt, as he was by the rejection by some of his peers in Hollywood. He was proud of his career in Hollywood and never thought of the acting profession as anything less important or prestigious than other careers.

Though he never received the honorary Oscar he wanted, it is worth noting here that Hollywood did honor their famous veteran at a star-studded salute to the president in 1985 that was televised on NBC and billed as *An All-Star Party for "Dutch" Reagan*. Among the entertainers in the audience were *The Godfather* actor James Caan, Sammy Davis Jr., Angie Dickinson, Glenn Ford, Robert Mitchum, John Ritter, Cliff Robertson, Telly Savalas, Red Skelton, Robert Stack, Jimmy Stewart, Alex Trebek, Robert Wagner, Betty White, *Dynasty* stars John Forsythe, Linda Evans, and Joan Collins, and a few members of the cast of CBS's *Falcon Crest,* which starred the president's ex-wife, Jane Wyman.

The Reagans attended the black-tie event with his daughter Maureen. Because she was Jane Wyman's child, not Nancy's, when I first started working in the White House I wondered about how welcome Maureen would be there. I need not have worried. She and Mrs. Reagan had a great relationship. I was struck by how vigorously Maureen defended her stepmother against detractors.

The president and Mrs. Reagan referred to Maureen affectionately as Mermie. She was smart, vivacious, loyal, and liked to laugh. Ronald Reagan respected his oldest child's opinions and advice. Though he never said so—and, as far as I know, never pushed Maureen into it—I sensed he was proud his daughter was pursuing a political career. And she was front and center at the Hollywood dinner, as usual, cheering her father on.

The dinner was hosted by a close friend of the Reagans, the one and only "Ol' Blue Eyes" Frank Sinatra—whom the president continually referred to, publicly and in their correspondence, by his full name: Francis Albert. Sinatra, now seventy and obviously reading from cue cards, was nonetheless a charming MC. As he was announced into the room, the audience, most of whom were celebrities, rose to their feet and applauded. Sinatra quipped, "You may be seated."[*] He saluted Reagan as "the only member of our community living in public housing."[†] He also noted to the audience that "rules of protocol have been relaxed." Referring to the president, he said, "Tonight he's Dutch. As for Nancy, do as I do: call her 'Beautiful.'"[‡]

---

[*] *An All-Star Party for "Dutch" Reagan,* December 8, 1985, CBS-TV, www.you tube.com/watch?v=1tnHMx9vmV8.
[†] Ibid.
[‡] Ibid.

The actor Burt Reynolds also spoke. Reagan had not known Reynolds well during his time in Hollywood, but some three years before, in March 1982, he joined the Reagans for dinner at the White House. That evening, the president came away surprised by Reynolds's "serious and sincere crusade spirit against drugs."* But on the night of the *All-Star Party*, Reynolds was in a lighthearted mood. Commenting on the tight security surrounding the event, he told the president, "Only Sylvester Stallone has more security than you."†

The actor Charlton Heston departed from the mood of the room with a tribute to the president that left him near tears. Praising his leadership, Heston, a well-known conservative, declared, "You speak to mankind in our name."‡ And he offered Reagan a prayer: "As you lead us into the uncertain, beleaguered future—the broad swell of continent between those shining seas—let me say for all of us, Mr. President, the words of a song you'll remember, 'God shed his grace on thee.'"§

At the close of the evening, a moved President Reagan rose to the microphones to thank everyone. "It's good to be 'Dutch' again," he said. He then said he wanted to borrow a line from the comedienne Lucille Ball, who'd spoken at a similar event honoring her: "To those who said such nice things about me tonight, I wish you were all under oath." Then Reagan added his own touch to the line: "I wish you were all members of Congress."¶ The proceeds of the event

---

*Ronald Reagan, *Reagan Diaries*, 117.
†Gerald M. Boyd, "Hollywood Stars Honor President," *New York Times* online, December 2, 1985, www.nytimes.com/1985/12/02/us/hollywood-stars-honor -president.html.
‡Ronald Reagan, *Reagan Diaries*, 117.
§Ibid.
¶Ibid.

were used for a Ronald Reagan Wing for children at the University of Nebraska hospital in Omaha.

The evening ended with Sinatra and Dean Martin leading the audience in a stirring rendition of "Auld Lang Syne." It wasn't an Academy Award, but the evening warmed Reagan's heart.

9

A GOLDEN OLDIE—
BEDTIME FOR BONZO

———◆———

Starring: Ronald Reagan, Walter Slezak,
Diana Lynn, Peggy (as Bonzo)
Directed by: Fred de Cordova
Viewed by President Reagan: June 22, 1984

———◆———

The Film That Helped Define a Career

On June 22, 1984, the military aide to the president boarded the presidential helicopter, Marine One, en route to Camp David, with two precious possessions: one was the "football" containing the codes the president would need to launch a nuclear strike. The other was a brown paper bag. When asked about its contents, the aide replied curtly that it was a "personal item" for the president. He did not elaborate further, which only added to the mystery.*

The mystery was cleared up a few hours later, when the gang

———

*Email to author from Marine One pilot Terrence R. Dake, June 5, 2015.

gathered at Aspen for the Friday night movie. Before anyone sat down, President Reagan said that he had been disappointed in the level of entertainment at Camp David. Tonight, he explained, he had brought his own selection. The face of the Camp David commander, whose most important mission was to keep the president happy while there, fell. No one wanted to disappoint a kind man like Reagan.

But then Reagan's eyes twinkled, and everyone knew he had something special in store.

By the time the group got to Camp David that weekend, everyone in the entourage was ready for a rest, except the president. He did not seem tired or worn out by what had been a busy time, even by White House reelection-mode standards.

At the beginning of the week, he and Mrs. Reagan hosted a state dinner for the president of Sri Lanka. A number of Hollywood legends were on the guest list, including Fred MacMurray, Robert Conrad, Rich Little, Tony Randall, Jane Powell, and Frank Sinatra, one of Mrs. Reagan's favorites, who provided the entertainment that evening.

Even though state dinners made for a long day, I liked working them. The First Lady's Press Office was in charge of coverage, but I was on hand to monitor what the president said to reporters. Around six thirty or so, I would close the door of my office, pull together the flimsy curtains on my window facing Pennsylvania Avenue—so as to spare tourists a horrifying (or thrilling) experience—and change into my tuxedo. I would then proceed to the North Portico of the White House to witness the president and Mrs. Reagan greeting the visiting world leader and spouse. Rarely, pretty much never, did anyone in the assembled press corps there shout a question at the president, but I was present just in case. We then moved inside to watch the Reagans pose with their guests at the foot of the grand staircase in the White House's main foyer, and then the press and working staff departed until it was time for toasts, mingling, entertainment, and dancing. During the state dinner itself, the staff in attendance would eat in the White House Staff Mess, usually with our counterparts on the staff of the visiting dignitary. At an appointed hour, we would escort the press pool to the State Dining Room, where they would cover the president and his guest exchanging toasts. Sometimes the toasts occurred at the beginning of the dinner so as to make news deadlines, but not always.

Whenever the dinner ended, the Reagans and their guests had coffee and liqueurs in the Red, Blue, and Green Rooms while the East Room was being set up for entertainment. It was a long-standing custom that a small group of reporters from the wire services, newspapers, and magazines mingled with the guests. Theoretically, the reporters were there only to observe and listen, but it rarely worked out that way.

My usual practice was to go into the White House usher's office, a few paces from the Blue Room, call the press duty officer just before the reporters were to arrive, and ask if there was anything the president needed to be aware of in advance. If there was, I would pull him aside and brief him. As soon as they arrived on the State Floor, the reporters rushed over to the president, who was always in the Blue Room. Sometimes they just hovered nearby to hear what he was saying. I always tapped him on the shoulder, raised my eyebrows, and gestured to the reporters nearby so that he would know he was being overheard. Many times they ignored the "rules" and approached him with questions.

After a few minutes of this mini press conference, I would say in a loud voice, "Mr. President, I believe some of your guests are waiting to chat with you." He understood and pivoted to a waiting guest, at which point the reporters would scowl at me and move toward the

East Room to cover the evening's entertainment. But if the president had "made news" during this encounter, they would be escorted back to the Press Briefing Room to file their stories and then be brought back up to the East Room. Likewise, if he had said something newsworthy, I would again retreat to the usher's office to call the press duty officer to tell him or her what the president had said.

After the evening's entertainment, everyone moved to the Cross Hall on the State Floor, including the pool of reporters. Usually the Reagans would escort their guests to the front door of the White House, bid farewell, and come back in for a dance or two. (Occasionally, but not too often, the visiting leader and spouse would dance before leaving, too.) The reporters present rarely approached the president. After their dances, the Reagans would very leisurely walk toward the elevator that would take them to the residence, talking with guests and posing for photos on the way. The second they were in the elevator on their way upstairs, I headed home.

The visit of the Sri Lankan president was only one part of what had been a busy week in the Reagan White House. The president spoke at dedication ceremonies for the new building of the National Geographic Society, at a presentation ceremony for a large group of recent high school graduates recognized as Presidential Scholars, and at bill signings designating wilderness areas. He also traveled to River Dell High School in Oradell, New Jersey, where he spoke about efforts to curb drunk driving. Giving a heartfelt and strong speech, Reagan departed from his prepared text, something he rarely did. Here's part of what he said:

> I'm going to depart from the main theme here to tell you that Nancy and I discussed what I would be saying here. And we want you to know that we're aware that the problem we have on our highways isn't just drinking and driving. It's also drinking and

drugging . . . I speak as one who has lived seventy-three years . . .
I've seen a lot. I lived a good part of my adult life in Hollywood and
Los Angeles. And I saw a lot of people who were living fast lives.
And I just want to tell you: don't take drugs. Don't abuse your
mind and body that way.*

Later that day, the president traveled to Connecticut to address the
National Sheriffs' Association. As he did often, Reagan used his Hollywood experience to establish a bond with his audience, telling the
sheriffs, "Back in those days when I was doing television, I once
played a sheriff, a western sheriff, in a TV drama. And the gist of the
story was that the sheriff thought he could do the job without a gun.
It was a thirty-minute show. I was dead in twenty-seven minutes."
The audience roared.

The day's schedule did not end there. That evening, he and
Mrs. Reagan hosted a Congressional Fish Fry on the South Lawn
of the White House, which featured the legendary southern rocker
and country singer Charlie Daniels as the evening's entertainment.

Even though the president had disagreements, some quite sharp,
with many members of Congress, he and Mrs. Reagan enjoyed hosting these events. The Reagans did not view such events as chores
and never rushed to get through them. They knew that the social
relationships built at such events could come in handy in business
situations down the road. They did a lot of that with state legisla-
tors when Ronald Reagan was governor of California. Similarly, they
liked to get to know members of Congress, from both sides of the
aisle, as people and never let politics get in the way of friendship.

*Ronald Reagan, "Remarks at River Dell High School in Oradell, New Jer-
sey, June 20, 1984," American Presidency Project, www.presidency.ucsb.edu
/ws/?pid=40073.

I think it surprised (and maybe even annoyed) some people on the White House staff that the Reagans were friendly with two Democrats from Massachusetts: especially Speaker of the House Tip O'Neill and his wife, as well as Senator Edward Kennedy and his wife. There were those who simply could not get beyond a person's politics and could not see any redeeming values in anyone who was not on the same side of an issue. Not Ronald Reagan. He meant it when he said politics ended at six o'clock. Political beliefs were not a factor in whether the Reagans liked or socialized with someone.

Despite such a rigorous schedule, Ronald Reagan was not tired when he arrived at Camp David for what was an unusual weekend in late June. Mrs. Reagan was not there. She was probably on a trip related to her campaign against drug abuse. I suspect that because he did not want to be lonely, the president invited guests who were close to him and Nancy: specifically, longtime close aide and Deputy White House Chief of Staff Mike Deaver and his wife and family, and longtime friend and colleague Senator Paul Laxalt of Nevada and his wife. This was a rare occurrence. The Reagans almost never had guests at Camp David. Sometimes they had family members there with them, and White House chiefs of staff James A. Baker III and Ken Duberstein occasionally came with their families. That was very much the exception rather than the rule. Most of the time it was just the Reagans and a very small group of staff in attendance.

Since the Aspen Movie Club convened at Camp David, we'd been bugging the president to screen one of his own films. He'd finally given in.

"Well, tonight we have a treat, or what I hope you will think is a treat," he said, "and that's one of my old movies. Now, I would like to remind you that you are the ones who've requested these, so here we go. Roll 'em." The president had picked one of the best-known of his films: the one his political opponents liked to make fun of,

Bedtime for Bonzo. Bonzo, of course, was a chimpanzee. Incredibly, this was the first time that Reagan had ever watched the 1951 film in its entirety.

It was a typical comedy of the era: light, appropriate for all ages, with many genuinely funny scenes. Contrary to popular impression, *Bedtime for Bonzo* got great reviews at the time, and some said it may have helped revive Reagan's popularity, which had been on the wane. Like all good comedy, the movie was based on a solid, believable foundation. Briefly, Bonzo was an experimental animal at a university where Reagan was a professor. His character, Peter Boyd, and a colleague embarked on the kind of experiment conducted at universities—Duke among them, I believe—to see what would happen if they raised Bonzo the chimp in a home like a child, to see what level of environment could enhance his ability to learn. Amanda Deaver, whose fourteenth birthday was celebrated at Camp David that weekend and was in Aspen when the movie was shown, remembers that President Reagan was "very spirited and animated," talking about what he called "that crazy chimpanzee." She told me he was "filled with joy" as he shared stories about making that movie.*

Admittedly, the movie was not deep or particularly thought provoking. But in rewatching it years later, I did notice something interesting. In a scene where Reagan was mad at a misbehaving Bonzo, he threatened the chimp by saying, "I will tan your hide." That struck me because the phrase Ronald Reagan used most often when angry with reporters who wrote negatively about Nancy (one of the few things that infuriated him) was "*Damn* their hides." And even that was infrequent.

President Reagan's alleged use of strong language was a key factor in one of the more sensational reports about his and Mrs. Reagan's

---

*Amanda Deaver email to author, May 31, 2016.

personal life. One weekend in December 1986, I was called at Camp David by the on-duty White House spokesman about a story claiming that Mrs. Reagan had been pressing her husband to replace White House Chief of Staff Donald Regan so relentlessly that the president finally snapped at her to "get off my goddamned back." I promptly called Mrs. Reagan and told her that there was a report circulating that the president had spoken "sharply" to her about Don Regan. She asked what I meant. I stammered a bit, saying the words were not so nice. She insisted that I tell her exactly, word for word, what was being reported, so I did. The First Lady said to me, "Ronnie would never talk to me that way." With that, I simply relayed that the report was to be flatly denied. I am sure she was telling the truth, as I never knew Ronald Reagan to ever curse at his wife. But I had a feeling from her tone that there had been a "vigorous" discussion about Don Regan's future.

Despite threatening on-screen to "tan his hide," Reagan had remained a good sport about Bonzo and the film they shared throughout his political career. He was once asked to sign a picture of himself with the chimp, and he did so, adding: "I'm the one wearing the watch." On another occasion, he told a group of business leaders, "I have to confess that I am amazed that a Hollywood actor who costarred with a monkey could ever make it in politics." From time to time, he also would mention the movie in speeches. At a campaign rally in Atlanta in 1984, he said to the applauding and enthusiastic crowd, "If you had done this a few years ago when I was making Bedtime for Bonzo, I'd still be there"—meaning Hollywood. And at another political rally in 1986 in North Carolina, he told the crowd to vote for the GOP opponent of Democrat Terry Sanford, quipping, "Believe me, when it comes to reruns, Bedtime for Bonzo is better than tax time with Terry." When President Reagan heard that a senior Soviet official had dismissed him as a "reckless cowboy" actor, he pointed out that he played in only a couple of Westerns and that maybe he should send the official a print of *Bedtime for Bonzo*—presumably to show the range of his acting skills!

Reagan would often say that while *Bedtime for Bonzo* was perhaps the most fun movie he ever made, he did sometimes wonder if he should have heeded the advice of a director who once warned him never to share the stage with animals or children. Also, though he did make self-deprecating remarks about his involvement in the film, it annoyed him when critics pointed to it as an example of silliness; specifically, his starring opposite a chimpanzee. He did not see it that way. In *Where's the Rest of Me?*, Reagan recalled the movie:

> Universal [Pictures Company], where I was supposed to realize my action ambitions, came up with another comedy. Diana Lynn, Walter Slezak, and I fought a losing battle against a scene-stealer with a built-in edge: he was a chimpanzee, and he even had us rooting for him. The picture was called *Bedtime for Bonzo*, and he was Bonzo . . . On the set, he learned our business so well that going to work was a fascinating experience. Naturally, his trainer was on the set, and the normal procedure called for the director, Fred De Cordova, to tell the trainer what he wanted from Bonzo. But time after time, Freddie, like the rest of us, was so captivated that he'd forget and start to direct Bonzo as he did the human cast members. He'd say, "No, Bonzo, in this scene you should—" Then he'd hit his head and cry, "What the hell am I doing?" [Interestingly enough, while Bonzo was portrayed as a male in the film, the chimpanzee that played him was a female named Peggy.]

Despite attempts to belittle Reagan because of the movie, he was not embarrassed by it. In August 1982 his costar in the film, Walter Slezak sent him a letter. Chatty and respectful, the Austrian-born actor recalled their work together on the movie; told the president that he collected literary, musical, and political manuscripts; and asked for a signed photo. In a reply hand signed "Ron," the president volunteered to Slezak that "when I see some of what is coming out of the industry today, *Bonzo* is looking better and better!" and inscribed a photo referring to the memories of their work together as "fresh and warm."

That was not the only time Ronald Reagan wrote in support of *Bedtime for Bonzo*. In a letter to my mother, he again made the case for watching it. I had been home to suburban Cleveland in January 1985. My parents and I had hoped to see a movie while I was there, but everything they suggested I had already seen at Camp David with the Reagans. That prompted my mother to write a note to the president in which she complained good-naturedly, "When Mark was recently home, we tried to find a movie to take him to, but no luck; he had seen them all with you!" The president felt bad and wrote back to her, "I'm sorry about the movies; we'll try to run some 'Golden Oldies' instead of the current crop so Mark can see one now and then with you. To tell you the truth, I'd like an excuse to do that because I'm partial to the ones we used to make. I got carried away one weekend and made them look at *Bedtime for Bonzo*."

Though not originally Republicans, my parents adored Ronald Reagan. My working for him was what drew them to him, but that was by no means the only reason. They supported and respected what he accomplished as president, and were struck by how kind and gracious he was to them every time they saw him. I remember that one time my mother thanked him for "taking care" of me, and he looked at her, smiled, winked, and said, "I think Mark thinks he is taking care of *me*!"

My mom and dad seemed amazed that their son had a relationship with a president of the United States and that the president was so unpretentious and welcoming. It was particularly exciting for my father, a World War II veteran, who could not quite believe he had talked with a commander in chief. My parents were also quite fond of Mrs. Reagan. My mother was bothered by news reports that were critical of the First Lady, and frequently reminded me to be kind to her. "It's not easy being a mother," she would say.

My parents and siblings came to Washington several times during the years I was in the White House. Each time, the president received them. If she was in town, Mrs. Reagan did too. And my parents saw the president whenever we traveled to Cleveland. On his final trip there as president, he gave them a shout-out from the presidential podium at the beginning of his speech before the prestigious City Club, saying, "A special hello to Clevelanders Herb and Judy Weinberg, who are the parents of my assistant press secretary, Mark Weinberg." They beamed for weeks.

My parents visited me several times during the two years I lived in Los Angeles and served as director of public affairs in former President Reagan's office there. On one trip, I arranged for them to come to the office and visit with him. He greeted them warmly and, after we took some pictures, invited them to sit on the couch for a chat. I hovered nearby. The conversation was pleasant, touching on a range of topics: raising kids, World War II, life in Southern California, movies, favorite desserts.

The next day, Mrs. Reagan called me about something and began the conversation by saying "When Ronnie came home yesterday, all he could talk about was how *nice* your parents were." I said, "Thanks, but it sounds like he was surprised." Mrs. Reagan laughed but did not dispute my point.

Not everyone in the president's inner circle was a fan of *Bedtime for Bonzo*. Stu Spencer, the legendary and blunt Republican strategist who'd managed Reagan's 1966 campaign for governor of California and the 1980 presidential campaign, was one of the few people who would tell his boss that he did not like one of his movies. Spencer told the president he did not think *Bonzo* was a very good movie.

The president launched into a lengthy defense of *Bedtime for Bonzo*, but Spencer would not be swayed, telling him, "Ever since I have known you, you've been bitching about playing second fiddle to Errol Flynn, and in this movie, you play second fiddle to a chimpanzee. How in the world can that be a good movie?"

At the end of the movie, the small group applauded and the president bowed. There was then a long talk about virtually every aspect of the movie. Reagan's memory of script issues, special effects, stunts, makeup, and even bloopers, was amazing.

According to the president, Bonzo could be a pain. Sometimes the chimp would disrupt the action by deciding to climb to the top of the studio. No amount of calling or cajoling could get the chimp to come down. Out of options, the president said, all of the lights were turned off, leaving the studio pitch black. Then someone would make a surprised grunt or yell as Bonzo, who was afraid of the dark, would follow the voice and land on the human he knew.

What an evening! Perhaps Terry Dake, the pilot of the presidential helicopter, Marine One (who would go on to become a four-star General and Assistant Commandant of the US Marine Corps), said it best: "It was a study in contrasts to see a youthful Ronald Reagan on the screen going through antics with a chimpanzee and a dignified President Reagan sitting on the couch, watching and laughing."*

*Terry Dake email to author, June 5, 2015.

10

GHOSTBUSTERS

◆

Starring: Bill Murray, Dan Aykroyd, Harold
Ramis, Sigourney Weaver
Directed by: Ivan Reitman
Viewed by the Reagans: July 14, 1984

◆

The Film That Energized the 1984 Campaign

On Tuesday, October 2, 1984, just over a month before the election in which the nation would decide whether to reelect Ronald Reagan to a second term, his supporters on the campus of Texas Tech University in Lubbock gathered for a rally. The guest of honor was Vice President George H. W. Bush, who had lived in Texas for many years and had represented a Houston-area district in the House of Representatives.

Before Bush spoke, the crowd in Lubbock was treated to a warmup act: the "Fritzbusters." These were members of the campus College Republicans chapter who performed a short song-and-dance routine mocking Reagan's Democratic opponent, Walter Mondale, who was also known by his longtime nickname "Fritz." Their song included lines such as:

If there's something strange in America,
Who you gonna call? Fritzbusters!
If your tax rates are high, way up in the sky,
*Who you gonna call? Fritzbusters!**

The song, of course, was a parody of the theme from *Ghostbusters*, recorded by the R&B artist Ray Parker Jr., which had spent three weeks at the top of the *Billboard* charts in August.[†] The movie itself was even hotter. The top movie of the summer, it was breaking studio earnings records on a pace to eventually be the second-highest-grossing movie of the year.

It was no wonder the folks in Lubbock loved the Fritzbusters routine. A College Republican member at Texas Tech told the *New York Times*, "I thought they were too laid back for this kind of thing on this campus. I was surprised that they really got worked up."[‡] Even the Fritzbusters logo, a cartoon worried-looking Mondale in a red circle with a line through it, brought the movie to mind. The Fritzbusters act popped up on college campuses throughout the fall campaign.

That *Ghostbusters* permeated the ongoing national political debate in 1984 is just one measure of how popular the movie was. And it wasn't just Republicans. Vendors at the Democratic National

---

*Elizabeth Wasserman, "After Dallas, Republicans Get Student Support," *SUNY-Stony BrookStatesman*, September 19, 1984, https://ir.stonybrook.edu /jspui/bitstream/11401/63713/1/Statesman%20V.%2028,%20n.%2009.pdf.
†Ed Hogan, "Ray Parker Jr.," *Billboard* online, accessed September 17, 2017, www.billboard.com/artist/364688/ray-parker-jr/biography.
‡James Barron, "Young Fritzbusters Are Reined In," *New York Times* online, October 4, 1984, www.nytimes.com/1984/10/04/us/young-fritzbusters-are-reined -in.html.

Convention in San Francisco that year sold "Reaganbuster" T-shirts with a similar logo featuring the president.*

Released nationwide on June 8, 1984, *Ghostbusters* starred eighties comedy icons Bill Murray, Dan Aykroyd, and Harold Ramis as Drs. Venkman, Stantz, and Spengler, respectively, three paranormal researchers who get booted from their university gig and go into business for themselves, snatching up and locking away troublesome spirits. The ghosts they encounter include a demonic librarian at the famous New York Public Library that will scare anyone into silence, and a chubby floating green blob with arms, known affectionately as "Slimer," who causes havoc at a luxury hotel.

Sigourney Weaver plays Dana Barrett, a concert musician with a haunted apartment. Something is growing in her refrigerator more dangerous than any mold. Rick Moranis plays Louis Tully, her hapless accountant neighbor. Their fashionable apartment building on Central Park West just might end up being center stage for a global apocalypse brought about by an ancient vengeful spirit—unless, of course, the Ghostbusters manage to save the day.

But the four heroes—Ernie Hudson rounds out the group as Winston Zeddemore, hired by the original three when the ghostbusting business booms—have to contend with another villain as they seek to rid the city of spectral pests. This monster, however, is not supernatural. He's about as monotonously down-to-earth as one can get. He's a government bureaucrat, Walter Peck of the Environmental Protection Agency, played straight by William Atherton.

Peck is a humorless parody of a federal functionary, stuffed into a three-piece suit and speaking bureaucratese. He first shows up at the Ghostbusters' headquarters (a dilapidated former firehouse) demanding to "assess any possible environmental impact from your

*Barron, "Young Fritzbusters."

operation—for instance, the presence of noxious, possibly hazard-
ous, waste chemicals in your basement." After Venkman throws him
out, he comes back bearing an arsenal of regulatory cudgels, including a "cease-and-desist-all-commerce order, seizure of premises and
chattels, ban on the use of public utilities for nonlicensed waste
handlers, and a federal entry and inspection order."

This walking copy of federal regulations was a perfect foil for the
freewheeling Ghostbusters. When Dr. Spengler protests that Peck
has barged into "private property," Peck threatens him with "federal
prosecution for at least a half a dozen environmental violations." He
even tries to push around an accompanying NYPD officer, who responds with one of the movie's many quotable one-liners: "You do
your job, pencil neck! Don't tell me how to do mine!" Peck's adher-
ence to the rule book leads to an even bigger environmental hazard
than he could have imagined: the possible end of the world.

Atherton was so good at playing the stiff that his Walter Peck
character caused him trouble for years. People would try to fight
him in bars or yell insults from the movie out the windows of passing busses.* And it has not been lost on the movie's more politically
aware viewers that the stifling hand of federal regulation was one of
its main antagonistic forces—aside from the ghosts themselves, of
course. As *National Review* summed it up in 2009 when it included
Ghostbusters on its list of "The Best Conservative Movies of the Last
25 Years": "[Y]ou have to like a movie in which the bad guy . . . is a
regulation-happy buffoon from the EPA, and the solution to a public

---

*Jeremy Kirk, "36 Things We Learned from the 'Ghostbusters' Commentary
Track," Film School Rejects, last modified August 9, 2011, https://filmschool
rejects.com/36-things-we-learned-from-the-ghostbusters-commentary-track
-423ccf3ca5c3/#.biizamujj.

menace comes from the private sector."* Not everyone thought that was a good thing. Thomas Frank wrote in *Salon* that the "Reaganism" in *Ghostbusters* was "fully developed"—and that wasn't a compliment.† The journalist David Sirota observed sarcastically that the Ghostbusters get "rich and famous," but "real problems only arise when the big bad government tries to put them out of business."‡ The movie's tone was probably not accidental, either. Director Ivan Reitman later told *Entertainment Weekly*, "I've always been something of a conservative-slash-libertarian. The first [*Ghostbusters*] movie deals with going into business for yourself, and it's anti-EPA—too much government regulation. It does have a very interesting point of view that really resonates."§

President Reagan watched *Ghostbusters* at Camp David on July 14, 1984, as his campaign for reelection was revving up for the fall. Despite being out for more than a month, it was still the number one movie in America. While I do not recall the film making a major impression on the president, or any of us gathered in his cabin that evening, at least one person remembered it differently.

---

*Steven F. Hayward, "#10: The Best Conservative Movies of the Last 25 Years—Ghostbusters (1984)," *The Corner* (blog), *National Review* online, last modified February 12, 2009, www.nationalreview.com/corner/177234/10-best-conservative-movies-last-25-years-steven-f-hayward.

†Thomas Frank, "Baby Boomer Humor's Big Lie: 'Ghostbusters' and 'Caddyshack' Really Liberated Reagan and Wall Street," *Salon,* last modified March 2, 2014, www.salon.com/2014/03/02/baby_boomer_humors_big_lie_ghostbusters_and_caddyshack_really_liberated_reagan_and_wall_street.

‡David Sirota, *Back to Our Future: How the 1980s Explains the World We Live In Now—Our Culture, Our Politics, Our Everything* (New York: Ballantine Books, 2011), 89.

§Jeff LaBrecque, "Ivan Reitman Revisits 'Ghostbusters,'" *Entertainment Weekly* online, last modified September 12, 2014, http://ew.com/article/2014/09/12/ivan-reitman-revisits-ghostbusters.

In an article about the campaign published in the *New Republic* in September 1984, the journalist Sidney Blumenthal (who later gained notoriety in the Clintons' service) includes this anecdote:

"About a month before the convention, according to a top political aide, Reagan screened the movie *Ghostbusters* at Camp David. 'That was great!' the president said. 'It was better than movies when I was making them. You know why? If they had made *Ghostbusters* back then, the whole thing would've been a dream, and the guy would've woken up at the end.'"*

I don't recall this and I doubt it ever happened. For one, it isn't something Ronald Reagan would say. It sounds odd to hear him say *any* movie from the eighties was "better than movies when I was making them." I often heard him state the exact opposite! It wasn't his own movies that he liked better, he just liked the movies from that era more than those that came later. He thought those movies were cleaner, more wholesome, and thus more entertaining. While the president enjoyed many of the modern movies we watched, in his mind it was hard to top the classics from his own time in Hollywood.

In addition, as I envision the small crowd of regulars who gathered in Aspen for movie screenings, I simply do not believe anyone would leak anything to Sidney Blumenthal. I can't imagine who the "top political aide" he mentioned might be. Blumenthal might have heard the story secondhand (or third- or even further back). It may be that the president did like *Ghostbusters*, but the details of his reaction got distorted by the time they found their way to the pages of the *New Republic*.

This July weekend at Camp David was a welcome occasion for

---

*Sidney Blumenthal, "The G.O.P. 'Me Decade,'" *New Republic*, September 17, 1984, in Blumenthal, *Our Long National Daydream: A Political Pageant of the Reagan Era* (New York: Harper and Row, 1988), 111–12.

the Reagans to rest and gather steam before the general election campaign kicked off at the GOP convention in Dallas that August. But plenty was going on even at this stage. The Friday before he left for the presidential retreat, he met with the speechwriter Ken Khachigian, who was helping draft Reagan's acceptance speech for the convention. "I remember when I did all such things myself," the president noted wistfully. "No way now—no time."* That was unfortunate because he was viewed by all the speechwriters and many others on the staff as "the best writer in the house." He devoted what time he could, but the sheer volume of speeches required of a president made it impossible for him to do them all himself. I think he missed that.

Even though it has been reported that there was some uncertainty on the part of the president and Mrs. Reagan about whether he would seek a second term, there was zero uncertainty on the part of the staff. None of us thought he would be a one-term president voluntarily. We knew he had the energy, drive, and desire to "finish the job," as he referred to it, and no one could imagine him walking away after only one term. We always believed the president would win reelection. But the first debate with former vice president Mondale, when Reagan seemed overprogrammed and uncertain in his answers, gave us a momentary scare. Mrs. Reagan was known to be upset about the prep for the first debate, and rightfully so. Rumor had it that she had made her displeasure known to either Mike Deaver or Dick Darman (White House Staff Secretary and deputy to chief of staff James A. Baker III), saying in a firm tone, "What are you doing to him?"

Despite the angst caused by the first debate, the campaign for reelection was fun. The president enjoyed traveling across the

*Ronald Reagan, *Reagan Diaries*, 368.

country, speaking at rallies and meeting voters. It was never routine to him. He liked people and was energized by how crowds at rallies responded to his speeches. Some of us in the traveling party—staff and press—however, did not always have the same level of excitement and enthusiasm. It was a lot of work, and at the end of some days, we were dragging.

At many rallies, the president would tell a joke about Republican puppies versus Democratic puppies, which the crowd always enjoyed. After all, it was the first time the crowd was hearing the joke. Not so for the traveling staff and press corps, who heard it several times a day. On one occasion, toward the end of the campaign, the pool of reporters, TV cameramen, and still photographers who were in the buffer zone between the stage and the first row of the crowd just in front of the presidential podium handwrote a sign that read: "Please, no puppy story!" and held it up, hoping the president would see it. He did, laughed, and told the crowd that "they" (meaning the press pool in front of him) asked that he not tell the story, but he did anyway. And, of course, the crowd loved it. As I recall, the joke went something like this: A child had a sign on her front lawn that said "Democratic puppies, one dollar each." The next day the same child had a sign that said "Republican puppies, two dollars each." When confronted by a potential customer who asked why there was a difference in price for the puppies, she replied, "Well, yesterday when the puppies were just born, they had their eyes closed. But today they're open."

And as much as the crowd loved hearing Lee Greenwood's "God Bless the U.S.A.," which was played at the end of *every* rally, several of us (myself included) were so sick of that song by Election Day that we prayed to never hear it again.

On the Democratic side, Walter Mondale had made history just days before this Camp David visit by announcing his running mate:

Representative Geraldine Ferraro of New York. It was the first time a woman had occupied a spot on a presidential ticket for a major political party. Mondale had been trailing Reagan by sixteen points in the polls. After this announcement, he enjoyed a bump that brought him temporarily even with the president.* Even while relaxing at Camp David, Reagan was aware of the wall-to-wall coverage the Ferraro announcement was getting.

Debate prep was a far-off concern on the Saturday the president watched *Ghostbusters* in July, however. That afternoon, he gave his typical radio address, speaking at 12:06 p.m. Interestingly, this week's topic was the environment, and he explained how his administration was working through the EPA to handle environmental challenges, while transferring some responsibility back to the states. He cited a billion-dollar initiative to refurbish national park facilities, remarking wryly that "our progress on protecting the environment is one of the best-kept secrets in Washington."† He may have chuckled when—just a few hours later—he sat down to watch a movie in which the main villain was a functionary of the EPA.

Ghostbusters held the top box office spot for seven weeks before finally being knocked off by Prince's film *Purple Rain*.‡ Perhaps it was inevitable that the popularity of the movie and the season's biggest news story—the presidential campaign—would eventually collide.

---

*Andrew Glass, "Ferraro Joins Democratic Ticket, July 12, 1984," Politico, last modified July 12, 2007, www.politico.com/story/2007/07/ferraro-joins-demo cratic-ticket-july-12-1984-004891.

†"Radio Address to the Nation on Environmental Issues, July 14, 1984," Ronald Reagan Presidential Library & Museum online, www.reaganlibrary.archives.gov/archives/speeches/1984/71484a.htm.

‡United Press International, "'Purple Rain' Ousts 'Ghostbusters' as No. 1," *New York Times* online, August 1, 1984, www.nytimes.com/1984/08/01/movies/pur ple-rain-ousts-ghostbusters-as-no-1.html.

The Fritzbusters were the product of that collision, the brain-child of some officers of the College Republican National Committee. Twenty-three-year-old Paul Erickson, the CRNC treasurer, who had seen the movie three times, wrote the parody song that poked fun at Fritz Mondale.* Also in on the act was the CRNC's president, a young Jack Abramoff, who went on to an ignominious lobbying career. Abramoff was convicted of corruption and served time in prison for mail fraud, conspiracy to bribe elected officials, and tax evasion. The Fritzbusters routine debuted at the Republican convention in Dallas, and reportedly sold seven thousand T-shirts bearing their cartoon logo that week before taking the act on the road.†

Erickson and the others would visit campuses for rallies, appearing onstage "wearing coveralls, black rubber gloves, and goggles—essentially the same outfit that the actor Bill Murray wore in 'Ghostbusters,' with students as backup dancers," the *New York Times* reported.‡ They even traveled in a repurposed ambulance, just as Murray and the other Ghostbusters did in the film.

The fusion of politics and popular entertainment worked, and showed no signs of diminishing as summer turned to fall. The *Times* reported that in September, one crowd of Michigan students was "roused to a pitch usually reserved for the football field," giving Vice President George Bush "one of his most organized and vibrant receptions of the past two weeks."§

Reagan was not comfortable with negative campaigning, though,

---

*Barron, "Young Fritzbusters."
†Ibid.
‡Ibid.
§Jane Perlez, "Michigan School Crowd Rallies for Bush," *New York Times*, September 28, 1984, www.nytimes.com/1984/09/28/us/michigan-school-crowd-rallies-for-bush.html.

and lead Fritzbuster Paul Erickson would later tell the press that Michael Deaver, deputy chief of staff and lead curator of the president's image, had reacted negatively "through a back channel." According to Erickson, Deaver sought to ensure "the campaign is pro-Reagan and not anti-Mondale," and worried that "this song is obviously anti-Mondale."*

I wish I had known that on Election Night 1984. As had been their practice throughout the president's political career, the Reagans went to the home of their dear friends Earle and Marion Jorgensen to have dinner and await the returns with a small group of close friends and family. While there, the president received the call from Walter Mondale conceding the election. He took it in a spare bedroom, where a small portable television had been set up. Mrs. Reagan, Mike Deaver, and I joined him in the room. The call did not last long. From the president's end, it was cordial and gracious. After the call, Mike, thinking of national unity, said to Reagan, "You really should invite him to the White House." Before the president could reply, I chimed in with "For what? A tour?" To my great pleasure, Mrs. Reagan laughed heartily. Mike, though, was not amused. At all. He shot me a look I will never forget. The president readily agreed to have Mondale over for a visit.

The convention, the Fritzbusters, and the charged atmosphere of the coming fall campaign were still a ways off when Reagan watched *Ghostbusters* at Camp David in July. It may have been made with some free-market, libertarian undertones that would delight commentators on the right, but while Reagan believed in the power of

---

*Ira R. Allen, United Press International online, "'Fritzbusters' Spoofing Mondale," September 13, 1984, www.upi.com/Archives/1984/09/13/Fritzbusters-spoofing-Mondale/3762463896000.

the free market, he didn't screen movies based on their ideology. That's not what our movie nights were about.

They were the opposite: an *escape* from politics. Movie nights were a diversion from the business of governing—or the business of campaigning—and a chance for the Reagans to relax and enjoy the art form that brought them together in the first place.

11

BACK TO THE FUTURE

---◆---

Starring: Michael J. Fox, Christopher Lloyd
Directed by: Robert Zemeckis
Viewed by the Reagans: July 26, 1985

---◆---

The Film That Left Us Speechless

At 11:28 a.m. on Saturday, July 13, 1985, Ronald Reagan ceased, for the second time, to be president of the United States. At that moment, he was placed under anesthesia for nearly three hours of surgery to remove a two-inch cancerous growth from his colon. A letter he had signed earlier that morning transferred power temporarily to Vice President Bush.

Just minutes before, the president had been transported on a gurney down the gleaming white corridors of Bethesda Naval Hospital toward the operating room as the First Lady kept pace alongside, holding her husband's hand. The growth in his large intestine had been discovered only the day before during a colonoscopy exam. The decision had been made to perform the surgery right away. At

the door to the operating room, the president and First Lady exchanged a final "I love you" and squeezed each other's hands once
more. Then the medical team took over.

Reagan's wit shone through just before he underwent anesthesia.
He told the surgeons that after his colonoscopy the day before, "this
ought to be a breeze."

And, as colon cancer surgeries go, that's what it was. President
Reagan emerged two hours and fifty-three minutes later after a
complication-free procedure, minus all traces of the problematic
growth—along with two feet of his large intestine. In another few
hours, once the anesthesia and pain medication had worn off, he
resumed his presidential duties after an absence of less than eight
hours altogether.

The summer of 1985 was a happy time for the Reagan presidency.
He had just been inaugurated for the second time, having carried
every state but one in the November 1984 election. The economy
was improving impressively. The sky-high rates of unemployment,
interest, and inflation that President Reagan had inherited when he
took office were quickly being replaced by record prosperity. On the
international front, there was also cause for optimism. In Mikhail
Gorbachev, Ronald Reagan found a Soviet leader with whom he
could work; a worthy partner in the games of statecraft that would
characterize the last stages of the Cold War.

In the summer of '85, the momentum was all Ronald Reagan's.
"Morning in America" was turning into a brilliant high noon. "Morning in America" was the opening line in a television commercial used
in Reagan's campaign for reelection. It was designed to highlight
how much progress had been made during the first Reagan term—
that the country went from darkness to light. When Ronald Reagan
died in 2004, coverage of funeral arrangements was sometimes referred to as "Mourning in America."

The surgery was only a minor hiccup. Everything had been taken care of so quickly and easily, with no complications, that it seemed nothing was going to slow down the Reagan revolution—not a would-be assassin's bullet and not a little bit of cancer. Reagan himself was fond of saying, "I did not have cancer. I had something that had cancer in it, and it was removed." I was understanding but always felt that this was an unrealistic denial. Only many years later, when I was diagnosed with prostate cancer, did I understand what he meant.

In fact, in a strange way, Reagan's cancer surgery in 1985 eerily foreshadowed my own treatment in 2007. The day of the president's colonoscopy, with the surgery looming over us the following day, I rode back to the White House from the hospital in the limousine with Mrs. Reagan. She was understandably upset. At one point on that ride, in what was clearly an effort to minimize what was happening, she said to me, "Anyone can get cancer. Even you, Mark." I didn't think much of it at the time—the young always think they're invincible—but it flashed back to the forefront of my mind when I received my diagnosis. At the time, I told my wife, Erin, "Well, Mrs. Reagan was right." When she found out, Mrs. Reagan was extremely supportive and wrote us letters often. Thanks to some very talented doctors at New York's Memorial Sloan Kettering Cancer Center, the disease is no longer a part of my life.

After President Reagan's successful surgery, everyone wanted to get as far away from thoughts and talk of cancer as possible. It was important for the president to have time to recover, but there was a lot of work to be done, and the business of running the country could hardly be paused or even slowed down. In the weeks following the surgery, Reagan continued his recovery, gradually increasing his daily schedule of meetings and events. His vital signs were monitored every day by the White House physicians, and he spent time working from the residence, sometimes walking in the hallways for exercise. On rare occasions, he took a nap. Mrs. Reagan was vigilant on this point. If all went well in the first two weeks of recovery, he (and the rest of us) had a treat to look forward to: a weekend at Camp David scheduled for July 26.

Among the items on the schedule during the week leading up to that trip were a state visit by Chinese president Li Xiannian; meetings on a variety of topics, including the deficit and budget, sanctions against South Africa, and the case of John Anthony Walker Jr., an officer in the US Navy who'd recently been arrested and charged with having operated as a Russian spy for more than twenty-five years. He'd even turned treason into the family business, recruiting his own son, a navy seaman, into his spy ring; as well as a Cabinet meeting and an interview with Hugh Sidey of *Time* magazine.

After such a busy week, we knew it was a possibility that the president's physician would veto the Camp David visit and order him to remain at the White House to rest. Nonetheless, we hoped and planned to go. On Thursday evening of that week, the White House physician approved the trip, saying, "It will do him a world of good."

Midmorning on Friday, the day we were due to leave, I left the office to collect one last provision. At a candy store across the street from the White House, I bought a big box of chocolates with smooth, creamy centers. We had been advised by the president's physicians that he was not allowed to eat anything with nuts, seeds, or kernels anymore. Movie nights would no longer include popcorn. I hoped these chocolates would make for an acceptable substitute.

By the time he boarded Marine One on the south grounds of the White House that Friday afternoon, Ronald Reagan was tired and ready for a relaxing weekend. But he hardly showed it. When he and Mrs. Reagan emerged from the diplomatic entrance, he beamed—clearly happy to be on the way to a place that remained one of his favorites throughout his eight years in office. A larger-than-usual press contingent had gathered to witness their departure.

As Marine One took off, the feeling set in that everything was back to normal. On the helicopter with the Reagans were the president's personal aide, Jim Kuhn; his army aide; a physician; two Secret Service agents; and me. After we landed at Camp David, we traveled in a mini-motorcade to Aspen Lodge, and just before the president entered, someone suggested that maybe he would prefer to have a quiet evening off instead of inviting the rest of us over for the usual movie showing. None of us wanted to tempt fate or tax President Reagan as he continued to recover from major surgery less than two weeks earlier.

Nothing doing. "No, no," the president said. "I've been looking forward to this and want you all to come."

"Yes sir," we said almost in unison, and that was that.

Even though the "call time" for the movie was 8:00 p.m. as usual, we gathered at the front door of Aspen at 7:45. It was a typically warm, muggy July evening. As always, Ronald Reagan opened the door at 7:50.

Everything about the seventy-four-year-old seemed to glow with vitality unheard of in most men his age, or any age. Instead of screening a movie, the man before us could have been preparing to star in one. Though six foot one, he seemed to tower above us with an easy confidence that allowed him to command a room and put everyone in it at immediate ease.

I always thought that was because he genuinely liked people and was comfortable in his own skin. Ronald Reagan was fundamentally a happy man who enjoyed life. He was rarely ill at ease, and not given to being uncomfortably self-conscious. Those qualities served him well. He was just as comfortable going head-to-head with

Gorbachev as he was riding the perimeter at his California ranch. He made both look easy to anyone watching. He had played many roles in his life. Tonight he was obviously delighted to play host.

Dressed in a short-sleeved polo shirt, blue jeans, and comfortable moccasin-type shoes, the president beckoned everyone in. "How do you do?" he said with a smile, and we all assembled near the unlit fireplace.

Mrs. Reagan, wearing a denim shirt, blue jeans, and sneakers, came over and welcomed everyone. It was clear she was very happy that everything was back to normal.

We made our way to our usual seats. Jim and I made a point of watching the president closely to see if he moved with any obvious discomfort or more slowly than usual, but he did not. It was confirmed: he was back to himself. Just before the movie began, Mrs. Reagan stood up and told everyone that "tonight we won't be having popcorn, but I think Mark brought something else you will enjoy." The lights dimmed, and the movie started.

The Reagans were looking forward to seeing *Back to the Future*, maybe because its star, Michael J. Fox, was already well known for playing a precocious Republican teenager on one of their favorite television shows, *Family Ties*, then entering its fourth season. They were far from alone in their admiration for the NBC comedy. Between the 1984–85 and 1985–86 seasons, it jumped in the Nielsen rankings from number five up to number two in its prime-time slot.

Fox played Alex P. Keaton, the son of two aging hippie parents growing up with his two sisters—and in the final seasons, a brother—in suburban Ohio. Young Alex, to the bafflement of his liberal mother and father, had grown up into a staunch conservative, fond of quoting the economist Milton Friedman (a Reagan favorite), wearing tailored suits and carrying his schoolwork in a briefcase. He yearned for the day he could take his place among the "yuppie" class. Though Alex's political views could certainly cause chagrin among other members of his family, by the end of most episodes, their mutual love and respect for one another had smoothed out any domestic fissures.

The popularity of Alex P. Keaton was itself very much a reflection of the Reagan era. Alex personified the resurgence that right-of-center ideology was making among young people at the time, thanks in no small part to President Reagan's own capacity for inspiring leadership. The Reagan Revolution had made it "cool" to be Republican.

Twenty minutes or so into the movie, the two Aspen presidential food service coordinators came into the darkened living room. They crouched down so as not to block anyone's view of the screen as they made their way to the couch. One handed the president the big box of chocolates I had brought, and the other handed him and Mrs. Reagan water in crystal glasses etched with the presidential seal. They then handed the rest of us water in plain glasses. No presidential seals.

The president and Mrs. Reagan each took some pieces of chocolate, and we all passed the box around until it wound up on the coffee table, once again in front of the Reagans. The chocolates, I noted thankfully, had proved a success.

In the film, which had just been released three weeks earlier, Michael J. Fox plays Marty McFly, a high school student from a loving but struggling family. Through his friendship with a local scientist, inventor, and all-around eccentric, Christopher Lloyd's Doc Brown, Marty is transported from the present year of 1985 back to 1955 in a time machine made from a converted DMC DeLorean sports car. As he adjusts to the shock of living in his hometown of Hill Valley, California, thirty years in the past—and falls in with a younger but no less wacky Doc Brown—Marty's unexpected mission is to help the teenage incarnations of his parents meet each other and fall in love before Marty and his siblings vanish from the face of the earth.

Both Reagans appeared engrossed in *Back to the Future*, often laughing heartily. The president got a kick out of the fact that when Marty first goes back to 1955 and walks past Hill Valley's movie theater, the marquee shows *Cattle Queen of Montana*, the 1954 film starring Barbara Stanwyck and Ronald Reagan.

At the time, Roger Ebert compared *Back to the Future* to Frank Capra's 1946 classic *It's a Wonderful Life* and speculated that executive producer Steven Spielberg was "emulating the great studio chiefs of the past." The timeless quality of the storytelling was not lost on the two veterans of old Hollywood sitting with us in the darkened living room.

But beyond that, I could not help but wonder if the president may have seen parts of himself in certain aspects of the film. Marty journeys back to a simpler time—when patriotism mattered, when the town square was kept a little cleaner, when everyone seemed to smile a little easier, and the music the kids listened to was just a little softer. Reagan often implored us to embrace the simple values that informed this earlier era, to recapture the grit and spirit of togetherness that helped win World War II and usher in the prosperity of the 1950s. Indeed, America's booming economy at home and unrivaled standing abroad, which characterized Ronald Reagan's 1980s, in some ways mirrored the country's similarly strong footing in the 1950s.

Of course, the 1950s were far from perfect—in reality or in the movie. Marty's goal is always to get "back to the future," back to 1985. It would have been far more difficult to make a movie chronicling a character's struggles to get back to the eve of Reagan's election in 1980, with its gas lines, stagflation, and the Iranian hostage crisis in full swing. Or even worse, back to the mid-1970s, when the Watergate scandal had ratcheted up national tension to nerve-wracking levels.

Marty knows he must get back to 1985 because his future is there, and while he can't see what it holds, he knows he must return to experience it. But to do that, he has to make sure his future parents get together so that Marty himself can be born in the first place. Marty's future father, George McFly, is a loner and a bit lost, but he is madly in love with Marty's future mother, Lorraine. When Marty encourages George to tell Lorraine that "destiny"—or as George famously flubs the line, "density"—has brought them together, he is speaking literally as a part of that destiny himself.

Ronald Reagan believed in the concept of destiny and the guiding hand of providence. It was plain to see in their everyday interactions that he and Nancy believed they were destined for each other. But he also had a long-standing vision of destiny for America and its people. As early as 1952, Reagan said to a graduating class at William Woods College that he "always thought of America as a place in the divine scheme of things that was set aside as a promised land."*

It was this unshakeable belief in the boundless future of that promised land that drove Ronald Reagan throughout his presidency. In his disdain for limits and his endless capacity to look ahead, he resembled the movie's Doc Brown. Like Brown, Reagan was a visionary, a dreamer, a man whose imagination was among his greatest assets—yet always a realist. As it turned out, both Brown and Reagan were right: there is such a thing as destiny, though sometimes it needs a little push.

In only one brief instance did the mood in the room darken. It

*David Brooks, "Reagan's Promised Land," *New York Times* online, June 8, 2004, www.nytimes.com/2004/06/08/opinion/reagan-s-promised-land.html?mcubz =3.

was during a scene after Marty McFly arrives in 1955 and meets the younger Doc Brown:

DOC: Tell me, Future Boy, who's president of the United
          States in 1985?

MARTY: Ronald Reagan.

DOC: Ronald Reagan? The actor? [Rolls his eyes.] Ha! Then
          who's vice president, Jerry Lewis? I suppose Jane
          Wyman is the First Lady?

MARTY: Whoa, wait. Doc!

DOC: And Jack Benny is secretary of the Treasury!

The movie continued, but for me—and, I suspected, those around me—it felt as if the air had gone out of the Aspen Lodge. Something lingered in the room. A discomfort. That evening was only the second time in all eight years of my service in the White House that I ever heard Jane Wyman's name mentioned or her referred to by anyone other than reporters. Mrs. Reagan rarely mentioned her husband's first wife, to whom he was married from 1940 to 1949, though she did once recall going with the president to Jane's house to visit their children, Michael and Maureen. "Jane was perfectly nice to me," Mrs. Reagan said, "but those visits were awkward. Not only had she been married to Ronnie, but she was *the star*, and it was her house and her children. I felt out of place, and I was a little in awe of her." She also noted that Jane "knew how to play on Ronnie's good nature" and had somehow managed to convince him not to remarry until she did. (Nancy convinced him otherwise: the couple wed on March 4, 1952, eight months before Wyman tied the knot for the fourth time.)*

---

*Nancy Reagan with Novak, *My Turn*, 100.

Still, the unspoken "taboo" about mentioning her was pretty clear. In 1983 a staffer was riding in the limo with the president after some routine event. For reasons that I will never understand, my colleague happened to ask the president if he had ever seen *Falcon Crest*, the popular 1980s prime-time soap opera that starred Wyman as the conniving wine baron Angela Channing. *Falcon Crest*, which began airing on CBS in 1981, the same year Reagan took office, was routinely a top-ten show in the Nielsen ratings. It was hard to imagine that it escaped either of the Reagans' attention.

The president did not get easily riled. But when he did, we knew to watch out.

He stared at his aide with an intensity the man had never seen before and said, in the iciest tone imaginable, "No. Why do you ask?"

There was no good answer to that question. The aide attempted none. The staffer told me later that he wanted to jump out of the moving car but instead resigned himself to shrugging his shoulders and looking out the window for the rest of what seemed like an interminable ride back to 1600 Pennsylvania Avenue.

That was the weird thing about Jane Wyman, at least to the Reagan staff: it was as if she didn't exist to the president anymore. He seemed as though he had willed himself to forget about that period of his life, and was startled and resentful when asked to return to it. Throughout his administration, he never mentioned her name publicly, and she never mentioned his, even though Ms. Wyman was given ample opportunities to do so over the years. Nonetheless, she let it be known that she voted for him both in 1980 and 1984.

Only once in all the years that I knew Ronald Reagan did he mention Jane Wyman to me. Shortly after he left the White House, we were in the back of a car in Los Angeles, on our way to some event. He was reminiscing about Hollywood, and particularly about the disparity between actors' salaries in his day and now. At one point, he said, "That's back when I was married to Wyman." *Wyman.* I was struck that he mentioned her at all and by the fact that he said just her last name. Never did I hear even that from him again.

Fortunately, at the *Back to the Future* screening, Doc Brown's reference to the president's first wife passed without comment, and our breathing returned to normal. The discussion after the movie was pleasant, and the Reagans seemed particularly impressed by Michael J. Fox's performance. The president commented on how clever the movie was and how this was the type of movie that Hollywood should be making, as opposed to some of the more controversial, violent, or adult-themed films that seemed all too common at the time.

Mrs. Reagan brought up Jack Benny, who had been a friend of hers. As Jane Wyman had been mentioned in the movie in almost the same breath as Benny, some of us were a bit perplexed. But Mrs. Reagan did not say anything about Ms. Wyman. Instead, she recalled a conversation she and Jack Benny once had about worrying.

"Jack told me," she said, "'I don't understand when people say "Don't worry." If you're a worrier, you're a worrier, and it's okay.'"

"Well, Mrs. Reagan, you *are* a worrier," her husband said with a smile.

Perhaps with the president's recent surgery lingering in her mind, Mrs. Reagan replied, "Yes, honey, I am."

We filed out into the still-warm July air and went our separate ways. Jim Kuhn and I hung back and talked in front of the now-closed Aspen front door.

"He seems great," Jim said. "Back to normal."

"I know. It's amazing. The guy is seventy-four. I hope I'm like that at sixty-four," I replied.

Six months later, on February 4, 1986, President Reagan

channeled Doc Brown in his State of the Union address, as he exhorted Americans to remember that the sky—not the street—was the limit.

"Never has there been a more exciting time to be alive," the president said, "a time of rousing wonder and heroic achievement. As they said in the film *Back to the Future*, 'Where we're going, we don't need roads.'" That was how Ronald Reagan saw America. It is how those of us who knew him and loved him see it still.

It turned out, however, that we weren't quite finished with *Back to the Future*. In 1989 I was working for the former president at his office in Los Angeles when the movie mogul Lew Wasserman, Reagan's agent many years earlier, contacted him. Wasserman told the president that the director Robert Zemeckis was working on the second sequel to the film, *Back to the Future III,* and apparently was considering Reagan to play the 1885 mayor of Hill Valley. Would he be interested in the part?

It would have been his first role since the historical TV Western *Death Valley Days* and part of me hoped my boss would take it. How fun it would be to see him on a movie theater screen once more, doing a job he had loved. And how much fun he would have, hitting his mark and delivering his lines, one last time. But part of me worried that it would be beneath the dignity of the Office of President of the United States. My opinion was neither sought nor offered.

The president, flattered, thought about Zemeckis's offer for a while. I suspect that a part of him wanted to do it. Perhaps he, too, worried about the optics. Or, just maybe, he figured that returning to his Hollywood past carried more risk than reward. After all, time travel hadn't worked out all that well for Marty McFly.

In the end, he declined. Ronald Reagan loved the past. But he never needed to live in it.

12

ANTI-COMMUNIST FILMS— ROCKY IV

◆

Starring: Sylvester Stallone, Dolph Lundgren, Talia Shire
Directed by: Sylvester Stallone
Viewed by the Reagans: January 31, 1986

REDS

◆

Starring: Warren Beatty, Diane Keaton, Jack Nicholson
Directed by: Warren Beatty
Viewed by the Reagans: December 8, 1981

RED DAWN

◆

Starring: Patrick Swayze, Charlie Sheen, C. Thomas Howell
Directed by: John Milius
Viewed by the Reagans: September 7, 1984

◆

The Films That Set the Tone for an Era

In May 1983 a filmmaker named Timothy Anderson met with the Reagan image guru Michael Deaver to discuss a project he claimed to have conceived, a sequel to the popular *Rocky* movies, in which the actor Sylvester Stallone, as world champion Rocky Balboa, takes on a Soviet boxer in what Anderson called "a very great motion picture with a wide range of positive results." Also in attendance at that meeting was Stallone himself.*

That Stallone was one of the most prominent Hollywood supporters of Ronald Reagan (Charlton Heston and Tom Selleck were others) was not a secret. He and his then girlfriend Brigitte Nielsen would later receive a coveted invitation to an October 1985 White House state dinner honoring Singapore's president, Lee Kuan Yew. That occasion would lead to an interesting interaction with Stallone: he called the White House to ensure that he and Nielsen would be seated together. (Apparently, she felt uncomfortable with strangers.) As it happened, I fielded the call. I told the actor I'd see what I could do, but made no promises. I called the social secretary, who conveyed the request to Mrs. Reagan. To encourage conversations with others around the table, Mrs. Reagan had a long-standing policy of separating guests from their spouses or dates at such dinners. But above all else, Mrs. Reagan wanted guests to be comfortable and enjoy the evening. In Stallone and Nielsen's case, she made an exception, and they sat together.

At the event, which the actors Raquel Welch and Michael J. Fox also attended, Stallone told reporters, "It's always flattering to have the highest person in the land admire your work."† He promised

---

*Letter from attorney Timothy B. Anderson to White House deputy chief of staff Michael Deaver, May 10, 1983, from archives at Ronald Reagan Presidential Library. †Jacqueline Trescott and Donnie Radcliffe, "White House Starscape," *Washington Post* online, October 9, 1985, www.washingtonpost.com/archive/life style/1985/10/09/white-house-starscape/2c60e9f1-5695-4384-ac5c-68663137 e219/?utm_term=.838edd704bd7.

Reagan a *Rambo* poster if the president would give him a poster of himself in return.* The president had quipped after dealing with a hostage crisis, "I saw *Rambo* last night, and now I know what to do the next time this happens."†

The *Washington Post* reported about another guest at that state dinner, in a note that can now be read only with tragic poignancy: "[Christa] McAuliffe, the teacher who is training for the Shuttle *Challenger* mission, sat next to the president last night. She said he had talked about his Hollywood career. 'He told us a lot of stories about when he was in films,' she said. 'He also said maybe I could take some papers to grade with me in space.'"

Later in 1985, Stallone invited the Reagans to attend his wedding and reception in Beverly Hills. The president, who liked Stallone but was not particularly close to him, was unable to attend, though he did send a telegram expressing his wish that "the joy of your wedding day always be yours to share and may God bless and watch over you."‡

Popular culture linked the president and Stallone's work. A bumper sticker showed up in the eighties that said, "Rocky was a Republican." The *Rocky* series did have more than a tinge of the conservative ethos. It emphasized hard work, personal responsibility and determination, and celebrated the hardworking American who dreams of one day doing something great. Which, of course, is why it made perfect sense to send the legendary "Italian Stallion," Rocky

---

*Helen Thomas, United Press International online, "Actor Sylvester Stallone Promised Tuesday to Give President Reagan . . ." October 8, 1985, www.upi .com/Archives/1985/10/08/Actor-Sylvester-Stallone-promised-Tuesday-to-give -President-Reagan/1721497592000.
†Ibid.
‡Ronald Reagan, telegram to Sylvester Stallone and Brigitte Nielsen, December 13, 1985.

Balboa's nickname in the films, to battle Communism in Russia. This was the plot of the fourth movie in the series.

In 1983, early in the development of *Rocky IV*, Timothy Anderson was concerned about the production schedule for the film. "I assume that you realize the positive impact that my version of *Rocky IV* could have upon the electorate should it be released in midsummer 1984," he wrote Deaver. "The story has a strong message of courage and confrontation of evil, in spite of the fact that the hero has periodic cause to question his own strength and durability. This runs very specific parallels to the basic tenets of the president's foreign policy as well as the manner in which he handles certain difficult domestic problems." Anderson urged Deaver to impress upon Stallone an "expedited schedule" to ensure that the movie premiered before the president's reelection.

I learned a lot from Mike, an unassuming man in horn-rimmed glasses whose official title was deputy chief of staff. He was an indispensable member of the Reagan team but never sought credit or attention. He also protected both Reagans. Once on the 1980 campaign plane, at the end of a long day, candidate Reagan wandered back to the press section and engaged in banter with reporters. Deaver raced to his side, looking nervous, but Bill Plante of CBS News whispered to him, "Relax, Mike. He's okay." At an off-the-record meeting with reporters shortly after the 1981 assassination attempt, Deaver beseeched the press not to report on Reagan's wearing a bulletproof vest. Reporters wanted to know why, and Mike said, with genuine worry, "Because it tells a person to shoot for his head." Silence followed. Though Deaver knew both Reagans far better than Jim Baker, the chief of staff, Deaver let Baker run the show. He and the Reagans knew Baker would be better at operating the levers of government.

Deaver concentrated instead on the Reagan image. He had an

ability to read the president's moods, knew what settings would work for him, and how he would react. He understood "stagecraft" and how to convey messages through symbols and events. He was always on the lookout for "moments" that would help cement Reagan's history, but he also knew when to say no. During a 1984 event with Michael Jackson, a staff member suggested to Deaver that the president shake the singer's hand while wearing a white "glitter glove" to match Jackson's trademark accouterment. That was going too far. The idea was nixed.*

I'm sure that Deaver, with his keen, searching eye for moments advantageous to the Reagan image, saw the potential of the fourth installment of the *Rocky* franchise to help the 1984 reelection campaign. Not that the president needed much help. And the White House wasn't above using Hollywood films, and celebrities, to support the administration's message. Such interplay between DC and Tinseltown was in its infancy, compared with today. For example, during the Reagan years, the White House Correspondents Association's annual dinner was so boring it was referred to as a "nerd prom." In recent years, it has become a Hollywood star-studded event, including press coverage of arrivals on a red carpet.

Despite Deaver's foresight in meeting with the filmmakers, the timing did not line up: *Rocky IV* didn't premiere until November 1985, a full year after Reagan's forty-nine-state landslide. To make matters even more interesting, the version that hit theaters was *not* the same one that Anderson, Stallone, and Deaver had discussed in 1983. A legal dispute arose later between Anderson and Stallone

---

*White House memorandum on Michael Jackson visit, from James K. Coyne (special assistant to the president) to White House deputy chief of staff Michael K. Deaver, on May 2, 1984, from archives at Ronald Reagan Presidential Library.

over who owned the rights to that particular story. It was ultimately settled out of court. Stallone wrote the final version of *Rocky IV*.

Rocky IV, which centers on tense, brutal confrontation between the United States and the Soviet Union in the boxing ring, coincided with the first real thaw in Soviet-American relations since well before President Reagan took office. The new Soviet leader, Mikhail Gorbachev, was widely credited for the change. With his Western mannerisms and intellectual-minded wife, Raisa, "Gorby" was a different kind of Soviet leader. Compared with his predecessors, he was more open about Communism's shortcomings. The president liked Gorbachev personally and enjoyed telling him jokes. Asked if he was concerned about the growing popularity of his Soviet counterpart, Reagan put the situation into proper perspective. "I don't resent his popularity or anything else," he said. "Good Lord, I costarred with Errol Flynn once."*

The same month of *Rocky IV*'s release, Reagan, Gorbachev, and their wives met for the first time at a crucial summit in Geneva. There was another Reagan in attendance as well: Ron Reagan, the president's son, a talented writer covering the 1985 summit for *Playboy*. He never asked for special access or favors. He worked hard at a small space in the Press Filing Center at the InterContinental Hotel there and never used his status to his advantage. Neither of his parents asked that he be treated differently, but since Ron and I knew each other, I checked in with him from time to time during the summit. One evening, after all of the events were done and he had filed his story, Ron joined me and two magazine photographers for dinner. Then we went to a casino. When he showed his driver's

---

*Tom Redburn, "Gorbachev Is 'Different,' Reagan Asserts," *Los Angeles Times* online, December 2, 1987, http://articles.latimes.com/1987-12-02/news/mn-17 267_1_president-reagan.

license to enter the casino, the security guard looked at the name and did a double take.

The Reagans were always especially happy when Ron was at Camp David. He sometimes came up with his wife, Doria, for a day of horseback riding. The rides, Ron told me later, were "my fondest memories." One reason was that he could see his dad in the best of spirits. "As you know, my father was seldom happier than when he was on the back of a horse," Ron said. But he also confided a secret.

When Nancy decided she wanted to marry Ronald Reagan, she realized that she'd have to fall in love with horseback riding, too. Yet for all of the times Mrs. Reagan joined her husband on horseback, she never truly enjoyed it. The president was blissfully unaware of this, even after decades of marriage.

"My mother was less than thrilled about this activity but would gamely participate to please her husband," Ron said. "She took pains to hide from him her anxiety about saddling up."

Once, while Ron and Doria were out riding with his parents, the president decided to have a little fun, going from a lazy stroll to a gentle canter. Everyone in the riding party did the same. As Nancy bobbed uncomfortably up and down on her horse, she called out to her husband, "Honey! Doria wants to slow down."

This, as Ron recalled, was accompanied by a nervous look in Doria's direction to ascertain whether her daughter-in-law (who was, in fact, quite content with the faster pace) would contradict her.

As Ron told it, "Doria, as usual, did the kind and sensible thing under the circumstances and let this little deception go unchallenged."

Movie nights were certainly less intense than the horseback rides. The Reagans were both relaxed as we prepared to view *Rocky IV*. The Reagans liked the *Rocky* films—and as far as I knew, they'd seen all of them. (We'd watched *Rocky III* together at Camp

David in 1982.) *Rocky IV* was a special iteration of the familiar saga of the poor-but-proud Philadelphia fighter who made his way to an improbable world championship. In this case, the film's stakes were far higher: it was literally a test of the free world versus the Soviet machine, which took the form of rival boxer Ivan Drago, played by Dolph Lundgren. (Drago's wife is played by Stallone's future spouse, Brigitte Nielsen.)

The plot of the film was simplistic. The Soviets boast of building the world's greatest fighter, a muscled warrior and Olympic champion who in manner and appearance seemed more like a machine than a human being. Lundgren utters forty-six words in the entire ninety-one-minute film.* A televised exhibition fight with the American boxer Apollo Creed, Rocky's friend and former opponent, goes awry when Drago beats Creed to death. For extra pathos, Creed dies in Rocky's arms in the middle of the ring. Rocky agrees to fight Drago at a match in the Soviet Union to avenge his friend.

As the rivals train for the upcoming bout, the differences in their conditioning styles showcase the wide gap between their characters and the worlds from which they come. In a trademark *Rocky* training montage, Drago flexes his muscles hooked up to all manner of computers and instruments while intent Soviet scientists look on, determined to craft the perfect fighting machine. And they have no compunction about cheating. Drago is shown being injected with a needle presumably full of steroids. Rocky Balboa, on the other hand, sequestered for his own training in a remote Siberian cabin, works out the old-fashioned way by lifting logs and rocks and scaling

---

*Will Robinson, "*Rocky IV* Turns 30: Here Are 4 Things You Never Knew About the Film," *Entertainment Weekly* online, last modified November 27, 2015, http://ew.com/article/2015/11/27/rocky-iv-30th-anniversary-things-you-didnt-know.

mountains—not to mention outrunning the sinister KGB agents who trail his every move.

That scene reminds me of one of Reagan's favorite stories about the difference between our societies, which he shared in a speech in Nebraska in 1987:

> "And you young people who are here, let me tell you a little true incident. A scholar from our country recently took a trip to the Soviet Union. He happens to be able to speak Russian fluently. In the taxi that was taking him to the airport in this country—a young fellow—and in conversation with him discovered that the taxi driver was a student, working his way through school. And he asked him what did he want to be? And the young fellow said, 'I haven't decided yet.' Well, by coincidence, he got another young fellow driving the cab in Moscow. And he got in conversation with him, in Russian, and found out that he was a student and working at the same time. And he said, 'What do you want to be?' Just remember this difference between two countries. This young man said, 'They haven't told me yet.' That's the difference."*

Rocky's fight with Drago became a metaphor for the ongoing battle with the Soviet Union, at least as it was seen in the West at the time. The Soviets are fierce, humorless, and aggressive. They boo Rocky when he appears to fight. The full politburo shuffles into the arena to watch the bout, including a grim-faced actor who resembles Gorbachev. Rocky, in turn, is all heart, emotion, and resilience. As the fight goes on, and he never gives up, he improbably turns the cheering Soviets to his side. Winning a come-from-behind victory,

---

*Ronald Reagan,"Remarks to Citizens in North Platte, Nebraska, August 13, 1987,"American Presidency Project, www.presidency.ucsb.edu/ws/?pid=34695.

the bloody but unbroken Rocky delivers a somewhat incoherent mini-lecture to the assembled crowd and, by extension, the Soviet Union:

> During this fight, I've seen a lot of changing. I didn't know what to expect. I seen a lot of people hate me, and I didn't know what to feel about that, so I guess they didn't like much nothin' either. During this fight, I've seen a lot of changing, the way yous feel about me, and in the way I felt about you. In here, there were two guys killing each other, but I guess that's better than twenty million. I guess what I'm trying to say, is that if I can change, and you can change, everybody can change!

In the film, even the Gorbachev-like character rises and applauds the American fighter. The other apparatchiks seated around him then stand and follow his lead.

It was easy to see why a number of conservatives hailed the film as the "greatest Cold War movie ever made."[*] (CNN recently listed the film as one of the top five Cold War films of all time.[†]) It was also easy to see why those who supported negotiations and coexistence with the Soviets were less enthusiastic. A reviewer in the *New York Times* lamented, "Outside the boxing arena, the greatest victory is compromise, a message Rocky refuses to learn, and a lesson his fans will never accept."[‡] Roger Ebert was unimpressed, calling the film the *Rocky* series's "last gasp, a film so predictable that viewing it is like

---

[*]Philip Klein, "*Rocky IV* Turns 20,"*American Spectator* online, last modified November 28, 2005, https://spectator.org/47738_rocky-iv-turns-20.

[†]Thom Patterson, "Top Five '80s Cold War Movies," CNN online, last modified April 21, 2016, www.cnn.com/2016/04/21/entertainment/eighties-80s-cold-war-movies.

[‡]Klein, "*Rocky IV* Turns 20."

watching one of those old sitcoms where the characters never change and the same situations turn up again and again."*

Rocky IV infuriated the Soviets. A group of cultural officials from the Soviet Union denounced the film by name (along with Stallone's Rambo series and Red Dawn). One, Yevgeny Yevtushenko—a poet, an ardent anti-Stalinist and a frequent critic of Soviet government, and a proponent of glasnost—grouped those movies together as "warnography."† The Soviet minister of culture expressed bafflement at why the films were being shown, since they seemed to contradict the Reagan administration's expressions of hope for improved relations. This stance demonstrated another difference between capitalist and Communist regimes. The Soviets controlled their media, along with the arts and entertainment industries, and assumed that the American government did the same. There was also more than a little hypocrisy in their comments. As the New York Times reported at the time, Americans were "often harshly depicted in Soviet films,"‡ citing a 1984 television miniseries that depicted Americans as murderers and a 1983 film that showed them to be "violent psychopaths."§

Paradoxically, as was often the case behind the Iron Curtain, films castigated by the Soviet government for anti-Communist sentiments were sought by its citizens. In Moscow, Rocky IV was said to be in high demand.¶ The American public clamored to see the film, which grossed $300 million, making it the highest-grossing sports

---

*Roger Ebert, review of "Rocky IV," November 27, 1985, RogerEbert.com, www .rogerebert.com/reviews/rocky-iv-1985.

†Philip Taubman, "Societ Pans 'Rocky IV' and 'Rambo' Films," New York Times online, January 4, 1986, www.nytimes.com/1986/01/04/world/societ-pans-rocky -and-rambo-films.html.

‡Ibid.

§Ibid.

¶Ibid.

movie of all time. It held that record for decades, finally surpassed by 2009's *The Blind Side.*

After *Rocky IV* was over, none of the viewers at Camp David were impressed by the depth of the plot. The president quipped, "It had a very happy ending. He beats the Russians."* He marveled at Stallone's physique—"the time he must spend in the gym!"—and said that both he and "the fella playing the Russian" looked like Mr. America.

Reagan the viewer soon gave way to Reagan the film industry insider. The president commented that the movie offered some of the most realistic fight scenes he'd ever seen. By way of demonstration, he treated us to a lesson in Hollywood stunt work. He showed us how, in his day, fights were staged on movie sets to make it look as convincing as possible without hurting anyone.

Of course, he reminded us, that didn't always work. Reagan shared about how he once accidentally landed a real-life punch on a stuntman while filming a fight scene. The following week, that stuntman was replaced by his roommate, who returned the favor to Reagan by "popping him in the left eye," according to Tom Carter, the military aide at Camp David that night, who remembered the story vividly.†

In Reagan's view, *Rocky IV* put the stunt-fighting techniques of his day to shame. "To me, it looked like they were swatting each other," he remarked. Then the president pointed out something that only a trained eye would notice: "They can dub in the sound for a blow, but you can't dub in the sweat flying all over the place from a blow."‡

Reagan's eye for filmmaking did not deceive him. *Rocky IV*'s fight scenes *were* realistic, even more than our little group gathered for movie

---

*"Ronald Reagan Talks about 'Rocky IV,'" February 1, 1986, www.youtube.com /watch?v=fCLFheknZEY.
†Author conversation with Tom Carter via email, November 2016.
‡"Ronald Reagan Talks about 'Rocky IV.'"

night could have imagined. The president had no way of knowing that while filming one scene in the boxing ring, Carl Weathers, who played Apollo Creed, was thrown three feet by Dolph Lundgren. He apparently threatened to quit the movie. Stallone himself was hit so hard by one punch that his breastbone slammed against his heart. Rushed to the hospital, he was in the intensive care unit for more than a week.*

Regardless of how much Reagan admired Stallone and the film, his generosity had its limits. When Stallone's people reached out to the White House offering to present the president with the gloves and robe worn by Rocky in the film, a young White House lawyer weighed in against the idea.

"*Rocky IV* is a current Christmas season release, and [United Artists studio head Jerry] Weintraub's offer seems a rather transparent publicity stunt to promote the film," he wrote in a memo. "With the Rambo comments and White House dinner invitation, the president has already given Stallone more than his fair share of free publicity." That young lawyer was associate White House counsel John G. Roberts, Jr., who went on to become chief justice of the United States Supreme Court.

By January 1986, when they watched *Rocky IV*, the Reagans had seen a number of other movies with a Soviet theme. One of the first of these was *Reds*, which was released in 1981, the year the Reagans moved into the White House. *Reds* told the story of John Reed, an American journalist and Communist activist, known for his firsthand, pro-Bolshevik account of the Russian Revolution of 1917, *Ten Days That Shook the World*. Warren Beatty produced, wrote, and directed the film. He also starred as Reed, while his off-screen girlfriend Diane Keaton played Reed's love interest, the political activist and writer Louise Bryant.

---

*Patterson, "Top Five '80s Cold War Movies."

sponsibility I had was to look after some of Mrs. Reagan's personal
make sure it got back to the residence posthaste. *Courtesy of the author*

Ronald Reagan had come to know Beatty when the younger man first arrived in Hollywood. They were friends despite their political differences. When *Reds* came out, the president invited Beatty to screen the movie at the White House. Beatty recalled that Reagan "was very complimentary about the fact that I had produced it, written it, acted in it, and directed it at the same time."[*] The president appreciated all of the effort involved with each of these elements of the filmmaking process and no doubt admired anyone who could juggle them all as effectively as Beatty did in *Reds*. He wasn't the only one who felt that way. *Reds* was nominated for twelve Oscars, winning three. Beatty himself had been nominated in the writing, acting, and directing categories, winning for best director.

Despite Reagan's appreciation for his friend's hard work, he found nothing romantic about the Bolshevik Revolution the movie portrayed. At a twenty-fifth-anniversary showing of the film in 2006, Beatty admitted that Reagan was "probably not sympathetic to the characters in the movie."[†] But that is not to say he viewed them hard-heartedly. After watching the doomed young leftists Reed and Bryant struggle through love and war for more than three hours, the president offered Beatty a characteristically Reaganesque comment: "I was kind of hoping for a happy ending."

It is thanks to Beatty's and Reagan's enduring friendship that we have one of the sharpest observations attributed to President Reagan. He once told Beatty, whom California Democrats often

[*]Deborah Solomon, "Questions for Warren Beatty: In the Picture," *New York Times Magazine* online, October 1, 2006, www.nytimes.com/2006/10/01 /magazine/01wwln_q4.html?ex=1317355200&en=e77f4eba98ee2c09&ei=509 0&partner=rssuserland&emc=rss.
[†]Roger Friedman, "Beatty: Reagan Wanted Happy Ending for 'Reds,'" *Fox News* online, last modified October 5, 2006, www.foxnews.com/story/2006/10/05 /beatty-reagan-wanted-happy-ending-for-reds.html.

fantasized about running for various offices, "I don't know how anybody can serve in public office without being an actor."* He was not, of course, suggesting that all politicians were empty suits who could bluff their way through by acting. Reagan's training as an actor gave him the skills and the style he needed to communicate effectively, whether it was working a small gathering of supporters, a tense Cabinet meeting, or a speech in front of tens of thousands. A politician must have vision, but an actor's particular skills can be a big help in sharing that vision with others.

If *Reds* was pro–Soviet Union, *Red Dawn*, which the Reagans watched at Camp David on September 7, 1984, was its opposite. This film, the product of the maverick director John Milius, presents the provocative, if unlikely, scenario of a Russian invasion of the continental United States, with assistance from its Communist allies in Latin America (some of whom infiltrate over the southern border posing as illegal immigrants). The movie opens with Soviet paratroopers landing on the football field of an all-American high school in an all-American small town: the fictional Calumet, Colorado. One of their first acts is to machine-gun a history teacher and then turn their fire on shocked students. It doesn't get much more nuanced from there.

A group of students led by brothers Jed and Matt Eckert (played by Patrick Swayze and Charlie Sheen, respectively) flee into the mountains and become resistance fighters against the occupying Communist forces. They call themselves the Wolverines, after their high school's team mascot (or, as one Soviet officer refers to it, "the local youth sports collective"). Other members of the group are played by 1980s teen movie stars C. Thomas Howell, Lea

*Marty Graham, Reuters, "Actor Beatty Shadows California's Schwarzenegger," *Washington Post* online, November 5, 2005, www.washingtonpost.com/wp-dyn /content/article/2005/11/05/AR2005110501651_pf.html.

One of my most important responsibilities as [...] Camp David was to make sure the president w[...] ments that had occurred over the weekend so he [...] questions when we landed back at the White Ho[...] before leaving for Washington, I spoke by phone [...] officer to get "guidance," which I would then p[...] were flying back. Nine and a half times out of [...] what was up and what to say before I talked to [...]

Reagan Presidential Foundation & Institute

The othe[...] luggage a[...]

The other responsibility I had was to look after some of Mrs. Reagan's personal luggage and make sure it got back to the residence posthaste. *Courtesy of the author*

One of my most important responsibilities as the press aide in attendance at Camp David was to make sure the president was briefed on any news developments that had occurred over the weekend so he was prepared to answer reporters' questions when we landed back at the White House. The routine was that shortly before leaving for Washington, I spoke by phone with the duty White House press officer to get "guidance," which I would then pass on to the president while we were flying back. Nine and a half times out of ten, the president already knew what was up and what to say before I talked to him on the helo. *Courtesy of the Ronald Reagan Presidential Foundation & Institute*

I like dogs, but did not love the Reagans' dogs during the White House years. Lucky, a Bouvier des Flandres, was big and unwieldy. She eventually was moved to the ranch. Before her relocation, she was a regular passenger on the helo to Camp David. I kept "paw-printed" pictures of her on display in my office as a contrarian thing to my colleagues who adorned their office walls with pictures of themselves with famous humans. *Courtesy of the Ronald Reagan Presidential Foundation & Institute*

Ronald Reagan would always comply with a request for his autograph—something he had done since his earliest days in Hollywood. The staff took a dim view of him signing things thrust at him, since it could have been a folded-up petition or some other inappropriate document. But he never worried about that. *Courtesy of the Ronald Reagan Presidential Foundation & Institute*

Usually, I flew aboard the White House press charter. The minute it was in the blocks, someone from the White House Communications Agency would race up the front steps to deliver me a telephone (with a long cord) connected to the White House switchboard. *Courtesy of the Ronald Reagan Presidential Foundation & Institute*

From time to time, I traveled aboard Air Force One. I would usually be in the staff section or hanging out with the small pool of reporters at the back of the plane. Occasionally, I made my way to the boss's cabin. *Courtesy of the Ronald Reagan Presidential Foundation & Institute*

A talented writer, Ron Reagan was hired by *Playboy* to report on his father's first Summit meeting with Mikhail Gorbachev in Geneva in 1985. He never requested any special access, and like every other reporter, he worked from a cramped space in the international press filing center. One of the nights there, he and I went to a casino with some magazine photographers. You should have seen the look on the face of the doorman there when, like everyone else seeking admittance, Ron showed him his driver's license! *Courtesy of the author*

Although not Catholic, I had great respect for Pope John Paul II and wanted to have a picture with him. I resisted the temptation to jump in the line during presidential visits to the Vatican, but when the pope came to Florida in 1987, Jim Kuhn—who had also never been photographed with His Holiness—and I conspired to have the president introduce us to the Pope. He did so with great pride.

Courtesy of the Ronald Reagan Presidential Foundation & Institute

Getting a dirty look from the leader of the Soviet Union could have been a death sentence for some, but I did not mind. I suspect Gorby was annoyed because I kept pestering him to sign the copy of his book I brought with us to San Francisco. He refused. He eventually relented when the Reagans went to Moscow after their years in the White House. *Courtesy of the author*

I knew Reagan had strong feelings about Errol Flynn, so when I saw this T-shirt, I couldn't resist getting it for him. Both Reagans laughed heartily when I unveiled it in their living room in Aspen Lodge one weekend at Camp David. *Courtesy of the Ronald Reagan Presidential Foundation & Institute*

Lots of interesting people came to the White House over the years, none more so than Michael Jackson. He did so at the very height of his popularity, and his visit caused quite a stir among the normally easygoing (read: jaded) White House staff. I had heard that he had never been there before, so I got the idea to get him a set of guidebooks, which I dutifully presented—but not before I summoned a White House photographer to record the moment. *Courtesy of the Ronald Reagan Presidential Foundation & Institute*

The Gipper meets Maverick (Tom Cruise). What struck me most about the meeting of these two Hollywood legends was how easily they got along. Their conversation was animated, friendly, and with no awkwardness at all. It was almost as if they had known each other for years. Both gentlemen of impeccable manners, they seemed genuinely happy to be with one another, and each had obvious respect for the other. *Courtesy of the author*

Thompson, and Jennifer Grey (who would star with Swayze three years later in *Dirty Dancing*). Some place *Red Dawn* among the so-called Brat Pack movies, except this time the Brats pack heat.

The violence of the film, and that much of it was committed by and against high school students, surprised a lot of people. The critics pounced. Bob Thomas of the Associated Press decried the violence, while the *Los Angeles Times* review remarked that "the battle scenes are neither dramatic nor convincing, merely brutal."* It was the first movie to carry the newly created PG-13 rating.† Condemned along with the violence was the movie's anti-Communist, even pro-war, stance. The *New York Times* called it "incorrigibly gung-ho," while the *LA Times* carped that director Milius "spent too much time playing to the rabid anti-Commies."‡

Audiences, however, were more receptive. *Red Dawn* earned $10.5 million in its first five days in theaters, taking the top box office spot away from *Ghostbusters*. A woman who saw the movie in Anaheim, California, reported, "I have never seen an audience reach such a fever pitch," while another theatergoer recalled "high moments where people were shouting 'Wolverines!'"§ A few weeks after *Red Dawn*'s release, the Associated Press wrote a feature story on the differing responses to the film from critics and moviegoers, which included the headline "Viewers Cheer It While Critics Jeer."¶

I cannot recall any specific cheering or jeering from the Reagans when they watched the movie in Aspen in September 1984, about a month after its nationwide release. They generally disapproved of

---

*Associated Press, quoted in "'Red Dawn' May Benefit from Renewed Patriotism," *Ocala (FL) Star-Banner*, August 24, 1984, 12B.
†Ibid.
‡Ibid.
§Ibid.
¶Ibid.

movies with over-the-top violence. *Red Dawn* did have some friends in Washington, however. Former secretary of state Alexander Haig, who had left the Reagan administration in 1982, had since joined the board of MGM/UA Entertainment Company, the studio that released *Red Dawn*. He called it "one of the most realistic and provocative films that I have ever seen," adding that it offered "a clear lesson to all viewers, and that is the importance of American strength to protect the peace we have enjoyed throughout history." To Haig, America's "military posture" was key to preventing events such as those depicted in *Red Dawn*.

Haig had even organized a private screening in Washington before the movie hit theaters. Several prominent figures in the defense and intelligence establishments attended, including General Edward Rowny, Reagan's chief negotiator on the Strategic Arms Reduction Treaty (START) between the United States and the Soviet Union. First proposed by President Reagan in 1982, the treaty limited and reduced strategic offensive arms. Signed in 1991, it went into effect in 1994. Also on hand was former Central Intelligence Agency (CIA) director Admiral Stansfield Turner; and former ambassador to the Soviet Union Walter Stoessel, who had also served in Reagan's State Department. At a reception before the screening, Rowny said he came out of loyalty to Haig and didn't know what the movie was about. When informed, he winced and said, "I hope he doesn't get me in trouble here," adding, "I want to go back and negotiate with the Soviets." Stoessel, before going into the screening, said he'd heard the movie was "a slam-bang thing," and commented, "I hope the good guys win."*

After the movie, however, the foreign policy experts had less to

---

*Elizabeth Kastor, "The Night of 'Red Dawn,'" *Washington Post* online, August 9, 1984, www.washingtonpost.com/archive/lifestyle/1984/08/09/the-night-of-red-dawn/cca31591-5559-491b-9127-6fd853ae94cf/?utm_term=.882f7d96470c.

say. Turner refused to speak to a *Washington Post* reporter on the scene, and Stoessel said simply, "It makes you think." Rowny called the movie "provocative" and made clear he wasn't saying anything more: "I'm going to be diplomatic. Silence is golden, and I'm going to glitter."*

Reagan watched *Red Dawn* at an interesting point in US-Soviet relations. He was in the midst of the 1984 reelection campaign, and committed to maintaining the strong stance against the Soviet Union that he had promised the American people in 1980 and held to throughout his first term. The year before, in 1983, he had referred to the USSR as an "evil empire" and announced plans for the Strategic Defense Initiative, later dubbed "Star Wars." He aimed to show the Russians that the United States meant to win the Cold War.

The very day of the *Red Dawn* screening, Reagan met at the White House with Secretary of State George Shultz to discuss a dramatic prospect: an upcoming meeting with Soviet foreign minister Andrei Gromyko, who would be in the United States later in September for the United Nations General Assembly session. That afternoon, as Reagan noted in his diary, it was "off to Camp David."†

But not without first facing the usual gauntlet of reporters gathered to witness his departure from the White House. The rest and relaxation (and *Red Dawn*) would have to wait. As we made our way to the helicopter on the South Lawn at about three thirty that afternoon, the press bombarded Reagan with questions. They asked him about his planned appointment of Edwin Meese III to serve as attorney general and about some comments made by Walter Mondale on the campaign trail. "Do you think that God is a Republican, as

*Kastor, "The Night of 'Red Dawn.'"
†Ronald Reagan, *Reagan Diaries*, 379.

Mondale charges?" To that, Reagan responded, "I have no answer to any of those things that what's-his-name said." He did banter with the reporters about the nature of religion and politics but soon continued toward Marine One. Among the last questions shouted after him were "Will you meet with Gromyko? Are you going to try to meet with Gromyko?"* The president kept the answer to himself. That evening, we watched *Red Dawn* in his cabin.

The next day, September 8, Reagan noted, was a "beautiful day." He took one of his beloved horseback rides around the mountain trails. He also delivered his "radio talk": this week, on education. When Reagan commented in his speech that "violence and disorder have no place in our schools," I wonder if he might have been thinking of the violence and disorder the high school resistance fighters had got up to in the previous night's movie.†

On Monday the 9th, instead of returning directly to the White House, the president took the helicopter north to Doylestown, Pennsylvania, to speak at a Polish-American festival held at the National Shrine of Our Lady of Czestochowa. He gave a rousing speech to a crowd that he later recorded as forty thousand.‡ The throng consisted mostly of Polish Americans whose ancestral homes had been overtaken by the Communists. Reagan's language was strong:

"Our country's days of apologizing are over. America is standing tall again, and don't let anyone tell you we're any less dedicated to peace because we want a strong America. I've known four wars—four

---

*"Informal Exchange with Reporters on Domestic Issues, September 7, 1984," Ronald Reagan Presidential Library & Museum online, www.reaganlibrary.ar chives.gov/archives/speeches/1984/90784b.htm.

†"Radio Address to the Nation on Education, September 8, 1984," Ronald Reagan Presidential Library & Museum online, www.reaganlibrary.archives.gov /archives/speeches/1984/90884a.htm.

‡Ronald Reagan, *Reagan Diaries*, 380.

wars—in my lifetime, and not one of them came about because we were too strong. Weakness is the greatest enemy of peace."*

The *New York Times* might have described this language the same way it described *Red Dawn*: "incorrigibly gung-ho." But the audience loved it. A few lines later, the president was interrupted by chants of "Four more years!"

Two days later, on September 11, President Reagan announced to the press that he would meet with Foreign Minister Gromyko later in the month. They met first in New York, and later had a three-and-a-half-hour discussion in Washington. It was the first high-level meeting with a Soviet official of Reagan's presidency. Some reporters noted that the announcement came just after Reagan had watched the stridently anti-Communist *Red Dawn* and reiterated his commitment to peace through strength in Pennsylvania. Even before his later successes with Gorbachev, Reagan knew that strength and diplomacy were not mutually exclusive. He also knew how to keep everyone guessing.

After one Friday night screening in Aspen of a movie that featured Communists—it may have been *Red Dawn*, but I can't be certain—we had our usual discussion at the fireplace. I spoke up and said something that sounded a bit "un-American." What it was and why I said it, I cannot recall, but it caused the president to quip, "You sound like those Communists in the movie we just saw." I smiled sheepishly and said, "I think he just painted me red."

Everyone, including the president and I, had a good laugh. I went back to my cabin, off to bed, and didn't give the incident a second

---

*"Remarks at a Polish Festival in Doylestown, Pennsylvania, September 9, 1984," Ronald Reagan Presidential Library & Museum online, www.reagan library.archives.gov/archives/speeches/1984/90984a.htm.

thought. During the president's radio address at Laurel Lodge the next day, everything was as usual. Good moods all around. But that night in Aspen, when the entire group gathered for the Saturday evening movie, the president spoke up.

"Say, last night I said something silly about Mark and Communists," he said to everyone. "I'm sorry if I implied he had the wrong ideas. Of course he doesn't. He's part of the family." I was touched but mystified. I hadn't been bothered at all by the joking the night before, and I hoped the president wasn't either. We all then took our seats and settled in for the weekend's second screening.

After the movie ended and the lights came up, I walked over to Mrs. Reagan and said in a low voice, "That was so nice of the president to say, but he did not need to at all. I was fine." She replied, "I know, but Ronnie felt very bad about it." I asked her why he did not mention it at the radio address earlier, and she explained, "We talked about that, but he thought it was important to say it in front of the whole group."

Of course he didn't think I was some kind of Communist. Casual banter like that was part of the fun of movie nights. But it showed how seriously Reagan took the Communist threat that he went out of his way to explain himself. Communism was no joke for a man whose job it was to go toe-to-toe with the Soviets. And it showed how much both Reagans cared about doing right by their people— by those who were, as he kindly called me, "part of the family."

13

TOP GUN

◆

Starring: Tom Cruise, Kelly McGillis, Val Kilmer
Directed by: Tony Scott
Viewed by the Reagans: May 30, 1986

◆

The Film That Became a Touchstone for the Reagan Years

As I left my office on the thirty-fourth floor of the Fox Plaza building in Los Angeles and rode the elevator down to the entrance to greet Ronald Reagan's guest, I wasn't sure what to expect. Since leaving the White House in January 1989, Reagan had returned to California and established his postpresidential office in Fox Plaza. This gleaming, barely two-year-old, thirty-five-story building in Century City had already earned its own place in movie history by this point; some might know it better as "Nakatomi Plaza," the setting of the 1988 action thriller *Die Hard*. A big part of its appeal was its proximity to the Reagans' Los Angeles residence, less than fifteen minutes away by car. The Reagans had come full circle, returning to live and work in this city that had been the scene of some of their earliest successes and most important events in their lives—not just their careers on the screen but also their meeting and falling in love with each other. The Reagans felt at home in Los Angeles and comfortable in the buzzing, celebrity-packed atmosphere.

I, on the other hand, a kid from Ohio, considered myself lucky to be there. It seemed like only yesterday that Ken Duberstein, then White House chief of staff, called me one day in the summer of 1988 and asked if I would be interested in going to Los Angeles as director of public affairs in Ronald Reagan's office once he'd left Washington. I was both stunned and thrilled. Like everyone else on the White House staff, I had been polishing my resume as the end of the Reagan presidency loomed. I told Ken I would love to do that, but he made no promises. A couple of weeks later, one weekend at Camp David, as we were sitting in the conference room in Laurel Lodge for the president's weekly radio address, Mrs. Reagan turned to me and said, "Ronnie and I are so happy that you will be coming with us to Los Angeles." That was that. The job of public affairs director entailed being spokesman, speechwriter, media advisor, and personal aide. (I found out years later that the Reagans had asked Ken to approach me about the job, because they did not want any awkwardness if I turned out not to be interested.)

Unlike the Reagans, I was new to Los Angeles's celebrity culture, but I was trying to learn fast. And this day was promising to be quite an education. The individual I was on my way to greet was one of the biggest stars in Hollywood.

Perhaps that's why I was a bit surprised when an ordinary-looking SUV pulled up in front of the building, and Tom Cruise hopped out of the driver's seat. He was recognizable, of course, with his hair parted and that famous smile. He had no chauffeur, no security, and no entourage, and was wearing a dark suit and tie to meet my boss.

I introduced myself, and he was as friendly as I had hoped. I told him my name as we shook hands, and he said, "And I'm Tom." "Yes, I knew that," I said. He chuckled. We walked to the elevator and rode it to the floor on which the former president's office was.

The idea to get these two stars together was born from an ongoing conversation among former president Reagan's staff, helped by Mrs. Reagan. Once we set up the LA office, she, the chief of staff Fred Ryan, and I tossed around ideas for interesting and fun things for the erstwhile chief executive to do, to liven up the staid duties that often typified the careers of past presidents.

One idea that appealed to all of us was that Reagan should get to know modern Hollywood. After all, he was an elder statesman not only of the United States but of Tinseltown. And we knew he would be interested in getting to know his successors as movie stars, as well as learn how the motion picture business had evolved. Cruise, one of the biggest stars of the 1980s, seemed an ideal person to approach. Reagan not only knew who he was, but also he had enjoyed watching Cruise's 1986 blockbuster *Top Gun* at Camp David several years ago, despite some interruptions.

I was unable to make the trip to Camp David on the weekend in the spring of 1986 when *Top Gun* was shown. Denny Brisley, a colleague in the White House Press Office, took my place. Since graduating from Stanford University in 1982, she had worked at the Office of Management and Budget (OMB), the largest office within the president's Executive Office, before joining the White House press staff in 1985. Denny had also recently joined the US Navy Reserve and was celebrating her twenty-sixth birthday the day she took off with the Reagans for Camp David on Friday, May 30—her first time filling in on this trip. It promised to be an eventful birthday weekend.

Also on board Marine One that day was Commander Vivien Crea of the US Coast Guard, the first woman to serve as a presidential military aide. As the chopper thundered over the National Mall, Commander Crea, the "football" case containing the nuclear launch codes held in her grasp, leaned over to the president and made a special request. She asked if Marine One could divert from the usual flight path to Camp David and fly over the Coast Guard headquarters at Buzzard Point on the Anacostia River in southwest Washington, DC.

Crea, who would go on to become vice commandant of the Coast Guard, explained that their headquarters was getting a special visit that day. The Coast Guard cutter *Eagle*, a nearly three-hundred-foot sailing vessel used as a training ship for cadets, was docked there on a visit from the US Coast Guard Academy in New London, Connecticut. The president liked the idea, and the pilots altered course for the southwest waterfront. When the brilliant white vessel with its three high masts and familiar Coast Guard emblem came into view, the helicopter began to circle as the president and Mrs. Reagan waved down at the cadets (who were no doubt surprised to be buzzed by Marine One). Rex, the Reagans' yappy and annoying Cavalier King Charles Spaniel, barked at the window.

Although a committed navy woman herself, Denny Brisley was proud of the salute to her fellow seafaring service members. After that detour, it was on to Maryland.

As the presidential pilot lowered the helicopter to land at Camp David, Brisley watched from the window as the presidential flag was raised to welcome the president. It hit the top of the staff just as Marine One touched down. One of her fellow naval officers greeted the president with a salute as the party disembarked. As it turned out, there was still more to come to stir Ensign Brisley's navy pride that weekend.

From the helicopter, the staff party transferred to the small motorcade of nondescript silver Chrysler sedans that would ferry them to their cabins. As everyone was getting in, President Reagan turned to Brisley and asked if she would care to join them for a movie later that evening. She had hoped this invitation was coming, but she knew the routine. You didn't just "show up" for movie night in Aspen; the Reagans had to invite you.

"Thank you, Mr. President, I would be delighted," she replied. "What are we going to watch?"

Brisley remembered that Reagan responded with a smile and a wink. "We are watching *Top Gun*," he said. He was clearly excited, and so was the young press aide and naval officer who was set to join him.

Top Gun had been out for only about two weeks, and already it was proving wildly popular. On its opening weekend, it brought in more than $8 million and shot to number one at the box office. Critics praised the action scenes but scoffed at some of the dialogue and story lines. No matter, it would become the top movie of 1986.*

The film centers on fliers at the US Navy's Fighter Weapons School, known informally as Top Gun, where the best aviators in the naval ranks receive advanced training. It opens with a tense aerial encounter in the skies above the Indian Ocean between F-14 Tomcat fighters from the aircraft carrier USS *Enterprise* and hostile jets from a never-identified country (but bearing a Communist red star). Lieutenant Pete Mitchell, played by Tom Cruise and known by his call sign "Maverick," performs a daring maneuver, managing to invert his F-14 above the enemy aircraft and give its pilot a less-than-diplomatic middle finger. The incident ends without gunfire, but the top pilot in Maverick's squadron cracks from the pressure of the encounter.

*"*Top Gun*," Box Office Mojo, accessed September 19, 2017, www.boxoffice mojo.com/movies/?id=topgun.htm.

Maverick and his radio intercept officer, Lieutenant Junior Grade Nick "Goose" Bradshaw, played by Anthony Edwards, become the squadron's top team, earning them a trip to Top Gun fighter pilot school, then located at Miramar Naval Air Station in California. They are sent off with a warning from their commander, who is well aware of the recklessness that earned Maverick his call sign. These include "a history of high-speed passes over five air control towers and one admiral's daughter."

At Top Gun, Maverick and Goose rival another hotshot team of fliers in their class, "Iceman" and "Slider," played by Val Kilmer and Rick Rossovich. Their instructors, "Viper" and "Jester" (Tom Skerritt and Michael Ironside), recognize Maverick's natural talent but try to tame his headstrong tendencies. After one training flight that didn't end well, Jester remarks that Maverick displayed "some of the best flying I've seen to date—right up to the part where you got killed." To further complicate things, Maverick falls for Charlotte Blackwood, a civilian air combat analyst attached to Top Gun (and bearing her own call sign, "Charlie"), played by Kelly McGillis.

Viper, the older instructor, holds a key to the secret that drives Maverick to fly the way he does: the unresolved disappearance of his father, also a naval aviator, during the Vietnam War. Maverick's "need for speed" eventually takes its toll, leading to tragic consequences. He must face the question of whether he has what it takes to fly with the best at Top Gun. And in the film's gripping final dogfight, when the black jets emblazoned with red stars are menacing a disabled American ship, he must rely on both his Top Gun training and his natural risk-taking instincts to survive.

Top Gun was made with the full cooperation of the US Navy, and real pilots performed the flying sequences. Dozens of naval aviators were thanked by name, including their call signs, in the credits for their help in making the film. The coordination wasn't always easy.

In one instance, when director Tony Scott was filming on an aircraft carrier, he realized the lighting would look better if the ship was traveling in a different direction. Informed that the effort to turn the massive vessel would cost $25,000, Scott cut a check then and there.*

The US Navy received a return for its efforts. Enlistment booths set up outside theaters showing the movie across the country led to a surge in recruitment, especially for the aviation program. One recruiting officer in Los Angeles told the Associated Press, "I've asked several of these individuals if they've seen the movie and if that's why they came down to talk to us again, and they've said 'yes.'" Another recruiter reported that her offices had received more than twice their usual number of phone calls in the weeks since *Top Gun* came out. When they interviewed applicants, "about ninety percent said they had seen the movie."†

Denny Brisley had already joined the navy, but that didn't lessen her enjoyment of the film when she watched it in Aspen with the Reagans. The president and Mrs. Reagan were settled on the couch together as usual, with their feet up on the ottoman and Rex nestled in between them. Brisley remembered the awkwardness during the "hot and heavy" love scenes between Cruise and McGillis that "seemed to go on forever"—the Reagans were well known to disapprove of too much adult content in movies. Incidentally, "Take My Breath Away," the song used in their famous blue-tinted love scene, won the movie's only Oscar, for best original song.

---

*Todd Leopold, "Director Tony Scott: An Appreciation," CNN online, last modified August 21, 2012, www.cnn.com/2012/08/21/showbiz/movies/tony-scott-appreciation.

†Mark Evje, Associated Press, "'Top Gun' Boosting Service Sign-Ups," *Los Angeles Times* online, July 5, 1986, http://articles.latimes.com/1986-07-05/entertainment/ca-20403_1_top-gun.

President Reagan was enthralled by the dogfighting scenes, which even the movie's critics had to praise. Roger Ebert called them "brilliant."* The president's dog apparently enjoyed them as well. During one intense aerial combat sequence, right as the movie's pumping eighties power-rock soundtrack reached its crescendo, Rex jumped up on the ottoman and started barking at the screen. The excitement must have gotten to him, too. The president, however, was less than amused to have his concentration on the action broken. Brisley remembered laughing to herself, amused at the spectacle of the most powerful man in the world struggling to quiet his barking dog.

The president enjoyed *Top Gun*, perhaps not least because it was one of the biggest Hollywood movies in a long time that was unabashedly pro-military. Since the end of the Vietnam War, Hollywood had taken a disillusioned attitude toward the military, focusing on the bitterness and brutality of war and portraying American fighting men in a morally ambiguous light. Movies such as 1979's *Apocalypse Now* and *The Deer Hunter* reflected this generally antiwar viewpoint. Movies about violent Vietnam veterans, like *Taxi Driver's* Travis Bickle (which reportedly inspired Reagan's would-be assassin, John Hinckley Jr.)† and Sylvester Stallone's character John Rambo, from *First Blood* and *Rambo: First Blood Part II*), were in vogue as well.

But *Top Gun*, released more than a decade after the end of the Vietnam War, was not afraid to portray the American military unequivocally as the "good guys," and that was certainly more in line

---

*Roger Ebert, review of *Top Gun*, RogerEbert.com, May 16, 1986, www.roger ebert.com/reviews/top-gun-1986.

†Laura A. Kiernan, "Hinckley, Jury Watch 'Taxi Driver' Film," *Washington Post* online, May 29, 1982, www.washingtonpost.com/archive/politics/1982/05/29 /hinckley-jury-watch-taxi-driver-film/783cde2f-1eea-4ec5-a36f-5ccf5d2a290f /?utm_term=.7e3aa890f502.

with Reagan's own thinking. He respected all men and women in the service, and the year before, during a Veterans Day service at Arlington National Cemetery, observed that "there is a special sadness that accompanies the death of a serviceman, for we're never quite good enough to them—not really; we can't be, because what they gave us is beyond our powers to repay."*

One aspect of Camp David that delighted the president was that it was a military facility, known officially as Naval Support Facility (NSF) Thurmont. He loved the troops and returned every salute directed at him. It was the president's idea to "drop in" at their mess hall and have lunch every so often. He would take a plastic tray and choose food from the cafeteria line like everyone else. A spot had been saved for him at a table with men and women of all ranks. He would ask them where they were from and was eager to learn about their families. After lunch, President Reagan would go over to an area where everyone could see him, usually in front of the milk machine, and give a few remarks about how grateful he and Mrs. Reagan were, how much they appreciated everything the troops did to make them so comfortable at Camp David, and so on, and then open it up for questions. The troops were silent at first, but after some coaxing, they would ask questions ranging from national security, war, and peace issues, to what it was like in Hollywood in his day, to what his favorite sports team was. He would have stayed in the mess hall the whole day if the staff had let him.

Around the holidays, at Mrs. Reagan's suggestion, every man and woman serving at Camp David was invited to meet the Reagans and

*"Remarks by President Reagan, Veterans Day National Ceremony, Arlington National Cemetery, Arlington, Virginia, November 11, 1985," US Department of Veterans Affairs online, last modified November 10, 2009, www.va.gov/opa/vetsday/speakers/1985remarks.asp.

have a picture taken, usually in front of the large fireplace in Laurel. The troops did not say much during their moments in front of the camera, but the Reagans enjoyed meeting and thanking them all.

The Reagans were similarly courteous to the military personnel with them at their ranch near Santa Barbara. There the on-duty military aide was assigned to a temporary housing trailer near the horse barn. The president would make the person feel welcome by walking over and offering a bottle of red wine on his or her first day of duty.

The members of the military who served at Camp David were complete professionals, who certainly did not display the flagrant (if endearing) disregard for higher authority shown by Pete "Maverick" Mitchell, Tom Cruise's character in *Top Gun*. Nonetheless, Maverick was a hero who, despite some flaws, wants to do his nation proud. He tells his commander, "[I] just want to serve my country, be the best pilot in the navy, sir." The line is delivered somewhat tongue in cheek as Maverick gets a dressing-down, but it's not all irony. Maverick may have been a hotshot and a reckless flier, but his intentions were good.

Top Gun did not single-handedly end the trend of antiwar movies in Hollywood. Director-writer Oliver Stone's *Platoon*, released the same year, depicted US soldiers engaging in war crimes in Vietnam. Three years later, Tom Cruise took on a different role as an antiwar Vietnam vet in *Born on the Fourth of July*. But in 1986 *Top Gun's* tremendous success showed that America was beginning to come out from under the shadow of Vietnam. In their own ways, both Ronald Reagan and "Maverick" helped us get there.

Soon after Ronald Reagan left the White House those two would get a chance to meet face-to-face.

As the elevator door opened on the thirty-fourth floor of Fox Plaza, and I led Tom Cruise into our office, the rest of the staff was shocked.

Only a handful of us knew that Cruise was coming in to meet with the boss—on the daily calendar, the time frame had been marked only as "Hold—Private Appointment." I considered getting a movie poster for him to sign but decided that would be rude.

Cruise could not have been more gracious as I escorted him around and introduced him to the people in the office. Paula Wagner, the actor's talent agent, joined us. Wagner had been instrumental in arranging this meeting. We approached her with the idea first, and she recognized its appeal. She promised to raise it with Cruise and got back to us within days to say that her client was in. Wagner would go on to become an acclaimed movie producer in her own right, sometimes partnering with Cruise.

After taking Cruise around to meet my colleagues, I took him in to see President Reagan, accompanied by Wagner and Fred Ryan. Reagan's personal office was modest by CEO standards, furnished with a desk, couch, armchairs, and coffee table. The walls were taken up by paintings and shelves. Amid the books were framed photographs of the Reagan family, world leaders, and sculptures, most with a Western theme. The office's best feature, by far, was the spectacular view of the Pacific Ocean. President Reagan never tired of taking visitors to the window to show them.

Reagan greeted his guests and offered them a seat on the couch. They were served water and jelly beans from a crystal jar bearing the presidential seal. Reagan and Cruise quickly engaged in an animated discussion about moviemaking and politics. Their conversation also touched on issues such as the environment and taxes. Reagan told Cruise that back in his day, his earnings had been taxed at a rate of ninety cents on the dollar. This astounded Cruise.

Comparing their own experiences in Hollywood seemed to be of the greatest interest to them. Reagan asked Cruise what it was like to be a star in the 1980s. For his part, the younger actor listened intently to Reagan's stories from the earlier days and how his acting experience had compared with serving as president. Reagan talked, longingly, to my ear, about the old studio system that used to run Hollywood, comparing working for a studio to being part of a big family.

The studios, Reagan explained, were run "like a Greek candy store, where they made it in the back and sold it in the front." They made the movies on their own lots and released them in their own theaters. Cruise was quite intrigued by that. Interestingly, just four years later, in 1993, he and Wagner would launch their own independent production company, something that would have been difficult, if not impossible, under the studio system of Reagan's time.

Wagner remembered Reagan as a "lovely, kind man." Despite her and Cruise traveling in the highest Hollywood circles, she told me later that they were amazed to be in a room with a man who had been president of the United States.*

When it came time for the nearly hour-long visit to end, Cruise and Wagner thanked Reagan for taking the time to see them. "No, thank *you* for coming by," he replied. He meant it. He appreciated and enjoyed their visit.

As they got up to leave, I could not help but think how interesting it was that two of the most talented, best-known men to make it as movie stars got along so well. They were both consummate professionals who enjoyed unmatched success. Even though Reagan was now a private citizen, he had left office earlier that year with the highest approval rating of any president up to that point in history. Cruise had costarred in *Rain Man*, the previous year's Oscar winner for best picture, and was about to secure his first Oscar nomination

*Author conversation with Paula Wagner via phone, August 9, 2016.

in his own right for *Born on the Fourth of July*. I had just witnessed a meeting between two of the most popular individuals in America.

Working in the White House was an experience like no other, but I will always have fond memories of those years in Reagan's Los Angeles office. He remained a great boss right up until the end. A few weeks before I was to leave Reagan's employ for good, he came into my office and said, "Well, Mark, is there anything you want?"

I had no idea what he meant, and said, "Sir, I must confess I do not know what you're asking me."

He chuckled. "Oh, well, I mean with regard to a position in Washington. I know when people left the White House, they sometimes arranged to be appointed to a position of some kind, and I'd be pleased to help with that, if you'd like."

I thanked him and said I would think about it and let him know. It had never occurred to me to seek an appointment to anything after I left the Reagans, but I was intrigued by the idea. So I did some research into presidential boards and commissions. Maybe it was paranoia on my part, but I suspected that people in the George H. W. Bush White House might resist a presidential appointment of a longtime Reagan aide. So I had to come up with something to which they could not say no for any reason. Specifically, that meant a position that did not require Senate confirmation, was uncompensated, and was on a board or commission with no limit on its membership. Those were few and far between. But one that checked all the boxes and genuinely interested me was the President's Commission on White House Fellowships, which interviews and recommends to the president candidates for appointments as White House fellows. Begun in 1964, the White House Fellows program identified high-achieving and high-potential young professionals, and invited them to come to Washington to work in close proximity to top executive branch officials. Elaine Chao and Colin Powell are among those who served as White House Fellows earlier in their careers.

Once I identified the position, I went in to see President Reagan and told him I had found something I thought would work. He said, "Great, just give me the information, and I'll call George." As in Bush. As in President George H. W. Bush. Alrighty, then.

So I went back to my office, wrote the usual "Recommended Telephone Call" sheet, printed it out, and took it in to President Reagan. He looked at it, winked, and asked his secretary to get President Bush on the line. A few minutes later, she came in and said, "He's on," and President Reagan picked up the phone.

"Hi, George. How are you?" After an exchange of pleasantries, President Reagan said, "Say, George, I'm calling because I wanted to ask that Mark Weinberg, who has been with us for a number of years now and is coming back to Washington soon, be appointed to the Commission on White House Fellows. I think he'd do a great job there." At that point, President Reagan stopped talking and listened to whatever his successor was saying. A few moments later, he said, "Thanks, George, I appreciate that. Nancy sends her love to Barbara. All right. Good-bye." With that, he hung up the phone, looked at me, and said, "I think they'll be in touch soon." I thanked him and returned to my office, still a bit stunned by what I had witnessed.

I can only imagine what it was like on the other end of that call. George H. W. Bush is sitting in the Oval Office, and his secretary comes in to tell him Ronald Reagan is on the line. Since they did not talk by phone often, the new chief executive had to be curious about the subject of the call. So he picks it up only to find that his predecessor is calling about . . . me. I hope he was not disappointed.

An hour or so after President Reagan spoke to President Bush, I received a call from the White House, telling me that my appointment was in the works.

14

KNUTE ROCKNE
ALL AMERICAN

---◆---

Starring:　Pat O'Brien, Ronald Reagan
Directed by:　Lloyd Bacon
Viewed by the Reagans:　October 2, 1987

---◆---

The Film That Created a Political Legend

The week of September 27, 1987, had been an interesting and un-settling one at the White House. On Tuesday, the president delivered a major economic address to the annual meeting of the Boards of Governors of the International Monetary Fund and World Bank Group, and later signed a bill to increase the federal debt ceiling.

But the real focus of the week was on Ronald Reagan's nomination of Robert H. Bork to become an associate justice of the US Supreme Court, replacing the retiring Lewis Powell. The nomination had been made on July 1, and it immediately brought equally strong support and opposition. No one doubted his intellect, but Bork's ultraconservative (some would say unyielding) stance on many issues and his absolute certainty of the correctness of his positions both delighted and infuriated many. Throughout the summer, supporters and opponents were in high gear, and by October, it was clear the nomination was in deep trouble. President Reagan did everything he could to support Bork, then a judge on the US Court of Appeals for the District of Columbia Circuit, including speaking on his behalf on three different occasions that week. He had given Bork his word that he would do whatever he could to ensure his confirmation.

When Ronald Reagan gave his word, that was it. It was gold. You could take it to the bank. I learned that the hard, yet reassuring, way a year earlier. In late January and early February 1986, I was in Asia on a pre-advance for an upcoming presidential visit there. A pre-advance takes a small group of White House staff, State Department aides, Secret Service, military support personnel, and representatives of the White House press corps to wherever the president is scheduled to visit overseas, so they can evaluate their respective logistical needs for the actual trip. I was in Tokyo on January 28, the day the space shuttle *Challenger* exploded. I returned to Washington a few days later and went to work as usual. On my first or second day back, Larry Speakes, the chief White House spokesman, called me to his office. At first, he was chatty, asking me how everything was, if there were any interesting stories from recent Camp David weekends, and so forth. Then he told me to have a seat on the couch opposite his desk. I was nervous. And I became even more so when he closed the door. He sat on a chair near the couch, looked *toward but not at* me, avoiding direct eye contact, and said, "Mark, you gotta find another job."

I thought I was going to pass out. I could not imagine my life without working in the White House for the Reagans. It was everything to me. I asked him what he meant, and he said that Don Regan, the current White House chief of staff, "told me you have to go." Larry claimed that he protested and asked Regan why, but was given no information. Larry was upset by this, but that was of little consolation to me. He asked me if my relationship with Mrs. Reagan was still good, thinking that perhaps she was involved. I assured him that it was good, that our most recent weekend at Camp David was fun as usual, and that I could not imagine she had anything to do with my being fired.

It bothered me that there was the tendency of some on the White House staff to blame Mrs. Reagan first for anything bad. It was unfair and almost never the case. Larry went on to say that "the plan" was that I would be assigned to be the spokesman for the recently named presidential commission investigating the *Challenger* accident, during which time I would look for a job and ultimately never return to the White House. I did not know what to say. I left his office and returned to mine. I immediately called my closest friend on the staff, Jim Kuhn, the president's personal aide, and asked if he knew anything. He didn't, but Jim had the wisdom to ask me if I had said anything derogatory about Don Regan. I said it would take less time to tell him what I *hadn't* said about Regan than what I had said.

I was among the very first people Don Regan met in the Reagan press operation. After he was announced as the incoming president's choice for secretary of the Treasury in December 1980, I shepherded him through some Washington, DC, interviews before Reagan's inauguration. I even remember going to the Treasury Department gift shop and buying a pair of cuff links with the Treasury Department seal and giving them to him one day, which seemed to delight him. On one of his visits to Washington, we had breakfast together at the Sheraton Carlton Hotel, and he offered me a job in the Treasury Department Press Office. I declined because I wanted to go to the White House Press Office.

I liked Don, but when he became chief of staff at the White

House in 1985, switching jobs with James A. Baker III, he seemed to forget that he was on *the staff* and that it was the *Reagan* administration, not the *Regan* administration. I do not deny that I made some unflattering observations about his imperial style to reporters. I suspect some of that got back to him.

I turned out the lights in my office and went home, where I threw a small party with four of my friends: Jim Beam, Jack Daniel, Jose Cuervo, and Johnnie Walker.

I was loyal to the Reagans, knew that I had done nothing wrong, and that Donald Regan's firing me was undeserved. I decided to fight back. First, I contacted Mike Deaver, told him what had happened, and asked him outright if I had done anything to offend the Reagans. Mike said, "No. If you had done anything to offend them, I would know." I was relieved, but still perplexed. Mike said he would see what he could find out. What I did not realize at the time was that Mike was among those urging the president to replace Regan.

I also contacted Maureen Reagan, who was my friend and informal advisor. She, too, was shocked by what had happened and promised to raise it with her father and Mrs. Reagan. True to her word, she did. A couple of days later, before I actually went to the offices of the Presidential Commission on the Space Shuttle Challenger Accident, I was in my office in the West Wing. The date was February 6, which happened to be President Reagan's birthday. It was around five o'clock in the evening, and with me was Dennis Revell, Maureen's husband. He had stopped by just to say hello, offer support as a friend, and urge me to hang in there. My phone rang, and I could tell it was a White House operator, as opposed to a call from outside the complex. I answered, and the operator said, "Mr. Weinberg, I have the president calling for you, sir."

I held my breath. A split second later, that familiar voice was on the line. "Mark, first of all, thank you for your birthday present, but

I'm calling today to say there must have been some misunderstanding. I just spoke to Don, and you aren't fired."

I said, "Well, sir, first of all, Happy Birthday, but I have to tell you that's what I was told. Larry said that I had been fired and was no longer to be on the White House staff."

The president said, "No, there must be some misunderstanding. I told Don that you are part of the family and that while it was fine for you to go over to the shuttle commission, and I would appreciate you doing that, I fully expected you to come back here where you belong." I almost cried. I said, "Mr. President, it seems like on your birthday you have given me the greatest present, and, sir, if that is your wish, I will go over to the commission and do the best job I can, *as long as I have your word that I can come back to my job here at the White House.*"

"You have it," he said without hesitation. That was that. I turned to Dennis and said, "You're here, and you are a witness." He smiled.

I walked up the hall to tell Larry what had happened. He seemed surprised by it. He went to Don Regan's office, came back a few minutes later, and confirmed what I had told him. So off I went to the office of the Presidential Commission on the Space Shuttle Challenger Accident, where I worked for a couple of months. But every day during that period, I made a point of stopping in my White House office to be visible, and I kept my White House pass. I did not want to be "out of sight, out of mind," and I did not trust Don Regan not to try again. But just as Ronald Reagan had promised, after my stint with the commission, I returned full-time to my duties at the White House as if nothing had happened.

I arrived just in time for the political firestorm of the Bork nomination.

Ronald Reagan was the eternal optimist and loyal. Some would say to a fault. Yet he was also a realist, and when Marine One landed at Camp David on October 2, the president knew it was unlikely Bork would be confirmed by the Senate. The votes were just not there. But he wasn't ready yet to give up, even though many on his staff urged him to do so. Mrs. Reagan, who had the best political instincts of us all, felt that the controversy surrounding the nomination had become something of a "circus," and she did not like the fact that there had been a pro-Bork rally, complete with signs, on the South Lawn of the White House when Marine One lifted off for Camp David that day.

She was right, of course. And after the Senate Judiciary Committee rejected his nomination, Bork should have asked the president to withdraw his name. But he did not. Why Bork did not have the common sense to spare the president further embarrassment remains a mystery.

I doubt Bork or Washington politics were on the president's mind when the lights dimmed and the screen lit up with the most iconic film of Ronald Reagan's career.

Knute Rockne All American is the 1940 film biography of former Notre Dame University football player Knute Rockne (Pat O'Brien), who returns to his alma mater in 1918 as the football coach. With star freshman halfback George Gipp (played by none other than Ronald Reagan), Rockne quickly takes the once lackluster team to great heights. Two years later, just days after his final game, Gipp contracted a strep infection which led to a terminal case of pneumonia, and died a few weeks later. He was just twenty-five. Gipp ends up doing even more good for the team as an inspiration than as a player.

Sometimes certain roles identify an actor in the public's mind. Sylvester Stallone will always be "Rocky," just as Carol Channing will always be "Dolly." Though not as successful as the *Rocky* series or *Hello, Dolly!*, *Knute Rockne All American* did the same for

Ronald Reagan. His portrayal of Gipp earned him a permanent place in the nation's mind as "the Gipper." To this day, newspapers sometimes refer to Ronald Reagan by that nickname. It's almost shorthand for his full name. Like most of his roles in the movies, he was proud of it.

So tied to the role of the Gipper was Ronald Reagan that "Win one for the Gipper" became a rallying cry at campaign events over the years. Not only did he invoke the phrase on his own behalf, but also he would often do so when campaigning for others. Only once do I recall that phrase becoming a potential issue. In 1989, as a former president, Ronald Reagan attended a University of Southern California (USC) versus Notre Dame football game in Los Angeles. He had been invited by both teams to visit their locker rooms before the game. Fred Ryan, the chief of staff and a proud alumnus of USC, was rightly concerned that the former president might urge the Fighting Irish to win one for the Gipper, which would have compromised his neutrality and been discourteous to the USC Trojans, who were his hosts.

Fred asked me to tell President Reagan not to utter the phrase when he visited the locker room, which I did, explaining why. The former chief executive nodded in agreement, but, truthfully, I was not certain he would comply. Fred and I were a little nervous when the president spoke to the Notre Dame Fighting Irish, and did not relax until he was done, having not said the famous five words—as much as he probably wanted to.

Everyone knew how important making the movie and playing George Gipp had been to Reagan. He expressed that eloquently when he visited Notre Dame in 1988 to participate in the unveiling of a commemorative postage stamp honoring Knute Rockne, who died in a 1931 plane crash. He shared how seriously he had taken the challenging role of George Gipp and how much it had meant to him to become part of the Rockne legend. "All I'd ever wanted was to play the Gipper if they someday made the film," he said. As he told the audience in South Bend, Indiana:

> [T]he role was a young actor's dream: it had a great entrance, an action middle, and a death scene right out of the opera. But it was more than that. I know that to many of you today Rockne is a revered name, a symbol of greatness, and, yes, a face now on a postage stamp. But my generation, well, we actually knew the legend as it happened. We saw it unfold, and we felt it was saying something important about us as a people and a nation.*

The role, Reagan explained, hadn't been handed to him. He went to the star, Pat O'Brien, who was playing Rockne, to put himself forward. His brazenness made an impression. "He told me bluntly that I talked too much," Reagan remembered. O'Brien told him it didn't look good. The studio wanted a "name actor" to play Gipp. But he decided to give Reagan a chance and put in a word with Warner Bros. studio head Hal Wallis.

But there were obstacles in Reagan's path. "Hal was, to put it mildly, unimpressed with my credentials," according to Reagan. He told the actor that he was too small for the role, but Reagan shot back with his knowledge of the George Gipp story. "I told him," he said later, "you're producing the picture, and you don't know that George Gipp weighed five pounds less than I weigh right now. He

---

*"Remarks at the Unveiling of the Knute Rockne Commemorative Stamp at the University of Notre Dame in Indiana, March 9, 1988," Ronald Reagan Presidential Library & Museum online, www.reaganlibrary.archives.gov/ar chives/speeches/1988/030988a.htm.

walked with a kind of a slouch and almost a limp. He looked like a football player only when he was on the field."

Reagan produced a picture of himself from his own college football days, where he played for coach Ralph McKenzie at Eureka College. McKenzie himself later described Reagan as "eager, aggressive, better on defense—overall, an average football player—but an outstanding talker." Wallis felt Reagan at least looked the part of a gridiron star and agreed to give him a screen test.

In some ways, the screen test was the easiest part. Reagan got a key assist from Pat O'Brien, who agreed to play Rockne opposite him for the tryout instead of simply having a crew member feed Reagan lines off camera. But Reagan left nothing to chance and came prepared: "I had known George Gipp's story for years, and the lines were straight from Knute Rockne's diary."

After filming was completed, Reagan brought an unexpected guest to the premiere in South Bend: his father. Jack Reagan, an alcoholic, had not been an easy man to grow up with, but in the run-up to the premiere, Ronald Reagan's mother took her son aside and shared what Jack himself could not: that as a good Irish Catholic, he loved Notre Dame and Pat O'Brien and would love to celebrate the movie's release. Ronald Reagan was concerned—he was still a young actor and he did not want his father to cause some drunken scene around the cast and crew and other guests. But Jack had vowed to stay off the booze during the trip, and so he accompanied his son to South Bend. Jack Reagan not only behaved himself but also shined on the Notre Dame campus. "His weakness was prosperity," his son said later, "and this was prosperity in capital letters." Jack even became fast friends with Pat O'Brien. After the whirlwind premiere, Jack came home and told his wife he'd had "the most wonderful time of his life." Shortly thereafter, he died—and among the mourners at his funeral was his newfound friend Pat O'Brien.

Reagan never shied from the less polished sides of George Gipp's character, admitting that "he played in some pool games and card games in his time." But he made sure to highlight that the real-life Gipper had a good heart. The legend in South Bend was that "he used his winnings from those games to buy food for destitute families and to help other students pay their way through Notre Dame." In fact, he contracted the pneumonia that killed him while doing a favor for a friend who was coaching high school football: Gipp had promised to give a special session to his friend's young players, and as Reagan told it, "it was during that training session in Chicago that an icy wind blew in across Lake Michigan, and the Gipper first felt the ache and sore throat that would lead to the illness that would take his life."

Being part of the Rockne story was important to Ronald Reagan. He maintained his deep admiration for the coach as an inspirational figure. "Rockne stressed character," he said. "He knew, instinctively, the relationship between the physical and moral." As a coach, he mastered the physical. Reagan observed that he was "remembered as the man who brought ingenuity, speed, and agility into this most American of sports." As a man, he mastered the moral. This is what Reagan said, quoting Rockne himself:

"You know all this hurry and battling we're going through is just an expression of our inner selves striving for something else. The way I look at it is that we're all here to try and find, each in his own way, the best road to our ultimate goal. I believe I've found my way, and I shall travel it to the end."

Reagan called Rockne's career "a sermon in right living."

He sought to use Rockne's example at a time when Americans needed the inspiration it could bring. When he spoke at the ceremony in South Bend, the explosion of the space shuttle *Challenger* two years before was still fresh in people's minds. But Reagan vowed that the same grit that sustained Rockne would sustain the American Space Shuttle Program:

> Rockne exemplified the American spirit of never giving up. That spirit is the reason why you and your generation are going to succeed. That's why we're not just going to compete, we're going to win. And that's also why this year we'll see the return of the American space shuttle, symbolic of America's tenacity. We never give up. And I cannot help but believe that the heroes of the *Challenger* will be cheering along with the rest of us when the United States reclaims its rightful leadership role in leading the conquest of this, the last frontier.*

When the movie ended in Aspen that night, there was applause, and then we had to shout over each other to ask questions. The president was more than happy to indulge us. He would tell the story of how he wanted the part and almost didn't get it, of how much he liked playing football, and how honored he felt to work with Pat O'Brien. He told us how Mrs. Rockne was often on the set during filming, and he made the point that Rockne's first name was pronounced "Ke-Newt," in two syllables, not "Newt." One of us asked him if he still remembered "the line." Without hesitation, he recited it perfectly, as if in the film:

"Rock, someday when the team's up against it . . . and the breaks are beatin' the boys . . . ask them to go in there with all they've got . . . and win just one for the Gipper . . . I don't know where I'll be then . . . but I'll know about it . . . and I'll be happy." For that moment, at least, the Gipper was back.

---

*"Remarks at Unveiling of Knute Rockne Commemorative Stamp, March 9, 1988," Ronald Reagan Presidential Library & Museum online.

15

THE UNTOUCHABLES

———◆———

Starring: Kevin Costner, Sean Connery, Robert
            De Niro
Directed by: Brian De Palma
Viewed by the Reagans: June 26, 1987

———◆———

The Film That Echoed One of Reagan's Lifelong Missions

"It's a heck of a way to start a weekend, but that's the way it goes."*

That's what Ronald Reagan quipped to his newest chief of staff,
Howard Baker (no relation to James A. Baker III), the influential
three-term senator and former majority leader from Tennessee who'd
succeeded Donald Regan in February, after he finished a colonoscopy exam on the afternoon of June 26, 1987. The president was
getting used to these procedures by now, having undergone several

*Helen Thomas, UPI White House reporter, "Two 'Benign' Polyps Removed
from Reagan," United Press International online, June 26, 1987, www.upi.com
/Archives/1987/06/26/Two-small-benign-appearing-polyps-were-discovered
-and-removed-from/3636551678400.

in the two years since his cancer surgery. This one was different in that it was able to be performed in the White House physician's office just down the hall instead of at Bethesda Naval Medical Center. Not only was it convenient but also it indicated that his recovery from the surgery had been as complete as everyone had predicted.

Still, top doctors took part to make sure everything went smoothly. In addition to the White House doctor, Colonel John Hutton, two surgeons from the Mayo Clinic, Dr. Robert Beart Jr. and Dr. Oliver Beahrs, performed the procedure. During the exam, which President Reagan watched live on a monitor—"first time I ever watched my insides on a screen," he wrote that day*—two more of the now-routine polyps were identified and removed. The physicians assessed them as benign and sent them off to pathologists for confirmation.

The visit to Dr. Hutton's office on the ground floor of the White House—"down the hall" from the Diplomatic Reception, Map, and China rooms—was the last item on the president's official agenda that day. Earlier, he had entertained a delegation of thirty-eight citizens of Dixon, Illinois, all of whom were volunteers at the Ronald Reagan Boyhood Home museum on Hennepin Avenue. After that session, which Reagan described in his diary as "warm [and] fun" and which included a photo shoot, the chief executive tackled more serious issues with Secretary of State George Shultz and Gaston Sigur, the assistant secretary of state for East Asian and Pacific affairs.

Sigur had just returned from a short visit to South Korea, which was, at that moment, rocked by massive student-led demonstrations urging more democratic reforms. Sigur had traveled to the key US ally to get a sense of the situation on the ground, and Reagan was greatly interested to hear what he had to say. Their meeting was cut

---

*Ronald Reagan, *Reagan Diaries*, 742.

short, however, when it came time to visit Dr. Hutton and the Mayo Clinic specialists.*

After the procedure, our Friday routine picked up right where it normally left off. We were off to Camp David. Walking out of the White House with Mrs. Reagan at his side, the president flashed the "okay" sign to the assembled reporters, who were calling out questions about the colonoscopy. As he made his way to the waiting helicopter, the president was in obvious good spirits—the *New York Times* reported he "took a tiny skip," while to Helen Thomas of UPI, it appeared he "started to dance a little jig."[†,‡] Reagan knew how to entertain an audience.

This trip, however, had an ending that differed from the usual procedure. Fog had enveloped the helipad at the compound higher up the mountain, making conditions too dangerous to attempt a landing. Instead, Marine One landed at the foot of Catoctin Mountain, where a waiting motorcade drove everyone up to the top.[§]

Getting back to the White House could sometimes be complicated, too. First of all, the time of return had to be determined. If it was a Saturday night, the conversation about the just-shown movie would be short, with the focus being on what time the Reagans wished to return to the White House the next day. The ritual was always the same. The Marine One pilot would ask, "What time tomorrow, sir, and ma'am?" and with that, the process began. The president would repeat "What time tomorrow?" and turn to Mrs. Reagan. "Honey, is there anything you need to be back for?"

---

*Ronald Reagan, *Reagan Diaries*, 742.
†Lawrence K. Altman, "2 Apparently Benign Polyps Found in Reagan," *New York Times* online, June 27, 1987, www.nytimes.com/1987/06/27/us/2-apparently -benign-polyps-found-in-reagan.html.
‡Thomas, "Two 'Benign' Polyps Removed."
§Ronald Reagan, *Reagan Diaries*, 742.

Almost always, her response would be "No, honey, any time is fine." Then the president would turn to the group and ask, "Does anyone have anything they need to get back for?" Everyone said no, of course.

So everyone just looked at one another for a minute or two until finally someone, usually Jim Kuhn or I, suggested a time. "How about two o'clock? That gives you time for lunch and to wrap up." The president would then say "Two? Seems fine. Honey?" Mrs. Reagan would say, "Sure, unless . . ." And then someone else would say, "Or maybe two thirty?"

PRESIDENT REAGAN: Two thirty? Honey?

MRS. REAGAN: Fine, honey.

PRESIDENT REAGAN: Or maybe three would be better?

MRS. REAGAN: Yes, three.

And then Jim or I . . . (in the first term, it would have been Dave Fischer) would say loudly, "Great! Three o'clock. See you all then!" And we would lead the gang out. When I got back to my cabin, I would call the weekend press duty officer and tell him or her the arrival time.

But in the winter, half the time it did not matter what had been decided, because weather conditions forced us to move up the time of departure. Usually wet snow was the culprit. In such weather, well before the agreed-upon time, I would get a call from Jim or sometimes the camp commander, saying departure would be earlier, often by several hours. I'd always have to scramble to be ready, but not before I would call the White House switchboard, ask to be connected to the weekend press duty officer in Washington, and inform him or her of the change in arrival time, so he or she could notify the press.

On all return trips to the White House, just before we landed—
as we were on what the pilots called the "short, final approach"
around the Washington Monument to the South Lawn of the White
House, I would leave my seat behind the president's, sit on the
couch across the tiny aisle from his seat, and attempt to talk to him
about what questions the press might ask as he made his way from
the helicopter to the White House. Usually he was reading either
the newspaper or briefing materials when I got there, so I would say
in a loud voice, "Mr. President, as you know . . ." and hope he would
turn toward me. Often he did. When he did not, Mrs. Reagan would
nudge him with a light tap from her foot to his. Then he would turn
to me, as would she, and listen to what I had to say. Nine and a half
times out of ten, the president already *knew* what I was going to say,
but he always let me go through it, and he always expressed his appreciation.

Back to the movie.

Luckily, neither the weather nor any other logistical inconve-
niences got in the way of that night's movie screening, and later that
evening, our little group settled in at Aspen Lodge, as we'd been
doing for years now, with the Reagans taking their usual places side
by side on the center couch.

That night's offering was *The Untouchables*, director Brian De
Palma's stylish look at the face-off between the underworld kingpin
Al Capone and law enforcement officers, led by the US Treasury
agent Eliot Ness, on the bloody streets of Prohibition-era Chicago.
The playwright David Mamet wrote the screenplay, basing it on
Eliot Ness's 1957 memoir, also called *The Untouchables*, which had
earlier inspired a 1960s TV series of the same name.

Kevin Costner, in the role that made him a superstar, headlines
the movie playing Ness, an earnest, hardworking Treasury agent
committed to cleaning up the bootleggers and putting away Capone.

He is also determined to fight clean and not lower himself to the gangsters' level of brutality. That brutality is on display from one of the earliest scenes, in which a little girl picks up a briefcase left behind in a drugstore by a mobster after the store's owner refused to buy his bootleg booze. The bomb inside blows up the entire corner store along with the child.

Ness starts his work with the Chicago police soon after that bomb attack rocks the city. But his first raid is a disaster. Capone's thugs knew Ness was coming, thanks to rampant corruption in the police department. Despondent over mocking headlines sneering "Crusader Cop Busts Out," Ness seems at a loss until he receives inspiration from an unlikely visitor. The mother of the little girl killed in the bomb attack shows up at his office and appeals to him parent-to-parent. "You see, it's because I know that you have children, too," she tells him, "and that this is real for you." Ness realizes he has to go after Capone using unconventional means.

Of course, with so many of the Chicago police taking Capone's blood money, Ness's immediate task is to assemble a team he can trust. The first member presents himself unexpectedly: the tough-talking veteran Irish cop Jimmy Malone, played by Sean Connery, nearly busts Ness for mere littering, but he has a deep well of crime-fighting wisdom gained from years of walking the beat. Ness and Malone soon recruit George Stone (Andy Garcia), also known as Giuseppe Petri, a sharp-eyed and sharp-witted kid from an Italian neighborhood on the South Side, straight from the police academy. As Malone tells Ness, "If you're afraid of getting a rotten apple, don't go to the barrel, get it off the tree." The final addition to the team is Oscar Wallace (Charles Martin Smith), a bookish but brilliant accountant convinced that Capone is guilty of tax evasion, and who also learns to handle himself well in a gunfight.

Their target, Al Capone, is played by Robert De Niro. De Niro's portrayal shows two sides of Capone: the suave media-savvy big shot who enjoys the finer things in life, such as lavish meals, manicures, and opera; as well as the brutal killer whose rage can erupt at any moment. The famous dinner scene in which Capone beats a disloyal associate to death with a baseball bat has since become iconic, but it is certainly an example of the gratuitous violence that the Reagans felt pervaded too much of modern Hollywood. Always at Capone's side is his dapper but deadly enforcer Frank Nitti, played by Billy Drago, who slinks through the movie as a sinister force, determined to hit the Untouchables where it hurts most.

From the back alleys of Chicago to the great plains of the US-Canadian border, Ness and his crew of Untouchables pursue Capone's bootleg liquor and his henchmen, inching closer to the kingpin himself. The rousing horseback chase scene at the Canadian border is reminiscent of the old-fashioned Westerns of which Ronald Reagan was such a fan (along with Kevin Costner). The lawmen learn more and more about Capone's organization, battling not only gangsters but also corrupt cops and city officials as the film builds toward its tense final scenes of confrontation.

While the critics praised *The Untouchables* and box office receipts made it one of the top-grossing movies of 1987, the film won only one Academy Award, thanks to Sean Connery's standout performance as Jimmy Malone. He won for best supporting actor, the only Oscar win of his career. The iron-spined Malone is a strong counterpoint to Costner's earnest but unsure Eliot Ness. When Malone offers Ness his help, he asks Ness a simple question: "What are you prepared to do?"

Malone explains that Ness won't be able to beat a thug like Capone by fighting by the book:

"You wanna know how to get Capone? They pull a knife, you pull a gun. He sends one of yours to the hospital, you send one of his to the morgue. *That's* the *Chicago* way! And that's how you get Capone."

Sean Connery's portrayal of Malone as the rock of the Untouchables squad resonated with critics, audiences, and the Academy members. The Scottish actor's biographer Christopher Bray suggested one reason was "because Jimmy Malone's no-nonsense heroics chimed with the 'Morning in America' vision of President Ronald Reagan." The character, according to Bray, tapped into a broader American mood inspired by Reagan himself: "Just as Reagan came to power promising to banish what he saw as the lily-livered America of the past two decades, Malone believed the job of toughening up the youngsters who were following in his footsteps was no more than his duty."*

Ronald Reagan probably would have objected to the idea of a "lily-livered America"—he was too much of a patriot for that—but it was true that he had little tolerance for weakness; political, personal, or otherwise. And that was true when it came to his efforts to fight organized crime, which I always felt was one of the more overlooked initiatives of his presidency.

Reagan's experience with the Mob went back long before he even entered politics. He was working in Hollywood when the Chicago Mafia attempted to get a piece of the movie business in the 1930s and 1940s. The Mob controlled a major union for film crews, the International Alliance of Theatrical Stage Employees and Motion Picture Operators. George Browne, the union's president, was a former Chicago mobster. Another key official in the same union was Willie Bioff, another Chicago gangster who had been personally dispatched by the real-life Frank Nitti to plant the flag of the Chicago Outfit, a secretive organized crime cartel, in Los Angeles.

*Christopher Bray, *Sean Connery: A Biography* (New York: Pegasus Books, 2011), 259.

The Mob also tried to take over Reagan's own Hollywood union, the Screen Actors Guild. "But," as Reagan would write years later, "through the commitment and efforts of people like my friend Robert Montgomery, then president of SAG, the Mob's attempted infiltration failed."*

The actors may have managed to hold off the Mafia, but "the impeccably dressed and courtly Willie Bioff" was more successful with the crew union.† He was the Mob's man in Hollywood for six years, and Reagan would later note that he and another corrupt union boss "split a million dollars with the Chicago underworld." But Bioff's ride ended when he was convicted under an antiracketeering law and sent to prison in 1941, where he began to, as the Mob movies put it, "sing like a canary." According to the *Los Angeles Times*, his information led to six more convictions of mobsters in the movie business, and "the syndicate's direct control of Hollywood craft unions came to an end."‡ Bioff's testimony also likely led to the real-life death of Frank Nitti, who committed suicide in Chicago before he could be indicted.§ Bioff himself was blown up by a car bomb in 1955, after his release from prison. He had been living in Arizona under a new identity.

After watching what he viewed as the Mob attempt to poison the industry he loved and in which he had earned his first success, it was no surprise that Ronald Reagan made it a priority to go after organized

---

*Ronald Reagan, "Declaring War on Organized Crime," *New York Times Magazine* online, January 12, 1986, www.nytimes.com/1986/01/12/magazine/declaring-war-on-organized-crime.html.

†Cecilia Rasmussen, "L.A. Then and Now: Mobsters Muscled into Film Industry," *Los Angeles Times* online, January 2, 2000, http://articles.latimes.com/2000/jan/02/local/me-50000.

‡Ibid.

§Ronald Koziol and Edward Baumann, "How Frank Nitti Met His Fate," *Chicago Tribune* online, June 29, 1987, http://articles.chicagotribune.com/1987-06-29/features/8702170754_1_frank-nitti-crime-syndicate-pulled.

crime across the country during his first term in office. On September 30, 1982, he convened a special session of the Cabinet to deal with the problem. Attorney General William French Smith laid out the plan his office had come up with to tackle the problem. Smith outlined how strong the Mob's influence remained in the United States, more than fifty years after the events of the Untouchables. He noted, according to Reagan's own recollection, "the growth and increasing sophistication of regional and national networks of professional criminals" who were "buying and bribing their way to the kind of official protection and respectability that would permit them to operate their criminal undergrounds with impunity."*

Smith's strategy involved setting up a national commission on organized crime, regional task forces to track Mob involvement in the drug trade, a "sweeping" legislative update of the criminal code, and beefed-up efforts against the Mob by Smith's own Department of Justice. A young assistant attorney general who had a hand in crafting this plan was Rudolph Giuliani, who later gained fame for prosecuting New York Mob bosses as a US attorney, eventually leading to his election as mayor of New York City in 1993.

Some at Reagan's Cabinet meeting objected to the cost of the plan Attorney General Smith had proposed. "I could sense the tension," Reagan remembered. But his was the most important voice in the room, and he knew where he stood: "I made it clear that financial considerations could not stand in the way; I approved of this plan, and I wanted it."†

The president got what he wanted and announced the plan to the nation the following month, speaking in the Great Hall of the Department of Justice. In his speech, he paid tribute to Eliot Ness,

*Ronald Reagan, "Declaring War on Organized Crime."
†Ronald Reagan, "Declaring War on Organized Crime."

among other "dedicated Americans [who] have broken the curtain surrounding this menace and successfully rooted it out." He made it clear he intended his government to carry on that tradition:

"We intend to do what is necessary to end the drug menace and cripple organized crime. We live at a turning point—one of those critical eras in history when time and circumstances unite with the sound instincts of good and decent people to make a crucial difference in the lives of future generations. We can and will make a difference."*

And the Reagan administration's efforts against organized crime made a difference. Investigative work intensified, helped by the 289 recording devices installed as part of federal investigations of mobsters by 1984.[†] In February 1985 he told the nation in his State of the Union address that the national crime index had gone down two years in a row, the first time that had happened in twenty years, and that drug and organized crime figures were being put "behind bars in record numbers."[‡] In October of that year, a preliminary report released by the President's Commission on Organized Crime found that the higher rates of prosecution were resulting in lower rates of Mob recruitment, stemming the flow of manpower into these criminal enterprises: the numbers of "made men" had fallen across twenty-four different Mafia "families."[§]

In 1986 the president wrote a lengthy article in the *New York Times Magazine* further detailing his work to root out the Mob

---

*Ibid.

†Ibid.

‡Ronald Reagan, "Address Before a Joint Session of the Congress on the State of the Union, February 6, 1985," American Presidency Project, www.presidency .ucsb.edu/ws/?pid=38069.

§Ronald Koziol, "Indictments, Convictions Hurt Mob Recruiting, Panel Reports," *Chicago Tribune* online, October 7, 1985, http://articles.chicagotribune.com/1985 -10-07/news/8503080232_1_organized-crime-trafficking-crime-families.

wherever they could be found. By that time, he could report that "organized crime convictions have more than quadrupled since 1981," and that those prosecuted were not just low-ranking foot soldiers but also major crime bosses.

The Reagan administration marked a turning point in the federal government's efforts against organized crime. John Kroger, a veteran prosecutor who brought a number of New York Mafia figures to court, said this success was directly inspired by Reagan's overarching philosophy:

> In the early 1980s the federal government reversed course and decided to take on the Mob. The primary catalyst was the election of President Ronald Reagan in 1980. Reagan and his team believed that Washington was a corrupt and inefficient cesspool. Though an oversimplification, this view came with one clear benefit: a willingness to reexamine existing government policies and to question the status quo. The Reagan Justice Department took one look at the government's Mafia policy and decided enough was enough. Virtually overnight, the new administration declared war on the Mafia.*

Kroger's difference with Reagan's "oversimplification" is understandable: Kroger himself was a committed Democrat who worked on Bill Clinton's 1992 campaign and later served as Oregon's attorney general. But that makes this bipartisan praise of Reagan's crime-fighting efforts all the more significant.

When Reagan launched his series of initiatives against organized

---

*John Kroger, *Convictions: A Prosecutor's Battles Against Mafia Killers, Drug Kingpins, and Enron Thieves* (New York: Farrar, Straus and Giroux, 2008), 142–43.

crime in October 1982, he led into the conclusion of his speech by presenting the audience with a simple hypothetical:

"It comes down in the end to a simple question we must ask ourselves: What kind of people are we if we continue to tolerate in our midst an invisible, lawless empire? Can we honestly say that America is a land with justice for all if we do not now exert every effort to eliminate this confederation of professional criminals, this dark, evil enemy within?"*

Though it was delivered years before *The Untouchables* was released, these words were notably similar to those spoken by Sean Connery's Jimmy Malone to Kevin Costner's Eliot Ness: "What are you prepared to do?" Over the next few years, mobsters brought to justice around the country learned how Ronald Reagan answered that question.

---

*Ronald Reagan, "Remarks Announcing Federal Initiatives Against Drug Trafficking and Organized Crime, October 14, 1982," American Presidency Project, www.presidency.ucsb.edu/ws/?pid=43127.

16

FERRIS BUELLER'S DAY OFF

———◆———

Starring: Matthew Broderick, Mia Sara, Alan
Ruck
Directed by: John Hughes
Viewed by the Reagans: June 21, 1986

———◆———

The Film That Reminded the Reagans of Yesterday

The president showed up at Bethesda Naval Hospital wearing a
black-and-white checked shirt, green pants, red argyle socks, and
black loafers.* He was in good spirits, as was Mrs. Reagan. When
the reporters assembled at the entrance shouted questions, asking

---

*Ira R. Allen, United Press International online, "Doctors Removed Two More
Small Polyps from President Reagan's . . . ," June 20, 1986, www.upi.com/Ar
chives/1986/06/20/Doctors-removed-two-more-small-polyps-from-President
-Reagans/7959519624000.

how he felt, the president flung his arms wide and answered, "Fine, fine!"*

This examination was to be routine, Reagan's fourth since the major surgery in July 1985 that removed a cancerous polyp and two feet of his intestines. For the most part, he had remained in good health since then. A few basal cell carcinoma skin cancer cells had been removed from his nose later in 1985, and in January 1986 three benign polyps were removed during another colon exam. But this visit was more significant: it was his one-year checkup.

The morning of Friday, June 20, had begun normally, with the president at work at the White House, but after a few hours, we boarded the helicopter for the short trip to Bethesda, arriving some twenty minutes after eleven o'clock. Inside, Dr. Edward Cattau, Bethesda's head of gastroenterology, and Dr. Dale Oller, who had performed the president's cancer surgery the previous year, greeted the Reagans.

The doctors conducted a number of tests, including X-rays, blood tests, and a colonoscopy. The procedure revealed two new small polyps, which the doctors removed. Both would prove benign. The medical team also checked the president's eyes and the skin on his nose to make sure no more cancerous cells had developed. The process was capped off with a CAT scan.

We waited it out, mostly confident, especially since the earlier exams had gone well. But there was always an undercurrent of nervousness when the boss was out of commission, however temporarily. If everything went according to plan, we would take the helicopter from Bethesda to Camp David.

---

*Gerald M. Boyd, "Doctors Remove Two Small Polyps in Reagan's Colon," *New York Times* online, June 21, 1986, www.nytimes.com/1986/06/21/us/doctors -remove-two-small-polyps-in-reagan-s-colon.html?mcubz=3.

More than five hours later, the Reagans were given the all clear to leave, all tests having been passed without incident (aside from the pesky polyps). Once again, the president and Mrs. Reagan passed the gauntlet of reporters, and once again they fielded shouted questions about how the president felt. "Fine," Mrs. Reagan said, and the president responded, "A-OK."

That was all they were going to get from the Reagans. Specific questions about what the doctors had found went unanswered. A short time later, the White House physician, Dr. T. Burton Smith, issued a short statement announcing the polyps removal, detailing the tests performed, and pronouncing the president "in good health."[*] The press would have to be satisfied with that. My boss, Larry Speakes, wasn't giving them anything else. We released the necessary information about the state of the president's health to keep the country informed, but beyond that, we wanted to respect the doctor-patient confidentiality to which Ronald Reagan, like anyone else, was entitled.

A thunderstorm was raging as all of us, including Rex the dog, piled back into Marine One. As we powered north through the rain toward Camp David, I could feel a sense of relief among the group. The colon cancer had not returned, just as the doctors had predicted after the surgery. Reagan would note in his diary that the doctor administering the CAT scan had especially encouraging words for him: "My insides were twenty-five [years] younger than my age," the president was told.[†] Nobody had expected any bad news from the morning's examinations, but after spending five hours at a hospital, everyone was ready for a quiet weekend at the presidential retreat.

[*]Boyd, "Doctors Remove Two Small Polyps."
[†]Ronald Reagan, *Reagan Diaries*, 611.

As it turned out, movie night the next night would deliver just the boost we needed. That Saturday we watched *Ferris Bueller's Day Off*, a gleeful, madcap teen comedy that was released on June 11 and has been lifting the spirits of viewers ever since.

Ferris Bueller was the latest offering from the director John Hughes, who by 1986 had already become famous for popular coming-of-age films such as *Sixteen Candles* (1984) and *The Breakfast Club* (1985), which focused on average American kids—from the jocks, to the nerds, to the unclassifiable eccentrics—managing the awkward ups and downs of high school life. An alumnus of the *National Lampoon* humor magazine, he had also written the script for the more "adult" comedy *National Lampoon's Vacation* in 1983 (if Chevy Chase's antics in that film can indeed be called "adult").

Hughes was also a ringmaster of the Brat Pack stable of young actors in the 1980s, casting actors including Molly Ringwald and Anthony Michael Hall in multiple movies and assembling many of the core Brat Packers for the ensemble cast of *The Breakfast Club*.

Ferris Bueller was not a Brat Pack film. Instead, it starred Matthew Broderick, then best known for 1983's *WarGames*, which the Reagans had also viewed, as the title character, a high school student determined to have one more day of extracurricular fun before his parents and teachers wise up to his habit of cutting class. The movie opens by making clear he's going for his *ninth* day of skipping school this semester, and his realization that making it an even ten would require him to "barf up a lung."

Ferris enlists the help of his best friend Cameron Frye (Alan Ruck), who is also staying home that day, apparently genuinely sick—even dying, in his own hypochondriacal estimation. Not only does Ferris convince the morose Cameron to get out of bed (his reasoning: "You're not dying, you just can't think of anything good to do"), but also he finagles him into taking out his father's red 1961

Ferrari 250GT California, one of only a hundred in existence, for their excursion.

The reason they need the fancy sports car? They need to spring Ferris's girlfriend, Sloane Peterson (Mia Sara), from school. Using an elaborate ruse, Cameron poses as Sloane's father on the phone, and Ferris plays the role in person, faking a death in the family to get Sloane out of class. As the three of them peel away from the school in the Ferrari, exulting in their freedom, they leave in their dust the dean of students, Edward Rooney (Jeffrey Jones), who escorted Sloane to the door. Rooney has had it out for Ferris for a long time. He resolves to catch him in the act of cutting class once and for all.

Ferris, Cameron, and Sloane leave their suburb—the fictional Shermer, Illinois, where Hughes set most of his movies—for a series of adventures in the "big city" of Chicago. Hughes, who grew up in the real-life suburb of Northbrook, thought of this movie as "my love letter to the city." He said later, "I really wanted to capture as much of Chicago as I could, not just the architecture and the landscape, but the spirit."* Tak Fujimoto's loving cinematography does just that, embracing the city with the camera lens.

The audience is treated to a rollicking good time as Ferris and friends take in a Cubs game, impersonate the "Sausage King of Chicago" to get seated at a fancy restaurant where they try the pancreas, and immerse themselves in the treasures of the Art Institute of Chicago. They are dogged all along the way by Ed Rooney, and Ferris's equally vindictive and jealous sister, Jeanie (Jennifer Grey). Ferris's well-meaning but bumbling parents threaten to spoil the fun at times, but he has a knack for finding his way out of even the stickiest situations.

---

*"Ferris Bueller: John Hughes and Chicago," AMC online, accessed September 19, 2017, www.amc.com/talk/2007/04/ferris-bueller.

Ferris Bueller found two immediate fans in the Reagans. Both the president and Mrs. Reagan enjoyed the movie from beginning to end and laughed at the antics of Broderick and company throughout. The group that had gathered in Aspen Lodge for the screening laughed heartily too. Afterward, we all agreed that it was nice to see a movie that didn't take itself seriously at all and just offered pure entertainment and unabashed fun. The president pointed out that in his view, that was the type of film Hollywood should be putting out, instead of movies filled with gratuitous violence and sex.

It was clear that one of the president's favorite scenes involved Ferris crashing the annual General Von Steuben German-American Appreciation Day Parade in downtown Chicago, which was filmed at the actual parade, with some ten thousand extras, according to Hughes.* Ferris winds up atop a float and entertains the assembled crowds with a lip-synched version of the Wayne Newton standard "Danke Schoen" ("Thank You" in German). Reagan and Newton were longtime friends, and the president was amused to see his pal's signature song from 1963 used as the centerpiece of a scene in a teen comedy in 1986.

Newton, also known as "Mr. Las Vegas," had known Reagan for years. "I met him about seven years ago in California," Newton told the *Washington Post* while in town for Reagan's first inauguration in January 1981.† That would have been about 1974, when Reagan was finishing up his tenure as California governor, and Newton was the highest-paid live act in the country. The connection was immediate.

---

*"Ferris Bueller: John Hughes and Chicago."
†Stephanie Mansfield, "Mr. Las Vegas," *Washington Post* online, January 17, 1981, www.washingtonpost.com/archive/lifestyle/1981/01/17/mr-las-vegas/783a 4658-2a1c-4c0b-97e5-b2846c5cceed/?utm_term=.20081dc8b298.

"I was very impressed with him," the performer remembered. "Something just clicked."

When Reagan ran for president in 1980, Newton jumped into action on his behalf, performing at seven fund-raisers that brought in millions in donations.* Newton was not just a celebrity attaching himself to a popular candidate for his own gain. He was a true believer.

"My motive with Reagan was altruistic," he told the paper. "I wanted to see him president. If I had a little bit to do with that, well, it makes me feel good." It went beyond that. "If Reagan had lost, I would have left the country," Newton remarked in the same interview. "I probably would have moved to Australia." Reagan's chief asset, according to Newton? His strength. "I'm one of those people who believe that strength will make this country what it once was," he said.†

Newton headlined the festivities at both of President Reagan's inaugurations, in 1981 and 1985. At the first, when the Reagans stopped by the ball that the singer was hosting at the Sheraton-Washington Hotel during their rounds of the celebrations, the new president made sure to thank Newton. "I'm so grateful to him," he told the crowd, "because Wayne, throughout the whole campaign, was just constantly working in our behalf."‡

The friendship went both ways. The day after he had been sworn in as president, Reagan sat down and handwrote a note to Wayne Newton. The entertainer kept it framed in the study of his Las Vegas

---

*Mansfield, "Mr. Las Vegas."
†Ibid.
‡Ronald Reagan, "Remarks at the Inaugural Balls, January 20, 1981," American Presidency Project, www.presidency.ucsb.edu/ws/?pid=43524.

home.* Reagan even visited Newton at home over the objections of some staff at the Republican National Committee.

Newton recounted to Larry King in 2005 that he had planned to have the president stay at his house during a visit to Las Vegas, but "the Republican Committee called and said, 'You know, he was going to come to your house, Mr. Newton, but we think that maybe it would probably be better for him to go somewhere else.'" Newton understood, but his feelings were hurt, until the same staffer called again a few days later. This time he told Newton, "We told the president what we had said to you, and I don't think I've ever been chewed out quite as nicely." Reagan's final word on the subject was: "I'm going to Wayne Newton's house, and get used to it, because he's my friend."

"And so that's the kind of guy he was," Newton told King.†

Newton was friends with the Reagans to the end. He was invited to both of their funerals.

President Reagan was thrilled to hear his old friend singing (even if Matthew Broderick was acting it out) in *Ferris Bueller's Day Off*. For his own part, Wayne Newton felt the same. Years later, he reflected that by the time *Ferris Bueller* came out, he "thought 'Danke Schoen' had run its gamut." Here was a chance to bring the song back into the public eye. "When I saw [Broderick] doing an impression and lip-synching to my version of the song, I just thought that was the coolest thing I'd ever seen."‡

---

*Chase Untermeyer, *When Things Went Right: The Dawn of the Reagan-Bush Administration* (College Station: Texas A&M University Press, 2013), 181–82.
†Wayne Newton, interview by Larry King, *Larry King Live*, CNN, January 18, 2005 (transcript, CNN.com, http://transcripts.cnn.com/TRANSCRIPTS /0501/18/lkl.01.html).
‡"Wayne Newton on Ferris Bueller and Bobby Darin," video, *Chicago Sun-Times*, June 18, 2014, www.youtube.com/watch?v=qcZL0rUsIVc.

Another Reagan ally, one of his few in the media, responded favorably to *Ferris Bueller* as well. The conservative columnist George Will, perhaps not best known for embracing popular culture, called it "the greatest movie of all time" when it came out. He explained: "By 'greatest movie,' I mean the moviest movie, the one most true to the general spirit of movies, the spirit of effortless escapism." Will devoted an entire column to praising the film, which despite being very much aimed at the teenagers of the day, also carried, in his view, an element of nostalgia. "Oh, carry me back to the olden days," he remarked, "when almost all movies were like 'Ferris Bueller'—no nonsense about seriousness."* I can imagine Ronald Reagan, himself a veteran of those "olden days" of movies, thinking much the same thing.

I think that a big part of what entertained the Reagans was that Ferris Bueller was trying to get away with something. Hoping he would not get caught. And I could relate to that—especially at Camp David.

On one of my early visits to Camp David, I woke up to my phone ringing. It was well before nine in the morning on a Sunday, so something had to be up. I rolled over, picked it up, and heard the Camp David operator announce, "Mr. Weinberg, I have the First Lady calling for you, sir." I had a nervous feeling.

"Good morning, Mrs. Reagan, how are you?" I said in a hoarse, sleepy voice.

"Mark, what do you think about it?" she asked.

"*It*, ma'am?" I replied in panic.

"The article," she said. I was the press aide in attendance, so naturally she'd expected I'd know about whatever she was referring to. I would routinely get three newspapers delivered to my cabin on

---

*George Will, "For Effortless Escapism, Take a 'Day Off' with Ferris Bueller," *Free Lance-Star* (Fredericksburg, VA), June 26, 1986.

Sundays, but they were still on the porch, covered in snow. So I took the phone—which fortunately had an extralong cord—to the porch and, in my T-shirt and briefs, scooped up the papers, brushed them off, and said to Mrs. Reagan: "It was interesting. What did *you* think?"

I hoped that would give me some indication of what she was talking about and buy a little time to find the piece. It did, and as she spoke, I tore through the papers and was able to locate and skim the article and offer an opinion, which I am sure was devoid of any intelligent analysis whatsoever.

From then on, I set my alarm to six o'clock on Sunday mornings and made sure to have read every paper by eight. She never called me for such a purpose again.

Of course, not all of the critics were buying into what the movie was all about, and some even managed to connect the movie to Reagan in a negative way. In *New York* magazine, David Denby sneeringly dismissed it as "John Hughes's nauseating distillation of the slack, greedy side of Reaganism."* Denby seems to take awfully seriously a movie whose clear, obvious guiding principle is frivolity, but he was not the only one conscious of some higher themes mixed in with *Ferris Bueller's* high spirits. Ben Stein, the former Republican White House staffer and actor (not a combination one often encounters), felt the same way.

Stein, who had served as a speechwriter in the Nixon and Ford administrations, appears in the movie as an economics teacher at Ferris Bueller's school, a small but memorable role that launched Stein's second career as an actor. First, we see him calling roll, and uttering in an unforgettable monotone, "Bueller . . . Bueller . . ." to no response. Later we listen in on a lecture he is giving to the class on, of all things, supply-side economics, or "Reaganomics." He covers

*David Denby, "Movies," *New York*, December 22–29, 1986, 142.

the "Laffer Curve," named for the Reagan administration economist Arthur Laffer, and even mentions the phrase George H. W. Bush used to attack Reagan's economic policies during the 1980 Republican primaries: "voodoo economics."

The role came to Stein in a roundabout way, as he explained in a 2006 interview with CNN:

"Richard Nixon introduced me to a man named Bill Safire, who's a *New York Times* columnist [and former Nixon speechwriter]. He introduced me to a guy who's an executive at Warner Bros. He introduced me to a guy who's a casting director. He introduced me to John Hughes. John Hughes and I are among the only Republicans in the picture business, and John Hughes put me in the movie."*

During the filming, Stein happened to be talking off camera to some of the extras playing his students about economics. The kids were delighted by his distinctive monotone style, and on hearing their laughter, the crew worked a lecture scene into the film. At the end, everyone applauded. "I thought they were applauding because they had learned something about supply-side economics," Stein said. "But they were applauding because they thought I was boring."†

As Stein noted, John Hughes was conservative in his own politics. In another interview, thirty years after the Reagans watched the movie at Camp David, he reflected on how Ferris Bueller, in his own goofy way, helped encapsulate the Reagan era:

America at that time was in the midst of the Reagan boom, so we were all in a pretty good mood. The end of the seventies were

---

*"Ben Stein Talks About Famous 'Ferris Bueller' Role," *Showbiz Tonight,* CNN .com, January 10, 2006, http://transcripts.cnn.com/TRANSCRIPTS/0601/10 /sbt.01.html.
†Ibid.

really bad economic times, and after the dark times of Watergate, I think Ferris was to some extent reacting to the fact that things were better. What was his mother's occupation? Luxury real estate broker. Those were happier days, a much more optimistic age—even though we were running large deficits. Ferris Bueller's optimism was very representative of the era, and it was very representative of who John Hughes was. He was an ardent Republican and extreme conservative. He believed Reagan could transform all of us into Ferris Buellers. Ferris was an artifact of a free era. Ronald Reagan was all about freedom. Ferris was an unregulated high school kid in an unregulated world. It was "morning in America," and it was morning for Ferris.*

Ronald Reagan may not have turned us into a nation of Ferris Buellers, but he and Ferris did share a common belief in freedom. And that included Reagan's own, personal freedom.

One of Ferris Bueller's most quoted lines, which I'm sure still appears in millions of high school yearbooks all across America, is this simple injunction: "Life moves pretty fast. If you don't stop and look around once in a while, you could miss it."

Reagan's weekends at Camp David were his chance to "stop and look around once in a while." And this weekend, after spending all of Friday morning in a hospital, that was especially important. He needed the swim and the walks he took that Saturday, and he needed the relaxation and laughter of a movie night with Ferris Bueller. We all did.

---

*Olivia B. Waxman, "Ben Stein: Ferris Bueller Represents the Reagan Era," *Time* online, June 10, 2016, http://time.com/4357446/ben-stein-ferris-bueller-ronald-reagan.

17

HELLCATS OF THE NAVY

---◆---

Starring: Ronald Reagan, Nancy Davis
Directed by: Nathan Juran
Viewed by the Reagans: September 7, 1985

---◆---

The Film They Starred In Together

When we first walked into Aspen, the president, wearing a mischievous look, greeted us with one of his trademark phrases, telling us we were in for a treat, or at least he hoped so. We knew what that meant. Reagan had used that line before to let us know we were about to watch one of his own movies. And as he made sure to remind us, we were the ones who had asked to see it.

It was true, of course. Reagan was always bashful about showing his own movies. But he had shown *Bedtime for Bonzo* the year before, and several of us managed to cajole him into showing the Oscar-nominated *Kings Row* a year later.

We all quickly took our seats and settled down for a time-travel journey unlike any other. This evening, the feature was a special one: *Hellcats of the Navy*, starring Ronald Reagan and Nancy Davis. We would be watching *both* Reagans watching themselves on the screen.

Hellcats, as the Reagans called it, was the only movie in which the two of them acted together, but it also happened to be the last picture that either made. Sharing the top billing was certainly a nice way to exit the business, but I have wondered whether they were happy about the way their Hollywood careers ended. I have a feeling that Ronald Reagan, at least, was not. In his first autobiography, *Where's the Rest of Me?*, published in 1965, he seemed a bit resentful, writing of his *Hellcats* experience:

"That ended pictures for me. Hollywood adopted an attitude that TV performers were *verboten* on the big screen, and once Hollywood starts believing its own cocktail party pronouncements, you just have to wait til they get off on a new kick. It didn't matter that my Sunday night stint [on G.E. Theater] was a quick forty-five seconds—I had a weekly show, and that was that."

More than twenty years later, that resentment had subsided at least enough for the president to consent to showing *Hellcats* that evening in Aspen Lodge.

We were coming off what had been a busy travel week for the president. On Monday he traveled from the ranch near Santa Barbara, California, to Independence, Missouri, where he spoke about tax reform at the thirteenth annual Santa-Cali-Gon days celebration. The Santa-Cali-Gon days celebration, according to the celebration's website, "commemorates the origin of the Santa Fe, California, and Oregon trails during the country's great westward expansion by early pioneers. More than 300,000 attendees spend Labor Day weekend at the region's oldest and largest festival." On Thursday, he traveled to Raleigh, North Carolina, to address students and faculty at North Carolina State University, again about tax reform. And on Friday he,

Mrs. Reagan, and Maureen hosted a luncheon for Elected Republican Women in the State Dining Room at the White House. Later that day, we left for Camp David.

In a relatively rare occurrence, the Reagans had a personal guest at Camp David that weekend: their longtime friend and acclaimed decorator, Ted Graber. He had been staying at the White House that week. Ted was always fun to be with. He had a great sense of humor, took an interest in whomever he was talking to, and, despite being one of the most successful interior designers of his time, was as down-to-earth and unpretentious as one could get.

That Saturday was a hot one, so after the president finished his weekly radio address, he and Mrs. Reagan spent most of the day at the pool. Of course, there was always more work to be done. President Reagan took an important call from Canadian prime minister Brian Mulroney regarding the Strategic Defense Initiative (SDI). The prime minister informed the president that the Canadian government had voted against teaming up with the United States for SDI research, but noted that he personally supported our efforts, and that there would be no blocks against private Canadian companies or other groups lending their assistance. Reagan understood and accepted the decision. A potentially awkward international situation was avoided by two world leaders who shared a warm friendship.

Ted Graber had joined the Reagans for dinner in Aspen, so he was already inside when "the gang" showed up at the front door at the usual time. Ted sat on the couch with the Reagans while the movie was shown. He was on Mrs. Reagan's left and the president was on her right. I'm sure no political symbolism was implied by that arrangement! The projector started up, and *Hellcats* began.

Made in 1957, *Hellcats of the Navy* was based on Vice Admiral Charles A. Lockwood's and Hans Christian Adamson's book *Hellcats of the Sea*. Ronald Reagan plays Casey Abbott, the commander of a

US Navy submarine in the Pacific in World War II. The mission—
to capture a new Japanese mine—encounters problems, and Commander Abbott must abandon a popular crew member on a dive attempting repairs. But Abbott's second-in-command thinks Abbott did so unnecessarily and, worse, for personal reasons. The diver was a rival for the affections of Nurse Lieutenant Helen Blair, played by none other than Nancy Davis. Though the Reagans were married by the time they made *Hellcats*, Mrs. Reagan was credited under her maiden name.

The movie's eighty-two-minute running time seemed to go by in much less. I was surprised at how few scenes Mrs. Reagan was in, far fewer than her husband, despite being billed as a costar. Her role in the film was crucial, yet I still did not see as much of her as I thought I would. As I watched, I kept waiting for her to appear!

I was around the man every day, yet the Commander Abbott I saw on the screen was nothing like Ronald Reagan at all. He was serious, even brooding, never smiling or appearing happy until the end. It was jarring. But, then, that's acting!

There was an extra flourish among the small group of us in Aspen whenever one of the president's own movies came to an end. There was always a round of applause, and the president would stand up and bow. Tonight it was a standing ovation, as we applauded both of our hosts.

We moved toward the fireplace for our usual postmovie discussion. These always went on a bit longer after a Reagan movie, because we had the chance to get their firsthand perspectives. We would pepper them with questions about every aspect of the movie: script issues, special effects, stunts, makeup, bloopers, and more. The president's and Mrs. Reagan's memories were amazing. They could recall everything and never tired of sharing anecdote after anecdote.

The big question we had for the president after *Hellcats*, of course, was what it had been like acting alongside his wife. He said it was special because they were together, and they would often hold hands on the set (as they still did). But once the director, Nathan Juran, shouted "Action!" they became professionals—an actor and an actress—and had no problems playing their roles. Mrs. Reagan nodded in agreement.

Interestingly, some years earlier, both Reagans had told stories about their time filming *Hellcats of the Navy* together that were slightly different from what they shared with us that night.

In her first autobiography, *Nancy*, published in 1980, Mrs. Reagan recalled things this way:

"What I remember best is a scene in which Ronnie is about to go to sea in his submarine, and we say farewell. The scene was shot on a dock in San Diego in front of a stack of explosive mines. I was sending him off to risk his life, and I couldn't stand it. The idea got to me. I kept breaking up in tears, and we had to reshoot and reshoot. However, I must say the love scenes in this film were the easiest I ever had to do."

Her costar had a similar recollection, writing earlier in *Where's the Rest of Me?*:

Nancy played a nurse, and the love interest. As I say, there is a tendency to get more involved when the atmosphere is for real rather than the make-believe of a soundstage. We have a moonlight farewell scene on the eve of my departure for the dangerous mission which was the climax of the story. The first thing we all knew, Nancy was crying instead of saying the script lines, and then she was giggling between sobs, laughing at herself for having gotten so carried away that she was really saying good-bye and sending me on a suicide mission.

Seeing Ronald Reagan in a US Navy uniform that night, even if only on film (in real life, he had served in the army), was undoubtedly especially fun for the Camp David commander, since Camp David is a navy facility. As it happened, the duty military aide that weekend was a navy commander, so there was another naval officer present who was probably happy to see the commander in chief in their service's uniform.

The Reagans had a good time. Any awkwardness about seeing themselves on-screen, or painful associations with *Hellcats* as signaling the end of their movie careers, were banished by the time Reagan recorded the evening in his diary the next day: "Sat. night we ran 'Hellcats of the Navy' starring N.D.R. and R.R. It was fun."

In *Hellcats,* Reagan's on-screen enemies were the Japanese. As president, of course, he enjoyed an excellent relationship with his Japanese counterpart for much of his administration, the conservative prime minister Yasuhiro Nakasone.

Just four years later, however, Ronald and Nancy Reagan would again find themselves facing a very real challenge involving Japan.

In 1989 the Reagans were paid $2 million for a series of appearances in Japan under the sponsorship of the Fujisankei Communications Group. That amount for multiple appearances by a popular former president and First Lady seems quaint by today's standards. Nonetheless, it was a lot of money and caused some to accuse the Reagans of "cashing in on the presidency."

Though I was working in the former president's office, I was not consulted on the original decision to make the deal with Fujisankei. Regardless, my job as director of public affairs was to do what I could to mitigate the damage to his reputation. Obviously, the easiest way to fix the situation would have been to cancel the trip.

Unlikely as it was, I decided to give that approach a shot in a conversation with former President Reagan. I was candid and told him that there were people who thought he was being "greedy" and was cashing in on the presidency. He listened to the points I was making but looked at me with a steely gaze. Finally, in a firm voice, he asked, "What are you suggesting we do?"

I gulped and then said, "Well, sir, one of two things: I suppose the easiest and most obvious would be to simply cancel the trip, and the second would be to donate all of the money from it to a worthy charity or worthy charities."

He paused for a moment, looked at me again, and said, "Well, Mark, I can understand why you say that, but, you know, with regard to the money, when I was making motion pictures years ago, they did not pay the salaries that a lot of the actors are getting today. And I'm not a young man, and we just bought a house, so I don't think there's anything wrong with wanting to build a strong financial base for my family. But even more important than that, I gave this company my word."

At that point, a voice inside my head said, "Game over, move on," because I knew that when Ronald Reagan gave his word, that was it. Period. I said, "Sir, thank you for hearing me out. I understand and respect your decision and will do everything I can to minimize any negative public relations impact." He responded with a smile and "You bet."

It wasn't often necessary for me to challenge my boss, but when I did, he handled it graciously. On a different trip, the former president, some advance people, and I were in a "holding" suite in a hotel, having dinner before he was scheduled to speak. Somehow the subject of sanctions against South Africa came up, and President Reagan said that what worried him about sanctions was "that they hurt the very people we're trying to help." For reasons I cannot explain now, I chose to challenge him on that and said that there are those who would argue that while in the short term sanctions might negatively impact those whose lives we sought to improve, the idea was that damaging the South African economy would force its leaders to abandon apartheid. Whatever temporary pain they might cause among the general population could well lead to a revolt against the government, which would also result in abolishing apartheid. Others at the table were stone silent and avoided eye contact with either of us.

After what seemed like an hour but was really only a few seconds, President Reagan replied by saying, "Well, that's an interesting point. I suppose it could well be that way. I just hope that whatever we do results in all the people there being treated fairly and not on the basis of their skin color." "Me, too," I replied.

My challenge regarding the Japan trip, while heard graciously, had been unsuccessful, so we began to work on a plan. We came up with several ideas: first was to schedule another foreign trip prior to his trip to Japan, so that the press could not report that "in his first overseas trip as a former president, Ronald Reagan went to Japan to collect $2 million."

Travel to London, Paris, and Rome was arranged. It was a trip on which there would be no paid engagements and on which he would receive multiple honors. For example, Queen Elizabeth II knighted President Reagan at Buckingham Palace, he was inducted into the prestigious Academy of Moral and Political Sciences in Paris, and he was received by Pope John Paul II in a rare private audience at Castel Gandolfo, the Pope's summer retreat. We arranged for high-visibility media interviews on the trip, and all in all, it generated good coverage. But it was not enough to blunt criticism of the trip to Japan.

When it came time for the Japan trip itself, we took two steps that we hoped would soften some of the edges. Working with the USO, we provided free air transportation for families of troops stationed in Japan on the airplane that Fujisankei chartered for the Reagans and their party to and from Japan. Of course, the Reagans greeted and posed for photos with all of the family members on board. And we arranged his Japan schedule so that he would participate in official governmental events before paid events, the theory being "honors before honorariums." He received an award from the emperor and empress of Japan at the Imperial Palace and had meetings with Japanese government officials.

But as popular as he was in Japan and as warmly received as he was during the trip, Ronald Reagan was still criticized severely in the United States for making the trip and accepting such a large fee. Oddly enough, his time in Hollywood even contributed to the controversy. He made a speech in Japan in which he criticized the US movie industry, offending a number of people in his former profession—so much so that he had to apologize in a speech in Hollywood after he returned home. I wish I had pressed harder on him to cancel the trip, even though I know that if he viewed it as a commitment to which he had given his word, there wasn't anything anyone could have done to dissuade him from going.

The speech in Japan was a rare instance of Reagan rebuking Hollywood, but it was not the only occasion. Another notable grievance with "the industry," as he called it, came about because of *Hellcats of the Navy*. He described some of the production difficulties in *Where's the Rest of Me?* by remarking that the film "could have been better than it was, except that the studio was more in love with the budget than the script."

The Reagans did not see eye to eye on the production of *Hell-cats*. Many years after we watched *Hellcats* at Camp David, I visited Mrs. Reagan at their home in Los Angeles, and we talked about movies. Her recollections of *Hellcats* were much warmer than what the president had written. I asked what went through her mind that night at Camp David when she watched herself and her husband acting together on the screen.

"I was very self-conscious, but I loved being in that picture with him. And he looked exactly the same!" she recalled.

I said, "You both did!"

She looked a little skeptical. "I did?"

"Yes. Definitely." It was true. I thought so then and still do now.

When I asked if she had any favorite films, she gave a false grimace and said, "Oh, my."

I offered some suggestions—*Night into Morning, Donovan's Brain,* or *The Next Voice You Hear*—all movies from the early 1950s, and all starring Nancy Davis.

She laughed and said, "Oh, no. But any that Ronnie was in." I pressed gently again for one in particular, and she gave me an answer: "*Hellcats of the Navy.*"

While the world may never know how far the Reagans could have gone in Hollywood had their movie careers not ended there, the world was lucky that they changed careers, setting Reagan on the path that would lead him to the White House. More people know them as president and First Lady than would ever know them as the costars of *Hellcats of the Navy.* But for Ronald and Nancy, the chance to finish their careers together was a special one—a memory that Mrs. Reagan carried with her until the end.

EPILOGUE

March 2016

I realized that Nancy Reagan had lived an amazing and long life, and wanted to be with her husband. She even once lamented to a former aide that she thought God had "forgotten" about her. Still, news of her death was especially sad for me, maybe even more so than when the president died in 2004. He had been ill and away for so long that his passing was "a merciful release," as Queen Elizabeth II described it in her handwritten letter of sympathy to Mrs. Reagan. But Mrs. Reagan was "with it" until the end, and was the last remaining link to him. With both Reagans gone, a very important chapter of my life ended.

Some members of her family referred to her funeral as "the event." And they were right. It was very carefully staged and choreographed, in accordance with Mrs. Reagan's wishes. But I have a feeling that calling it an event was not entirely a term of approval, at least on the part of the Reagan children, Patti and Ron. For their entire lives, they had to share their parents with the country and the world, and now, even as they said good-bye to their mother, they were forced to do so in public with hundreds of others—many

of whom they probably did not know—not to mention a television
audience of millions. Ronald and Nancy Reagan made a choice
that theirs would be public lives, which had to be hard on Patti and
Ron. Funerals for most people are held in churches, synagogues,
or funeral parlors with a small group of family and close friends in
attendance. But most people were not First Lady of the United
States.

Nonetheless, the event was a wonderful tribute. I was struck
by two things. First was the size of her casket. Matching that of
her husband, it was quite large and impressive, but since she was
neither tall nor robust, it seemed disproportionate. And, second, to
hear the eulogizers speak, one might think that the Reagans did not
have children. It was odd. But Patti's and Ron's heartfelt words more
than made up for that.

The funeral was held in a large tent at the Reagan Presidential Library in Simi Valley, and the rain held off until just before
Mrs. Reagan's casket was taken to the burial site, where she was to
be laid to rest next to her husband. The irony was not lost on me.
For as long as I knew her, Nancy Reagan was always worried about
the weather, sometimes calling aides several times a day for updated
forecasts. Once, I got one of the calls and told her optimistically,
"Mrs. Reagan, it's not that bad," to which she replied, "Well, Mark,
it's not that good."

It was just drizzling when the ceremony ended, and guests were
invited to pass by the casket to pay final respects. Family members
and VIPs such as First Lady Michelle Obama, former president and
Mrs. George W. Bush, Hillary Clinton, Rosalynn Carter, Caroline
Kennedy, Tricia Nixon Cox, former Canadian prime minister Brian
Mulroney, among others, went first, of course. By the time my wife
and I got close, it was raining pretty heavily, and we did not have
umbrellas. I turned to her and said, "If anyone would understand not

standing in line in this kind of weather, it would be Nancy Reagan. Let's go inside." Which we did.

As we were walking under an awning to the postceremony lunch inside the Air Force One pavilion, I ran into colleagues I had not seen in years. First was the renowned speechwriter and prize-winning columnist Peggy Noonan. We looked at each other, she said "Oh, Mark," and we embraced. Peggy had been quite close to Mrs. Reagan in her later years. A few seconds later, I saw my friend Jon Huntsman Jr., the former Utah governor (and onetime Reagan advance man), and we shared memories of some of our Reagan travels together.

The buffet luncheon was a lovely reunion of Reagan aides, friends, and family. Of course, Hollywood was well represented by stars such as Tom Selleck, John Stamos, Gary Sinise, Bo Derek, Wayne Newton, Arnold Schwarzenegger, Anjelica Huston, and Mr. T (Laurence Tureaud), the latter of whom had been an active supporter of Mrs. Reagan's antidrug abuse campaign. In 1983 he came to a White House Christmas party, at which he dressed as Santa Claus, and Mrs. Reagan sat on his lap and kissed his head. Many people at the luncheon had their picture taken with Mr. T, though none sat on his lap. I suspect Mrs. Reagan was looking down and laughing.

Erin and I were among the very last people to leave the Reagan Library that day. I think I was reluctant to let go.

I did not know it at the time, but I would have one more opportunity to bid the Reagans farewell.

September 2016

In accordance with their wishes, most of the household possessions from the Reagans' home in Los Angeles were sold at auction, with proceeds benefiting the Ronald Reagan Presidential Foundation.

Looking through the glossy catalog was fun at first and brought back many fond memories, but I found myself gradually slipping into sadness at the realization that the Reagans were really gone. Both of them. Forever. And yet, especially because of Erin, I was reminded of how the movie memories they shared managed to echo all the way to the present.

I recalled that President Reagan told us stories about working with Virginia Mayo and Eddie Bracken on the 1949 comedy *The Girl from Jones Beach*, and recalled how he and Eddie had to hoist Virginia on their shoulders for some of the publicity shots. Many years later, as a former president in Los Angeles, he invited Eddie and Virginia to visit him in his office, and the three reminisced for more than an hour about the movies they made together. No attempt was made to hoist Virginia. When I learned that Virginia and Eddie were scheduled to come in to see former President Reagan, I contacted a dealer in vintage movie memorabilia and bought an original poster from *The Girl from Jones Beach*, which all three stars were kind enough to autograph when they were together in the office. Ironically, several years after that, I began dating—and ultimately married—a native Long Islander who had spent many summers at Jones Beach. When she saw the signed and framed poster hanging in my apartment, she could hardly believe it. Talk about fate!

Before the auction, my own "girl from Jones Beach" and I attended a reception where the Reagans' possessions were displayed for would-be buyers, most of whom had never been in their home but were happy to eat sushi and drink sparkling wine as they looked over the lots. The staff from the famed Christie's auction house had essentially re-created 668 Saint Cloud Road in Bel Air, California, in Rockefeller Center, New York. It was eerie. The couches, paintings, books, china cabinets, and other objects were arranged just as they had been at the Reagans' home.

Everything was there, exactly as I remembered it.

Only Nancy and Ronald Reagan were missing.

I almost wish I had not gone. The finality of their deaths was profound. But I did notice one thing as I wandered through the gallery made to look like their den. I could finally see the top of the coffee table. The stacks of videocassettes of Ronald Reagan's movies, which had been piled atop the table as recently as my visit to their home just months before, were not there. Nor were they listed in the catalog. I hope they found a good home.

ACKNOWLEDGMENTS

When Ronald Reagan was writing his postpresidency memoirs, *An American Life*, he would sometimes refer to doing so as having "a monkey on my back." I did not understand what he meant—until I set out to write this book. And while I never viewed this book as being a monkey on my back, I eventually came to share some of his feelings about such an undertaking. That said, the truth is I enjoyed taking a trip down memory lane and committing to paper what I had experienced.

That's because I had the support and assistance of the greatest personal and professional team ever.

First and foremost, I am grateful to my family, starting with my father, Herbert C. Weinberg, a World War II veteran, and my dear late mother, Judith L. Weinberg. Always loving, supportive, and exemplary, they hoped I would tell "my story." Backing up a bit, my parents were not especially enthusiastic when, as a high school student, I told them I wanted to pursue a career in politics. Law, medicine, or real estate were what they had in mind for their firstborn. But they accepted it and never pressured me to abandon my goal. And they were quite happy that I knew exactly where I wanted to go to college (the George Washington University), rather than put them through the agonizing and expensive prospect of touring every college in the country. Whatever misgivings they may have had about my being in politics melted away the minute they met the Reagans. They loved Nancy and Ronald Reagan and the fact that I worked for them. I wish my mom had lived to see this project completed. She and my late stepfather-in-law, Jim Garvey (the definition of a swell guy), are probably badgering everyone in Heaven to buy a copy!

It was my wife, Erin, who urged me to write a book about my experiences with the Reagans, an urging I resisted for a long time. She insisted I had an interesting story to tell and owed it to the Reagans and to history to do so. As usual, Erin was right. She is truly the light of my life and was unfailingly supportive and encouraging throughout every minute of writing this, painstakingly reading every word many times. There is no way I could—or would—have done it without her. Our daughter, Grace, and our son, Jake, were equally excited, supportive, and encouraging. Grace, a high school student, wanted to know if she could get extra credit in her social studies class if I came in to share my experiences. (No.) And knowing that I am now often an uncredited ghostwriter for corporate clients, Jake, an elementary school student, asked if, finally, my own name would be on the cover of the book. He was beyond thrilled to know it would be. Throughout this process, while excited about my being an author, my sister, Mary Ellen Feinstein; my brother, Michael, and his partner, Eddie October; my mother-in-law, Gwen Garvey; my father-in-law, Bob Davy, and his wife, Anita; my aunts Sally Isenstadt and Susan Lipton; my brother-in-law Robert Davy and his wife, Genevieve; my sister-in-law Lauren Davy; my brother-in-law Sean Davy and his fiancée, Kate Dewan; and Erin's and my nephews and nieces: Zack and Jessie Feinstein, Ryan and Jackson Davy, and Annie and Rocco October-Weinberg, wondered about only one thing: whether I was done yet.

I am. (For now.)

Now, on to the others. Before doing so, however, I want to confess that I am desperately afraid of having left out someone. Which reminds me of when President Reagan wrote his first postpresidency book, *Speaking My Mind: Selected Speeches*, in 1989. He did not include me in the acknowledgments, nor should he have. After all, the book was just a compilation of speeches, with which I had nothing to do. But Ronald Reagan felt bad about the exclusion, and one day shortly after the book was published, he walked into my office and said, "Mark, I want to tell you how sorry I am I did not mention you in the book. It's like having a party and forgetting to invite your best friend." I told him I appreciated his kind words, but that I was not bothered in the least (I was acknowledged in his autobiography, *An American Life*).

That said, I apologize if I left anyone out. But if I did, I hope they will remember the sign that Ronald Reagan had on his desk that read "There is no limit to what a man can do or where he can go if he does not mind who gets the credit."

The men and women of the Office of the Press Secretary to the president were/are valued colleagues and trusted friends during my eight years in the White House and to this day. Led by Jim Brady, Larry Speakes, and Marlin Fitzwater, they all served their country with dedication and distinction. I have fond memories of our work together. Many—including Marlin, David Prosperi, Flo Grace, Sandy Sidey, Kim Hoggard, Denny Brisley, Jeannie Winnick Brennan, Mary Kayne Heinze, Dale Petroskey, Leslye Arsht, Rusty Brashear, Pete Roussel, Anson Franklin, B. Jay Cooper, Ben Jarratt, Bill Harlow, and especially the incomparable Connie Gerrard—the latter of whom served in the White House during eight administrations and was rightfully regarded as indispensable—were helpful in providing memories and advice, for which I am grateful. Veteran White House press advance man and Congressional Press Secretary Hugh O'Neill, who was my first boss in politics when I joined the fledgling Connally presidential campaign in 1979, showed me the ropes of working with reporters, and was a sounding board throughout this process.

In addition to my colleagues in the Press Office, I worked with many other White House aides, a few of whom came to Camp David on weekends, too. David Fischer, the president's personal aide in the first term, Jim Kuhn, his personal aide in the second term, (the late) Shirley Moore, Mike Deaver's executive assistant, and several White House physicians were also regular members of the Aspen Movie Club.

Sheila Tate, Mrs. Reagan's press secretary, a PR powerhouse who has a wonderful sense of humor and kept me laughing throughout and after our years together in the White House, and White House Chief of Staff Ken Duberstein, whose extraordinary savvy about how Washington works kept the Reagan ship of state sailing smoothly, kindly shared memories.

A special assistant to the president, Morgan Mason, Hollywood "royalty" himself, who may have had the greatest insight into the Reagans' relationship with the movie business, also generously shared his memories and thoughts.

Stu Spencer, the undisputed best political strategist of modern times, honored me by sharing memories of watching movies with the Reagans, as did Amanda Deaver.

So, too, did some of the officers who served as military aide to the president of the United States during the years Ronald Reagan was in the White House. He respected them all. Specifically, from the US Army: Jose Muratti, Casey Brower, Bob Ivany, Ron Thomas, and Jim Reynolds; from the US Marine Corps: John Kline, Pete Metzger, Pete Peterson, and Duane Hegna; from the US Navy: Bill Schmidt, Woody Sutton, Pat Dunne, and J.J. Quinn; from the US Air Force: Bill Drennan, Tom Carter, Steve Chealander, and Gary Dylewski; and from the US Coast Guard: Vivien Crea, and Woody Lee. I spent many weekends at Camp David with them watching movies with the Reagans.

Same for the US Navy officers who served as commander(s) of Camp David during the Reagan years: Ralph Cugowski, Bill Waters, Jim Rispoli, Jim Broaddus, Mike Berry, and Terry Dake, a pilot of Marine One.

No one from the Reagan White House Military Office was more helpful than Joni Stevens, the office manager, who knew everything and everyone, and was always unflappable.

Senior agents of the US Secret Service also watched movies with the Reagans at Camp David and several shared some fun stories, including Doug Cunningham, Bob DeProspero, Denny Finch, Dick Griffin, Steve Harrison, Garrick Newman, Joe Petro, Ray Shaddick, Gary Wiestrand, and (the late) Gary Yauger.

And so did Tessa Taylor, the legendary leading man Robert Taylor's lovely and articulate daughter, who practically grew up with the Reagans. She was so close as to call them Uncle Ronnie and Aunt Nancy.

After eight years in the White House, I had mixed feelings about moving to Los Angeles. I liked it when we visited there during the White House years (who wouldn't like staying *for free* in the Century Plaza Hotel?) and was thrilled to still be with the Reagans. But living and working there was an entirely different case, and I was not sure if it was for me.

Long story (not so) short, my time as director of public affairs in the Office of Ronald Reagan was not only special and cherished but also among the most happy years of my life. Our chief of staff, Frederick J. Ryan Jr., who had served in the White House as assistant to the president, and is now publisher and chief executive officer of the *Washington Post*, made what turned out to be a highly successful effort to create a feeling of unity and camaraderie among the staff. I did not know Fred super-well during our years together in the White House, but when I worked with him in former president Reagan's office, I quickly came to realize he has one of the sharpest minds as well as the best instincts and manners of anyone I have ever met. Fred remains a valued and trusted friend and is that rare person in Washington about whom *no one* has an unkind word. No one. (He and I do *not* have that in common.)

My other colleagues on the staff in former president Reagan's office, especially Joanne Drake, who is the most steadfastly loyal Reagan aide ever; Cathy Busch, who succeeded me as President Reagan's spokesperson and is the embodiment of class and good judgment; the savvy Sandy Warfield; the always real Sheri Lietzow; the hardworking Jon Hall; the competent and good-natured Paula Franklin; the sage and down-to-earth (late) Dottie Dellinger; the devoted and discreet Kathy Osborne; the witty and urbane Robert Higdon; the impressively smart and poised Michael Busch; the earnest and gracious Peggy Grande; Lisa Cavelier, Mrs. Reagan's worldly and wise top aide; and the indefatigable correspondence team of Janine Chase (Mathias), Kerry Geoghan (Perlow), Keri Douglas, and Bernadette Schurz, among others, helped create a family feeling among the staff. It was like when Ronald Reagan worked at Warner Bros.

The staff at the Ronald Reagan Presidential Library, especially director Duke Blackwood; archivist Jennifer Mandel; AV archivists Steve Branch and Michael Pinckney; executive director of the Ronald Reagan Presidential Foundation & Institute John Heubusch;

chief administrative officer Joanne Drake; and chief marketing officer Melissa Giller were of great assistance.

I am grateful to the extraordinarily talented and professional team at Javelin DC. Without them, this book would not be. My agent, Matt Latimer, a founding partner of Javelin DC and himself a *New York Times* bestselling author; his partner Keith Urbahn; Dylan Colligan, Javelin's editorial director and a gifted writer; and media relations director Vanessa Santos, took my vague and disjointed "proposal" for a book and turned it into something that actually made sense and appealed to publishers and (hopefully) readers. They provided invaluable guidance, advice, reassurance, and support. It was my friend and mentor, Peter Barnes, former White House correspondent for Fox Business, CNBC, and Hearst Television, who suggested I contact Javelin DC with my idea for a book, so, he, too, deserves much of the credit.

The unequaled professionals at Simon & Schuster were nothing short of amazing. At the top of the list is executive editor Ben Loehnen. There are no words to adequately describe how smart he is and how much his "suggestions" made this a significantly better book than what I submitted originally. Assistant editor Amar Deol, who made this book a reality, was unfailingly patient and attentive. Special thanks, too, to production manager Brigid Black, copyediting manager Jessica Chin, associate director of design Ruth Lee-Mui, senior publicity manager Erin Reback, associate director of marketing Dana Trocker, deputy general counsel Emily Remes and attorney Lisa Rivlin, and copy editor Philip Bashe.

I am indebted to the Reagan family. The Reagans' son, Ron, Mrs. Reagan's brother, Dr. Richard Davis, and Dennis Revell, who was married to Maureen Reagan, all shared recollections.

I would not have written this book without Mrs. Reagan's permission. Not only did she give me the "green light," she encouraged me to do so. She kindly granted me a lengthy interview at their home in Los Angeles, during which she shared stories and insights about her husband, our weekends at Camp David, the movies we watched, and her and her husband's experiences in Hollywood.

Finally, I want to thank the Gipper. The first draft of this book submitted to my brilliant editor, Ben Loehnen, was returned to me with his meticulous handwritten notes and a gentle admonishment to guard against hagiography. I had to consult a dictionary for the definition of hagiography. Ben was right. My first draft made Ronald Reagan seem like a saint. He wasn't, of course. (As far as I know—now.) That said, Ronald Reagan was a uniquely decent, kind, gentle, principled, exemplary, and wise man. I respected him, I learned from him, and I miss him.

INDEX